Graceful
EVANGELISM

Graceful EVANGELISM

CHRISTIAN WITNESS IN A COMPLEX WORLD

Frances S. Adeney

BakerAcademic

a division of Baker Publishing Group
Grand Rapids, Michigan

© 2010 by Frances S. Adeney

Published by Baker Academic
a division of Baker Publishing Group
P.O. Box 6287, Grand Rapids, MI 49516-6287
www.bakeracademic.com

Printed in the United States of America

Library of Congress Cataloging-in-Publication Data

Adeney, Frances S.
    Graceful evangelism : Christian witness in a complex world / Frances S. Adeney.
       p.   cm.
    Includes bibliographical references and index.
    ISBN 978-0-8010-3185-4 (pbk.)
    1. Evangelistic work. 2. Missions. 3. Christianity and culture. I. Title.
BV3790.A34 2010
269′.2—dc22
                                                          2010024422

10   11   12   13   14   15   16   7   6   5   4   3   2   1

For Terry

Contents

Acknowledgments

The idea for this project began with an invitation to do a weekend leadership seminar for First Presbyterian Church in Charleston, West Virginia. They were in between pastors and it seemed a good time to evaluate evangelism and forge some new directions. The weekend began with tension among those with differing perspectives on evangelism but ended with people talking across the room to one another, comparing notes on some of the dreams they had for ministries still "in the briefcase." Rather than tension between more conservative and more liberal session members, there was respectful listening, excitement, and affirmation. With a broader understanding of what Christian evangelism could be, barriers broke down and even those with differences headed down the road together.

I left that church with a great sense of excitement. This was a group of people dedicated to the work of the gospel. They had been divided falsely between caricatures of evangelism that were not really incompatible when understood as full-orbed theologies. Each group could find a place for its deeply held convictions. Each could see the other's views in the biblical narrative. Each could grasp how changing contexts became crucial in planning approaches for witness and presence. Conflict had been transformed into cooperation, lethargy into motivation. A graceful evangelism was taking shape.

As with any book project, many people helped and encouraged me along the way. Thanks go to colleagues at Louisville Presbyterian Theological Seminary. Colleagues Marty Soards, Dianne Reistroffer, and Cliff Kirkpatrick each read parts of the manuscript and gave invaluable advice. Faculty member Elizabeth Walker and President Dean Thompson gave chapel sermons that elegantly demonstrated graceful evangelism. Dean David Hester gave unstinting support as did the LPTS Board of Trustees, which generously gave me a sabbatical to work on the project. Students gave feedback on chapter contents as we struggled together to devise a way through the evangelism impasse that plagues the churches. Thanks also go to Baker editor Jim Kinney for his invitation to write this book, for his enthusiasm, and for the skill and patience of the editors who worked with me to bring it to publication. To my husband, Terry Muck, goes the biggest thank you, both for his wonderful support and for the integrating theme of *graceful evangelism*.

To readers and critics, I thank you beforehand for your comments and dialogue, which I hope will lead to greater understanding about the role that a graceful evangelism can play in today's church and world.

Frances S. Adeney
William A. Benfield Jr. Professor of Evangelism and Global Mission
Louisville Presbyterian Theological Seminary

Introduction

What This Book Is About

The word *evangelism* evokes strong reactions from Christians and non-Christians in American society today. To many Christians it is a word full of hope. Evangelism is the way to spread the good news that Jesus Christ came into the world to save us. Evangelism is the way to fulfill Jesus's injunction to "go into all the world and preach the good news to all creation" (Mark 16:15). It is our mandate, and we should pursue it vigorously.

To other Christians evangelism is "the E word." Evangelism is the way to alienate non-Christians and embarrass the church. Evangelism is an outdated way of announcing that Jesus Christ came into the world to inaugurate the kingdom of God. The church should find other ways to demonstrate the paths of justice that Jesus came to show us. After all, when Jesus announced his ministry in the synagogue, he focused on preaching good news to the poor, proclaiming freedom to the captives, and releasing the oppressed (Luke 4:16–19).

To some non-Christians evangelism is the way superreligious Christians push their views onto others with equally valid religions and ways of understanding the world. To others evangelism is a way some people protect themselves from the harsh realities of a world where every person looks out for his or her own interests, where resources are grabbed by those who can get them, and where political wrangling often gives way to open conflict. To still others evangelism is an irritating way people who haven't kept up with the times try to get others to follow an outmoded religious tradition.

How did we get to this impasse? Conflict about evangelism—what it is, whether we should do it, how to go about it, what results we seek—is dividing our churches. Where did this conflict come from, and how can we address it? The battle among views of evangelism rages and exacts a toll from congregations and denominations as they argue over definitions and strategies of inviting others to follow the Christian way. Should the church attempt to evangelize around the world, or should we concentrate on our local situation? Should we try to bring people of other religions to Christ, or should we affirm the religions of others? Should congregations try to grow numerically, or should we nurture our life together and hope that others will be attracted to the church?

In the wider society, the battle takes the form of arguing over religion in the public sphere, including debate about prayer in schools, posting the Ten Commandments in high school hallways, and announcing Christian holidays in schools, shopping malls, or town squares. To protect freedom of religion, our society is moving away from specific Christian references about Christmas, for example, to more general ideas that don't push Christ as "the reason for the season." Coke ads replace Christian symbols with snowflakes, "Merry Christmas" becomes "Happy Holidays," and Tiny Tim's famous line from Charles Dickens's *Christmas Carol* morphs from "God bless us every one" to "Bless us every one" on street banners in San Francisco. There are good reasons to protect people from having religious views foisted upon them and to be careful not to offend the religious sensibilities of others. But Christian evangelism no longer has the cultural support of general consensus and struggles to find a fit in our pluralistic society.

This book attempts to assess this situation and move toward a more graceful approach to evangelism. We will analyze the past, take stock of the present situation in evangelism, and find a way forward—a way that will reduce conflict and infuse energy into practices of Christian evangelism. We begin in chapter 1 by looking at some contemporary definitions of evangelism—definitions that bring people together and definitions that divide. We examine the inclusive definitions of church councils and denominations, both evangelical and ecumenical. We look at definitions of evangelism that have grown out of people's lives and their actions. How we define evangelism influences ways we are likely to cooperate and compete with other churches, denominations, and mission organizations. As times and circumstances change, definitions of evangelism are reformed. New alliances of Christians are formed around those changing definitions. Sometimes new ways of understanding evangelism and new configurations of organizations working on evangelism lead to conflicts. Those conflicts arise not only from changing definitions of evangelism but from our history.

Part 1 of this book deals with evangelism as shaped by biblical and historical models. It asks the question: "Where did we come from?" Where have we come from as a church, and as Christians who love God and want to share God's love with others? Has evangelism always been understood in the ways that we in American society today understand it? How has the church navigated the issues of plurality, conflicts of interest, and diverging theologies of evangelism in the past? We will examine patterns of evangelism used in the church over the centuries. We will focus particularly on crucial transitions in the ways the church has responded to the surrounding culture—the Reformation, the Great Awakenings, the nineteenth-century worldwide mission movement, and the fundamentalist/modernist controversy in the early twentieth century. Understanding the past helps us recognize where our own views came from and how they might be reordered to address current situations and foster future possibilities.

Chapter 2 examines five biblical models of evangelism. During Jesus's lifetime he showed again and again what it meant to evangelize. He spoke words of hope; he declared a new day; he insisted that the way to God was through him. Jesus himself is a model for evangelism. As we follow the paths he walked during his life, we will become light to the world. Relieving oppression as a declaration of Christian faith is another biblical model of evangelism. Jesus stood up in the temple and declared that his mission in life was to loosen the bonds of oppression, heal the lame, and give sight to the blind. For Jesus, declaring the time of salvation meant changing oppressive structures and bringing healing to the world. A third model—the Great Commission—finds its source in words that Jesus reportedly said after his death and before his ascension into heaven. He charged his disciples to follow him in preaching, teaching, and calling all nations to follow his way. The apostle Paul adds another model to this list of ways to evangelize when he instructs Christians to live their daily lives as a witness to the love of God. Finally, the apostle Peter reminds Christians to be ready to give an answer to anyone who asks why they live with hope in a world filled with suffering. These five biblical models each result in different approaches to evangelism.

In chapter 3, we look at how these biblical models were carried out through the centuries that followed. Evangelism began in a persecuted church, but its shape evolved with changing situations. New Testament models were adapted and transformed by the church fathers. Evangelism of a different kind was practiced by monastics in the fourth and fifth centuries. Medieval modes developed as the church ascended to a place of power in European society. The Reformation saw renewal and a changing focus on what it meant to live one's life as a witness to Christ. Modern philosophical frameworks have influenced evangelism, and colonial expansion took Christian witness in new directions. Today various liberation and contextual models address Christian witness in a time of postmodern thinking and globalization.

Current denominational and congregational conflicts about evangelism can be understood only against the backdrop of the history of the Western missionary movement of the nineteenth century. Chapter 4 takes a more in-depth look at nineteenth-century models of evangelism, particularly in the American context. As we look back two hundred years, we see changes in the shape and scope of evangelism and its relation to the role of Christianity in America. We see differences in the way denominations understood and practiced evangelism, in the United States and in other countries. We see different results in various locations.

As we get a grasp on where we have come from, we begin to better understand the complex situations we face today. Part 2 of the book is devoted to the question: "Where are we now?" What concepts of evangelism guide our thinking, and what emotional responses does the word evoke for various sectors of society? We will examine where the real conflicts are and outline areas of compatibility among varying views. We will look at the situation of churches and analyze some current theologies of evangelism that deepen congregational life and foster unity in denominations. We will look at the diversities of culture in the United States and ask what theologies and strategies of evangelism might fit into those diverse settings.

Chapter 5 begins by outlining the situation for evangelism in the twenty-first century, again from an American perspective. A world of cultural diversity and religious pluralism confronts a church that is no longer the dominant voice in public life that it may have been a century ago. Philosophical understandings of relativism and the limited nature of all knowledge have influenced views of Christian faith. Postcolonial critiques of Christian mission cause us to take seriously the potential harm some approaches to evangelism may have in certain contexts. The fundamentalist/modernist controversy, rather than ending, has taken new forms—forms that pit Christians with different theologies of evangelism against each other. Finally, the mishandling of evangelism by charlatans and well-meaning but naive proponents of wealth through Christian faith have turned some Christians away from doing evangelism in any form. This chapter addresses each of those issues, finding that they yield both positive and negative results for evangelism.

Christian evangelism links us to the worldwide church. Chapter 6 describes how mission trends around the world influence evangelism patterns in the United States. The growth of the church in Africa and Latin America has produced missionary activities from those continents to the United States, Asia, and Europe. An increased focus on national church leadership in countries that have previously been "mission fields" of the West has resulted in fewer missionaries going to those places. A decline in support for US-based denominational missions has corresponded with a growth in congregationally based mission and evangelism efforts. The recognition of women's leadership roles in evangelism and mission has also changed the face of Christian evangelism. Those changes are reordering, refocusing, and realigning US mission efforts around the world.

Addressing today's mission trends along with our history results in a number of contemporary theologies of evangelism, the topic of chapter 7. For some Protestants, proclamation—preaching the Word—takes a central place in approaches to evangelism. For others, justice and service have become key ingredients to evangelism and mission. Some Catholic churches take a "threshold approach," sharing Christianity with anyone who crosses the threshold of the church building. Orthodox churches evangelize by their presence in a community proclaiming the gospel through performing liturgical services. A liturgical approach to evangelism claims that the worship of the congregation is, in and of itself, evangelism. To others, welcoming all into the community as part of the human family speaks eloquently of God's love for the world.

Monumental changes for both the American and the global church press us to ask the question, "Where are we going?" which we take up in part 3. What is it we are aiming at when we speak of evangelism? What goals do we set as Christians for evangelistic activities? Perhaps we are not trying to achieve the same goal as the nineteenth-century mission movement, reaching the world in one generation. Perhaps our goal has changed since the middle of the twentieth century, when the worldwide Christian movement began to work for unity as the World Council of Churches. What is it that we want to accomplish through Christian evangelism for the twenty-first century? Perhaps God is doing a new thing, or many new things. We want to attune ourselves to what God is doing in the world, gaining insight into God's plans for the future. And we may not all come up with the same insight. We will look at reasons for diverging goals and ways to foster peace among those with different convictions about the future of Christian evangelism.

Chapter 8 refocuses the goal of evangelism to fit the current situation under the umbrella of seeking abundant life. Jesus's promise of abundant life provides a good metaphor for the good news that the world seeks and that God, through Christ, longs to provide. Abundant life begins with relationship with God. It includes good news to the poor and joyful fellowship among God's people. As we experience abundant life in ourselves and in our communities, we want to bring it to others.

As churches and individuals devise approaches to evangelism that recognize the uniqueness of each situation, they must come up with a mission statement for evangelism, the subject of chapter 9. The process of discernment that results in a concise statement on evangelism includes looking around us, assessing needs, and cooperating with others. We strive to be open to others' opinions about what the good news is and how it might be shared. We learn to listen across difference. We learn to reach into our own congregations, developing the spiritual life of our community. We learn to receive good news from sister churches, community organizations, and missionaries sent to us.

Chapter 10 reminds us to pay attention to our context. As our context changes, we need to name present realities and stop operating as if past realities are the norm. Through recognizing the importance of our history and assessing the dangers and uses of it, churches can move forward into new dreams. Christian traditions provide us treasures from the past. Imagining new possibilities for the future keeps us in touch with our current situation. As we struggle to experience, articulate, and share abundant life with others, it becomes clear that Christians in the United States are not just sharing the good news. We are *receivers* of the good news of the gospel as well. We can develop an appreciation of new contexts that can help transform Christian mission. This chapter presents exercises to help congregations explore their history and current context in order to devise forms of outreach that will bring abundant life to others.

Reformulating evangelism must be done in each generation. There is no one way that will suit every situation or fill every need. Part 4 asks the "how to" question: "Can we craft a graceful evangelism?" The church is not a static entity, either in its institutional structures or in its universality. Fulfilling the purposes of God in the world is a task too big for us. And yet it is a task to which we are called. We need to find ways of moving beyond our "evangelism wars." We need to come to a new and more graceful way of approaching the gospel in our settings, learning to appreciate how others might do evangelism *differently* in their own settings. The next crucial task, then, is developing theologies and methods of evangelism that address contemporary realities with a sensitivity to tradition while remaining true to the biblical models.

Chapter 11 describes how insights from contemporary theologies of evangelism can move congregations into a more graceful modus operandi in evangelism. Tacking between theologies of evangelism, finding our calling in an array of approaches, discerning a fitting response to the needs of a culture or community—all these steps can be taken as we discover a plethora of approaches to address particular needs.

Challenges in our pluralistic society also confront congregations as religious pluralism becomes more evident in our communities. Chapter 12 outlines some of those challenges and how they can be addressed. Interfaith marriages, a young person joining another religion, political questions in the public realm regarding other faiths, a pastor's relationship with religious leaders in the community—these and other challenges are discussed in this chapter.

Some of those challenges are currently being addressed by new movements and religious institutions, and chapter 13 outlines several of these approaches. A graceful evangelism can find roots in community movements and outlets in new mission directions fostered by congregations and denominations. Although change proves difficult for some groups, others are at the vanguard of new contextual theologies and strategies for reaching contemporary people with the good news of Christ's gospel.

Change can be just as difficult on a personal level as it is on an institutional level. How does a person gain knowledge and begin to understand those who have different and sometimes offensive views of evangelism? Chapter 14 focuses on how to see through the eyes of others who are different. It outlines a spiral of knowledge for understanding what confronts us in our congregations, communities, and the contexts of our evangelism efforts. Beginning with a recognition that our perspectives are shaped by our experiences, we move on to meeting a new situation with open eyes. Can we talk about evangelism despite our differences? Can we lay aside our convictions about the "only way" to do it? Having ears to hear, both from our sisters and brothers and from churches to which we minister at home and abroad, can alert us to new situations that demand refashioning our approaches to evangelism. Listening to what our culture is saying and to how others frame the issues of life's meaning also requires openness. We may need to recognize our inability to understand the viewpoints of others. We may need to reevaluate our own views on the basis of contemporary needs or as a result of the ideas of Christians with whom we associate. Going around the spiral of knowledge brings us to new understandings—then we go around again.

As we recognize multiple biblical models of evangelism in changing and varied contemporary contexts, our practices of evangelism need clarification. We need to devise an approach to living that fosters graceful evangelism. Chapter 15 suggests that a metaphor of gift giving and receiving may be apropos for doing evangelism in today's contexts. This chapter outlines seven "radical habits" for evangelism that show how the giving and receiving of gifts can be lived out in Christ's way. They can be used in multiple settings, with different evangelistic approaches. Recognizing the universality of the gospel message, putting hospitality first, honoring the free choices of others, respecting oneself and others, communicating the gospel in a myriad of ways, learning to love, and practicing ecumenism in evangelism are practices that can lead us into graceful evangelism. Taken together these seven practices reflect attitudes and actions that are consistent with the biblical message of Jesus as the Way, the truth, and the life.

As we explore the past, recognize the complexities of contemporary contexts, discover the goodness in theologies not our own, and form radical habits of acceptance and love toward others, not only the world but the church can hear the good news of the gospel. We can develop an evangelism that holds deep convictions while respecting the convictions of others, an evangelism that is both determined and patient, vigorous and tolerant. In short, we can imagine and craft a graceful evangelism.

PART I

Where Did We Come From?

1

What Is Evangelism?

Perspectives and Problems

Where Do We Start?

Before we can look back to see where we came from, we need to be clear about what we are looking *for*. What is evangelism? What does it include and exclude? Who defines it and for whom? How do we recognize evangelism when we see it in action?

When it comes to evangelism, everyone wants a piece of the pie. Missiologists, statisticians, ecumenical associations, denominations, congregations, and individual Christians all get into the act. Some claim universality for their view of evangelism; others insist their ideas are just personal opinions. Some people want to evangelize the world; others, their neighborhood. Some claim that evangelism is irrelevant to today's society or even harmful to American culture.

Sorting out the myriad perspectives, opinions, definitions, and biases of people using the term *evangelism* in American society today can be quite a challenge. In this chapter we will order definitions into three categories: inclusive definitions, ideological definitions, and lifestyle definitions. In the first category, inclusive definitions, we will look at the World Council of Churches and the Lausanne Covenant statements on evangelism, seeing how they define the turf and what differences can be seen between them. Next we will turn to ideological definitions, seeing how various groups understand evangelism in their context and discovering how their definition helps shape their identity and goals. Finally, we will look at lifestyle definitions, investigating how people act on their idea of evangelism, what activities they undertake, and what results they hope for.

Inclusive Definitions

Looking at the statements of denominations and church councils in the twentieth century, one might think there was unanimity in the church on the issue of evangelism. When I first began teaching evangelism at Louisville Presbyterian Theological Seminary in 1999, I had students in my Evangelism and Modern Society class compare statements on evangelism by denominations and umbrella organizations like the World Evangelical Fellowship and the World Council of Churches. Much to the students' surprise and chagrin, the statements were surprisingly similar. While ordered somewhat differently, they each included the idea that the gospel must be preached in word and deed. People's needs must be met, the poor should not be forgotten, justice must be served, and the witness of the church must include teaching and making disciples.

Yet sharp disagreements about what constitutes evangelism and how it should be practiced were as rampant among this class of eighteen students as they are in the Protestant church in the United States today. Most students assumed that their opposing views of evangelism were rooted in their denominations and the umbrella organizations with which they affiliated. But when they analyzed statements of those organizations, they found little disagreement.

What was going on here? Most students get their impressions of denominational teachings from their congregations. And in most Protestant denominations today, there are congregations that practice traditional forms of evangelistic outreach and those that use indirect strategies or even reject evangelism altogether. As students absorb those theologies and practices, they learn to oppose, on both theological and practical grounds, practices that differ from their own.

For example, in the Presbyterian Church (USA), the denomination of the majority of the students in that class, some congregations support Frontier Fellowship, a mission outreach that focuses on evangelism in a pointed way. Working with Kurdish refugees in England and seeking people who want to join the church is one of Frontier Fellowship's evangelistic outreaches. The Lafayette/Orinda Presbyterian Church in California, as a "mission-minded" congregation, supports such outreach. Other Presbyterian Church (USA) congregations would not dream of doing evangelism so directly. Montclair Presbyterian Church in Oakland, only thirty miles from Lafayette, is one. They sent a group of congregants to Indonesia in 1996. Their mission was to visit churches and seminaries, explore the cultures of Indonesia, and get a better idea of the role of Christianity in Indonesia. Montclair Presbyterian Church did not even consider this effort evangelism, but rather considered it a goodwill tour that put congregants in touch with Indonesian Christians and their diverse cultures. This is as close to evangelism as Montclair Pres wants to get. Both congregations are Presbyterian. Both have very different ideas of how to spread the good news of Jesus's way. And they consider those views incompatible with each other. The Lafayette congregation seeks to convince people from many countries to become Christians and join the church; the Montclair congregation wants to understand churches and cultures of other lands but not attempt to change them in any way.

Yet the PC(USA) policy statement on mission asserts that "the message we are called to bear is the Good News of salvation through Jesus Christ. The PC(USA) claims responsibility for bearing the Good News in this way: 'The Church is called to be Christ's faithful evangelist going into the world, making disciples of all nations . . . ministering to the needs of the poor . . . engaging in the struggle to free people from sin, fear, oppression, hunger, and injustice'" (George 2004, 121). That denominational statement on evangelism includes both proclaiming the good news and struggling against injustice, both making disciples and serving the poor. Because some congregations focus on one part or another of that inclusive statement, it is not surprising that seminary students from Presbyterian churches disagree vehemently about evangelism. And both sides think they are doing what the denomination teaches.

Statements crafted by other denominations gathering together to work on Christian evangelism exhibit a similar inclusivity. The World Council of Churches continues to affirm its 1975 statement on evangelism "that the Christian community should be assisted to proclaim 'the gospel of Jesus Christ, by word and deed, to the whole world to the end that all may believe in him and be saved'" (Scherer and Bevans 1992, 75). It also states that,

> Since our mission serves the coming reign of God, it is concerned with bringing the future into the present, serving the cause of God's reign, the New Creation. . . . We are called to exercise our mission in this context of human struggle, and challenged to keep the earth alive, and to promote human dignity, since the living God is both creator of heaven and earth and protector of the cause of the widow, the orphan, the poor and the stranger. To respond to all this is a part of our mission, just as inviting people to put their trust in God is part of that mission. The "material gospel" and the "spiritual gospel" have to be one, as was true of the ministry of Jesus. (74)

Statements by the Lausanne Committee on Evangelization show a similar inclusivity. Despite differences between the two organizations on eschatological issues, the Lausanne Covenant (1974), reaffirmed at subsequent regional and international meetings, connects evangelism with the kingdom of God, as the church is a sign of his kingdom (Scherer and Bevans 1992, 300). At Manila in

1989, Lausanne II stressed ecumenical cooperation in evangelism and linked social work and political action with evangelism that was committed to the biblical gospel (301). "Jesus not only proclaimed the Kingdom of God, he also demonstrated its arrival by works of mercy and power (Matt. 12:28). We are called today to a similar integration of words and deeds (1 John 3:18)" (297).

Both the conciliar and the evangelical global statements on evangelism focus on the broad themes of working for God's future, proclaiming salvation through Christ, seeking justice through socially responsible action, and serving the poor, sick, and needy. Both groups stress the importance of ecumenical cooperation in these evangelistic efforts.

The inclusivity of those statements is sometimes overlooked by Christians who feel a strong allegiance to one side of the Christian movement or the other. Sometimes congregations focus on either seeking justice and serving the poor or preaching the gospel and making disciples.

Ideological Definitions

With such broad, biblically based, and theologically sound definitions of evangelism, why are the churches so divided on this issue?

The problem of definitions of evangelism occurs in part because inclusive definitions of denominational statements are neglected by congregations. Instead, congregations either favor a narrower definition of evangelism or, if using an inclusive definition, focus on one aspect of that definition. The result is ideological definitions that divide.

Ideologies are simplified views of the world that are useful in many ways (Adeney 1994). They serve as a kind of map that highlights the most important features of the landscape or worldview of the group espousing the ideology (Geertz 1973, 220). They show the most clear and direct routes to a chosen destination. Ideologies of evangelism direct us to the goals of doing God's will, showing the way to salvation, and bringing God's justice to the world. Ideologies also serve to motivate people to action. When we understand that the God of the universe wants us to act to make disciples of all nations, to bring good news to the poor, and to announce the coming reign of God, we want to act decisively to bring about those changes in our world.

Ideologies focus on clear motivational aspects of a subject, ignoring complexities and tangential issues. Ideological views of evangelism motivate congregations to act in a particular direction, for example, for social justice or for church growth. By focusing on a narrow sphere of action for evangelism, oppositions develop among congregations.

One often hears the statement "This is a very mission-minded church." That usually implies a traditional view of evangelism. The congregation sends missionaries to the inner city or overseas to make disciples of Christ in those places. It is concerned for all people everywhere to name the name of Christ, and it is proud of its efforts to make that happen around the world.

Another common statement is "This is a peace and justice church." Despite the inclusive positions on evangelism and mission taken by the denomination or ecumenical affiliation, that statement usually implies that traditional mission and evangelism is unnecessary or even harmful. Chapter 4 explores convincing postcolonialist critiques that show that Christian mission work and Western colonialism went hand in hand in many countries during the nineteenth century. Congregations influenced by those critiques see proclamation evangelism as an outmoded way of relating to people of other cultures and different faiths. What is needed, in their view, is mutual understanding and dialogue. Such congregations may send educators, health workers, or political activists to other countries and are proud of their efforts to bring peace with justice to others at home and abroad.

Inclusive denominational and ecumenical statements broaden views of evangelism. What produces conflict in denominations and sometimes in congregations are those narrower views that pit one view of evangelism against another view. Peace and justice views can exclude preaching and teaching about the gospel. Proclamation and making disciples views can exclude working for peace and justice in structural and political forums. Those ideological definitions can be balanced and expanded by a study of ecumenical and denominational policy statements on evangelism.

Lifestyle Definitions

A narrow ideological definition of evangelism does not necessarily lead to a narrow sphere of action. The lives of persons doing evangelistic or mission work illumine a different picture. Studying the biographies of missionaries or interviewing missionaries in various locations shows a more complex "lived" definition of evangelism (Adeney 2009).

"The Call," a story in the *New York Times Magazine*, highlighted Mark and Barbara Blank of Baptist Mission to Kenya (Bergner 2006). This evangelical couple's main concern is the salvation of a small tribe in North Kenya. They long for the tribe to accept Christianity and live in the freedom of the gift of eternal life through Jesus Christ. As their ministry is described, however, it turns out that healing the sick, helping the poor, and working for the rights of women occupy most of their time. Their lives fit the inclusive definitions of denominations and ecumenical organizations better than they fit either of the ideological definitions described above.

Albert Schweitzer, one of the pioneers of health missions to Africa, illustrates the complexity from the other side. Mistrusting his theology of the person of Jesus, the Paris Missionary Society rejected his candidacy as a missionary to the Congo (Marshall and Poling 1971, 97). It did not recognize his calling to a ministry of healing as Christian mission. After much struggle, it finally agreed to allow him to go to the Congo but would neither support his work nor allow him to preach. Schweitzer assured the society that he only wanted to be a doctor and, as to preaching, he would be "mute as a fish" (103). After showing fellow missionaries on the mission field that he was not interested in foisting his theological views on them, Schweitzer was released from this promise (133). But his ministry continued to be one of living out his faith by serving the medical needs of the African community. He also built an organ and played hymns every evening for the community. Soon a congregation formed. One photo shows a Christmas communion service with thirty to forty Africans participating (Marshall and Poling 1971). The gospel was preached through service and worship. Schweitzer's "lived definition" of evangelism included Christian worship with people who somehow heard and believed the good news of the gospel through his work.

Knowledge and Context

Besides differing definitions, the *location* of those doing the defining also influences understandings of evangelism. Our social and historical location informs both the parameters and the goals of our understanding of evangelism.

Many Christians think that their way of understanding evangelism is the way it has always been understood. A study of church history shows that multiple understandings have operated over the centuries. Chapter 3 describes ways that the early church, Reformation thinkers, and others during the past two thousand years understood and practiced evangelism. Their contexts—what was going on in the societies of their day—influenced them. They could not see beyond their own time, although they could learn from the past. The same is true for our understandings today. Studying our contexts and appropriating our historical heritage aids our understanding of evangelism. Study of other contexts and experiences of Christianity in different cultural, economic, and social locations also broadens our understandings. But we cannot get away from the basic fact that our experience and milieu greatly influence how we understand evangelism.

H. Richard Niebuhr put it this way: "We are in history as a fish is in water" (1960, 48). The fish is not conscious of the water as a habitat. The fish does not realize how thoroughly its life depends on the water and cannot imagine life without that secure environment. As people, we depend on our environment too—the context in which we grew up and presently live is like the water around the fish. We are not always aware of the life-giving sources of our knowledge and our security: our family upbringing, our congregation, the neighborhood in which we live, the schools that shaped our thinking, the media that influences our understanding of the world around us. These things in our context are so familiar, so close to us, that we rarely think of them as crucial to our knowledge.

We rather like to see ourselves as independent thinkers who figure out problems, analyze situations, and decide what to believe. But actually our knowledge is dependent on our context—our experience of the world close to us. That context includes not only economic and cultural factors but also social factors—who we know and are influenced by.

Knowledge, rather than coming from objective sources, is inherently social. "All knowing involves an acknowledgement of other knowers" (Niebuhr 1989, 40–41). To learn, one must hear from someone; one must trust someone. And so knowledge is bound up with imperfect people who might be in error, and with promises they tacitly make to speak truth, although they may not always do so (40–41).

Garrison Keillor describes his upbringing in a strict Plymouth Brethren sect. He remembers the first time he questioned the wisdom of the elders. He was young, a preteenager. And he surprised himself by questioning the veracity of the Christian doctrines he was being taught. It was a *kairos* moment—a moment when he knew that the knowing being passed on to him was partial and just possibly in error.

We begin in a social context. That context shapes us. The ways we perceive and understand are influenced by those around us. Because our knowing is so connected to our social location, we end up mirroring the perceptions and opinions of others. And because we are often *unaware* of the influence of our context upon our ideas, we often see our perspective as the only valid one.

Our context, then, limits us. We cannot see beyond the boundaries of our experience, including our experience of the biblical texts, the church, and our faith as we know it. To understand more, to broaden our views, we need to expose ourselves to different perspectives and seriously try to learn from them rather than simply opposing them.

In that way we can begin to influence our context. We are not passive recipients only. We actively engage in life in our world. As our horizons expand, we can put forward a new way of thinking about and practicing evangelism. Sidebar 1.1 gives you a chance to explore how your view of evangelism has been shaped by your context, how it has been limited by that context, but also how your response can change that situation. If we are not open to new ways of looking at an issue, conflict can easily arise because Christians have not all had the same background of experiences with evangelism.

Sidebar 1.1 Context Worksheet

Location, Location, Location!

Break into small groups of four to five, discuss your location. Illustrate each of these points with an example from your own life, the life of your congregation, a social or ethnic group you belong to, your society, or even the world context. Choose a scribe and jot down ideas on flip chart paper. Spend about ten minutes on each question and then regroup to share ideas for twenty minutes. This exercise takes about one hour.

1. "We are in history as a fish is in water." *Location*: Our location includes our past and the traditions of our faith as well as family and cultural heritages. Give an example of how your history influences the way you understand the world.
2. Our context shapes us. *Formation*: Share an experience of how some facet of your context influences your thinking and behavior, for example, a changing neighborhood, a new job or retirement, recent political events, news of natural disasters, a new pastor at your church, or a change in your family through birth, death, illness, or relocation of a loved one.
3. Our context limits us. *Limitation*: Talk about how a recent choice, of your own or of your congregation, narrows your possibilities for the future. Discuss the pros and cons of that focusing process.
4. We shape our context. *Transformation*: Recall a decision that changed the direction of your life, as an individual or as part of a group. Brainstorm about decisions your session could make, pathways that could be created, that would transform your congregational life in some way.

Evangelism Shaped by Context

Current views of Christian evangelism are a prime example of contextual framing. Every year in my evangelism classes, I ask students to recount an incident in their lives that helped shape their view of evangelism. I hear stories of wonderful models of Christian love and witness. I hear stories of inept models of witness that resulted in pain and a rejection of Christian evangelism altogether. When we get to definitions of evangelism, it isn't surprising that people with positive experiences and those with negative experiences define evangelism differently.

In *Shadow of the Almighty*, Elisabeth Elliot describes the death of her husband, Jim, at the hands of the South American Auca tribe when he and fellow missionaries attempted to bring the gospel to them. She describes him as a martyr for the gospel (1958, 12). So that his sacrifice would not be in vain, she continued to reach out to those tribes, and eventually they were brought to Christ. Despite the loss of her husband, Elliot holds a positive view of assertive evangelism. Practices linked to that view include going to places where the Christian gospel has not been heard, translating the Bible, preaching and witnessing to the love of Jesus, and planting churches.

By contrast, Barbara Kingsolver recounts her negative experiences with assertive but inflexible evangelism in *The Poisonwood Bible*. She describes a rigid and controlling father who could only practice as he had in the United States. He planted his garden, organized his family life, and preached the gospel without adjusting to his new context. His efforts to evangelize tribes in Africa met with tragic results for both himself and his family. Kingsolver's rejection of Christian evangelism is tied closely to this family history. She has not lost her concern for the people, but instead of traditional evangelism, she has turned to political witness to foster human flourishing among the Congolese.

A third response, one of total rejection of Christian faith, has been taken by Darcey Steinke. In her memoir, *Easter Everywhere*, Steinke recounts her childhood experience with devoted Christian parents who sacrificially gave of themselves to others but neglected to address her questions about God. Her Lutheran pastor father eventually lost his faith while continuing to don the cloth. Steinke's devastation has led her to a vague spirituality that couldn't satisfy her deep longings (Metcalf 2007, 11).

Each of those responses—joyfully continuing traditional patterns of evangelism, turning from traditional evangelism to other forms of witness, or leaving Christianity altogether—is common in our society. Understandings of evangelism necessarily differ markedly among those who experienced evangelism in such differing ways.

Students at Louisville Seminary are still in the church and thus split between the first two options. Their definitions of evangelism vary widely, reflecting a deep divide among churches today. Some want to joyfully preach the gospel; others want to spread the gospel without words. All are concerned for the world, but their ways of reaching out seem diametrically opposed. The divide among student opinions reflects their positive or negative impressions of evangelism. Those responses are often learned in their families and congregations.

If it were simply a matter of discord between a few Presbyterian students at a seminary in Kentucky, this wouldn't be a problem. But the positive and negative responses to traditional evangelism have grown strident and oppositional in the Protestant churches of the United States. Some Protestant churches define themselves as "evangelical," others as "peace and justice" churches. Some churches have individuals of both persuasions within a single congregation. That often leads to conflict about how evangelism should be conceived of and practiced.

American Individualism and Evangelism

Views of evangelism become even more complex when we consider the individualistic turn that American society has taken over the past century. A significant characteristic of our US culture is a focus on the individual as the source of achievement and the reference point for gauging success and happiness. Although families and associational organizations like churches influence us, we Americans tend to look to ourselves in seeking meaning and making life choices. Rather than appeal to ecumenical or denominational policy statements, or even to congregational leaders, many Christians want to define and practice evangelism in their own way.

Robert N. Bellah, with a team of researchers, did a study on the character and habits of middle America (mainly white middle-class or upper-middle-class folks on both coasts) in the 1980s. Unlike most sociological studies and much to the surprise of the team, the book became very popular. *Habits of the Heart: Individualism and Commitment in American Society* was widely read and was sometimes used in church discussion groups. The study struck a chord with a certain class of Americans, many of whom populate our Protestant churches.

The study focuses on four cultural traditions: the biblical tradition and the republican tradition upon which the nation was founded, and two kinds of individualism that have grown up since the Enlightenment in Europe. Expressive and utilitarian individualism have become the first languages of our society, according to Bellah. Although the biblical and the republican traditions still operate, they have become secondary to the claims of individualism on the lives of Americans (Bellah et al. 1985, 51).

The American frontier attracted people who sought a better life and were willing to risk everything to find it. A "bootstraps" approach to living, which insisted that each person find strength in himself or herself to succeed, became attractive, and stories of the "self-made man" in America became popular. This was the "promised land" where with diligence and hard work one could realize "the American dream." Success depended not on family connections, social conditions, or even economic status but on a do-it-yourself determination that defied all obstacles.

It is not surprising that in such a climate, utilitarian individualism became the creed of many. Benjamin Franklin epitomized this philosophy with his emphasis on saving time and money and doing what works to succeed. His daily notebook of goals and steps to meeting them became the inspiration for the popular Franklin Covey calendar system used by efficiency-minded Americans today.

Expressive individualism was a reaction to this daily duty and disciplined approach to life. According to this view, industrialization was making humans into machines. The steel industry was only one instance of how people became subject to incredibly oppressive working conditions and were forced to accept low wages that put them permanently in debt to a company. The reaction of poets, like Walt Whitman, and people who lived experimentally, like Henry David Thoreau, focused on getting back to nature and experiencing the joys that life had to offer. The focus was still on the individual, but rather than ask, "What works for me?" they asked, "What feels good and fulfills me?"

That emphasis on the individual has grown stronger in American society in the last century. Utilitarian and expressive individualism have become "first languages" in our society, relegating traditional biblical and republican foci to the status of "second languages." Ambiguities result from the strengthening of these "first languages" of utilitarian and expressive individualism. Since values increasingly find their source in the individual, they become separated from traditional communal values. Even if "what works for me" in business is a dishonest practice, for instance, if it works it is still good. Reference to the biblical tradition that has fostered trust by emphasizing honesty in business dealings is undermined. The individual becomes less accountable to a community. The standards for behavior that one develops individually are standards that are "good for me." The idea is that no one else, and no community, should be the arbiter of my values. In this way the individual becomes autonomous and separated from moral obligation in community.

Another result is that people are drawn away from communities and any commitment to them. Robert Putnam's book *Bowling Alone* uses bowling as a metaphor for this trend in American society. Putnam notes that although there are more individuals bowling today, there are fewer league bowlers. More often, people bowl alone. This isolating trend makes contributing to public life, or the life of the church or other voluntary organizations, less attractive as individuals lead their "private" lives.

The trend toward individualism and the resulting ambiguities for societal life have influenced Christian views of evangelism. Rather than focus on inclusion in community, much evangelism focuses on individual gain or fulfillment. "Come to Jesus and he will fulfill your desires for wealth," for example. Paula White's ministry, The Seven Promises of the Atonement, reflects that utilitarian individualistic emphasis. She promises that if you follow a certain pattern of approaching God during the season of the Jewish New Year, God will give you material blessings. One of the steps is to send money to her ministry—an essential step, as it turns out. She discourages people from giving the money to their pastor or church because, as an individual, you must find your own way to God. In this way, the evangelist separates the Christian from her or his congregation. The appeal is one of utilitarian individualism—follow these steps on your own and God will bless you.

Expressive individualism also influences evangelistic content and messages in our society. Finding fulfillment, realizing your potential, and experiencing peace through knowing Jesus are emphasized in many evangelistic outreach programs. You will "become who you are meant to be," "get in touch with your true self," and "experience peace and joy" if you come to Christ. Again, the emphasis is on the individual, quite apart from his or her context in community, church, or family.

Evangelism that is disconnected from biblical sources and church tradition leaves the individual without the support of a congregation and without the nurture of the biblical texts. Salvation becomes getting what I want or feeling the way I want to feel. Such emphases in evangelism have attracted many people but have also dismayed many others. If evangelism is simply getting people to send money to an evangelist, if it is merely a ploy to get rich, or if it is simply a feel-good fix, evangelism becomes so narrow that it becomes un-Christian.

This is not a new problem, although it takes new forms in our society. The apostle Paul dealt with the same problem in his letter to the Philippians. It seems that church leaders were concerned that some evangelists were preaching Christ out of selfish ambition rather than to spread the good news of God's salvation in Christ. Paul recognized that "some preach Christ out of envy and rivalry, but others out of goodwill" (Phil. 1:15). He tells them to let those preachers alone because, whether they preach Christ from false motives or true, Christ is preached (1:18). When we think about evangelistic techniques that seem abusive or those that are practiced by charlatans for material gain, we cringe. But in God's grace even such imposters can reach a person hungering for God.

Calling and Evangelism

Individualism can have positive effects also, as it helps a person focus on her or his calling by God. Many Christians called to special ministries have faced huge problems. Their independent spirit and conviction that God's Spirit has called them strengthened their determination to follow God's call. *Sisters of the Spirit* recounts the autobiographical writings of three African American women called to be evangelists in the late nineteenth-century United States. Their strong individualism helped them to persevere in their very special callings.

Because evangelism taps into our personal gifts and sense of call, it takes many forms. A person called to a healing ministry may define evangelism by focusing on wholeness and well-being. One who is called to preach may use a more proclamation-oriented definition. In 1 Corinthians 14, the apostle Paul outlines the gifts and callings of Christians in the church. He mentions evangelist and teacher, healer and encourager. Each of those gifts aids the spreading of the gospel and the growth of the church.

In the broadest sense, every Christian calling spreads the gospel as the lives of Christians and Christian communities show the love of God to the world. June Rogers' book, *And God Gave the Increase*, tells the stories of Christians from around the world who are called to work in theological education. The witness of their lives and the educational institutions they support combine with the powerful witness of the leaders they train to demonstrate God's grace. As we grapple with relevant forms of contemporary evangelism, we may want to revisit the gifts listed in 1 Corinthians and see whether a more inclusive definition of evangelism relating to calling might arise.

Sometimes a person's calling leads him or her to an attraction for one definition of evangelism over another. One's background, context, and theology may predispose one to define evangelism as proclamation, witness, seeking justice, social service, making disciples, presence, or worship, to name a few options. Those definitions need not be mutually exclusive but can build upon one another collaboratively. The next chapter describes biblical models of evangelism, showing how evangelism can cover a breadth that makes the definitions given above collaborative and not exclusive.

Context and Conflict

Nonetheless, conflict over evangelism increasingly poses a crisis in US Protestant churches. Opposing definitions of evangelism are just the tip of the iceberg in this conflict. David Barrett and Todd Johnson list seventy-nine definitions of mission in their study of mission trends (2001, 42–45). Other factors in this crisis include a diffused authority for evangelism, criticisms of traditional evangelism from scientific and postmodern critiques, the increasing presence of other religions and confusion about how to address them, and a perceived irrelevance of traditional approaches to the contemporary felt needs of many Americans. Those issues will be taken up in chapter 5.

Our context shapes us, our context limits us, but we also influence our context. We are not passive recipients of cultural change but active agents in the world. How we respond changes the situation around us. In the next three chapters we will look to our past for wisdom in understanding how evangelism has been understood over the centuries and how we have arrived at the perspectives and problems that face evangelism in our Protestant churches today.

2

---○---

What Does the Bible Say?

Biblical Models of Evangelism

The Basis for Evangelism in the Early Church

Looking back into our history to discover how evangelism was thought of and practiced, we begin with the biblical text. The Christian faith grew out of Judaism. At Advent Christians celebrate the story of the birth of a baby boy born into a family in the line of King David. As Jesus grew, he preached and healed; he admonished his people to follow God; he sought economic justice and demanded allegiance to the true meaning of the law. Jesus focused his attention on the people of Israel, reading Torah in the synagogue, preaching to the people in the open air, healing those who sought his help, training his disciples to follow the ways of righteousness.

After all, Israel was carrying the message of God through its community. The Law of Moses, encrypted on tablets of stone, was carried in the ark of the covenant. The movable tent of meeting had been replaced by a great temple in Jerusalem. The people gathered to hear the Word of God in their synagogues. This was the world into which Jesus brought his message.

The universality of the message of the good news began to be felt during Jesus's lifetime. When a Canaanite woman asked Jesus to heal her daughter, he told his disciples that his work was with the Israelites. She insisted, however, that some of the benefits of his power should fall to those outside the circle of Judaism. And he healed her child (Matt. 15:22–28).

It was as though a crack of light pierced through an opening door. After his death and resurrection, that door widened and the light poured through. Paul, a high Jewish official who had been persecuting the followers of Jesus, suddenly encountered God on the road to Damascus. The light blinded him; his life turned around. He became a follower of Jesus.

Paul wanted the Jews to accept Jesus as the Messiah. But he kept finding himself drawn to preaching to those outside the house of Israel. Athens, Corinth, Rome, Philippi—Paul preached the gospel of Jesus Christ in all those gentile cities. He realized that he had a special calling to take God's good news to the gentiles. The message itself was a universal message: "All have sinned and fall short of the glory of God and are justified freely by his grace through the redemption that came by Christ Jesus" (Rom. 3:23–24).

Evangelism through the work of the apostle Paul took on a number of new dimensions. Part of Paul's ministry became explaining the way God was now working with humanity through Jesus Christ. The book of Romans is a treatise on the new thing that God was doing in the world through the life, death, and resurrection of Jesus. The law shows us that we have sinned and can never measure up to God's standards (Rom. 3:19–20; Gal. 3:10). But the grace of God overcomes the law, reconciling us to God and giving us access to God's grace (Rom. 5:1–11).

Rather than seeking to follow the law to the letter, the task of Jesus's followers became accepting God's grace through Jesus Christ. A new freedom entered the lives of the followers of Jesus. No longer bound by the law, Christians became free to practice the goodness that the law enjoins (Gal. 5:13–14).

Those new revelations became part of the Christian way in those early days. Spreading this new good news to all who would hear became a major focus of early Christianity. Paul took three missionary journeys, traveling throughout the Middle East regions, taking the message with him wherever he went. As a prisoner on his final journey to Rome, Paul continued to speak this universal message of grace to all he encountered.

Christianity from its inception was a missionary religion. The truths about the one God became available to all peoples through the work of Christ. God's plan of bringing all things together in Christ had taken a giant step with the birth of Christianity (Eph. 1). The emphasis on carrying God's truth through the community of the Israelites broadened into a focus on teaching and making disciples of all nations, a task that had been given to the disciples after Jesus's resurrection (Matt. 28:19).

Many features of the ethical mandates given to the Israelites became features of the outreach of Christians in those early days. The Jews were instructed to give hospitality to the stranger and not to oppress the alien (Exod. 22:21). Like the three visitors to Abraham and Sarah, and like the foreigner Ruth, whom the widow Naomi took back to her Israelite community, many strangers were welcomed, given food and shelter, and some of them became permanent members of the community.

The early church followed this pattern of hospitality, holding all things in common and caring for those in need (Acts 2:44–45; 4:32–35). Communities of Christians helped one another across the miles as well, sending monetary aid to the church at Jerusalem during a time of economic upheaval. Caring for

Sidebar 2.1 Five Biblical Models of Evangelism

Evangelism, witnessing to God's love in word and deed, is a basic calling of the church. Throughout Christian history, evangelism has been practiced in different ways, using Scripture as a basic guide, interpreting biblical passages in their own unique contexts. The following five models of evangelism are tied to their biblical contexts. Note when, where, and to whom each passage is written. Think about how these models might be used in the contemporary context of our congregation, denomination, and society.

1. **The Great Commission**. Matthew 28:18–20: "And Jesus came and said to them, 'All authority in heaven and on earth has been given to me. Go therefore and make disciples of all nations, baptizing them in the name of the Father and of the Son and of the Holy Spirit, and teaching them to obey everything that I have commanded you. And remember, I am with you always, to the end of the age'" (NRSV).
2. **Jesus as Model**. John 17:18, 22–23: "As you have sent me into the world, so I have sent them into the world. . . . The glory that you have given me I have given them, so that they may be one, as we are one, I in them and you in me, that they may become completely one, so that the world may know that you have sent me and have loved them even as you have loved me" (NRSV).
3. **Daily Living**. Philippians 2:12–15: "Work out your own salvation with fear and trembling; for it is God who is at work in you, enabling you both to will and to work for God's good pleasure. Do all things without murmuring and arguing, so that you may be blameless and innocent, children of God without blemish in the midst of a crooked and perverse generation, in which you shine like stars in the world" (NRSV).
4. **Speaking of Hope**. 1 Peter 3:15–16: "In your hearts sanctify Christ as Lord. Always be ready to make your defense to anyone who demands from you an accounting for the hope that is in you; yet do it with gentleness and reverence" (NRSV).
5. **Relieving Oppression**. Luke 4:18–19: "The Spirit of the Lord is upon me, because God has anointed me to bring good news to the poor. God has sent me to proclaim release to the captives and recovery of sight to the blind, to let the oppressed go free, to proclaim the year of the Lord's favor" (NRSV).

the poor, the orphan, and the widow became part of the witness of the early church. In these and other ways, seeking economic justice—a common theme of the prophets of Israel—also became incorporated into Christian witness.

The early church modeled its ethical behavior on the pattern of the revelation to the Jewish community. The Old Testament was still a guide, although the message of salvation through Jesus broadened to include all humanity. The task of explaining God's wonderful grace shown through Christ, the mandate to make disciples of all nations, and the assertive outreach to communities that were not part of the house of Israel were added to the types of witness already practiced by the Jewish community: hospitality to strangers, care of the poor, economic and political justice, and the witness of the community itself.

Biblical Models of Evangelism

Jewish and early church facets of witness become incorporated into New Testament models of evangelism that we practice today (see sidebar 2.1).

The Great Commission

The Great Commission provides the most overarching biblical model for evangelism. So much is included in this mandate of the risen Christ that it gives a very full picture of the missionary task of the early church. "And Jesus came and said to them, 'All authority in heaven and on earth has been given to me. Go therefore and make disciples of all nations, baptizing them in the name of the Father and of the Son and of the Holy Spirit, and teaching them to obey everything that I have commanded you. And remember, I am with you always, to the end of the age'" (Matt. 28:18–20 NRSV). Matthew tells us that after the resurrection and before Christ's ascension into heaven, he gave this mandate to his disciples. In this passage, Jesus promises his presence even as he assigns to the disciples the task of spreading the news that he is the way to salvation, to knowledge of God, to heaven. But the passage does more than that.

It describes the disciples gathered on a mountain in Galilee, a place that Jesus had told them to go. Their response is obedience—they gathered on the mountain. When they saw the risen Christ, they worshiped, but some doubted (Matt. 28:17).

Matthew's Gospel emphasizes the continuity between the Jewish faith and the disciples of Jesus. So it is not surprising to see the authority of the risen Christ emphasized by this rendition of the disciples' obedience, their worship of the risen Lord, and his words that he has, indeed, been given the authority of God. The church is established by that authority, and the words of the Christ are instructive not only to individual disciples but to the com-

Sidebar 2.2 The Mission of the Church

Using the term *mission* broadly to include the work of the church in the world, the following five facets describe the church's mission in a productive and integrated way.

1. A unified, engaged praxis:
   - Engagement (spiritual, intellectual, and practical) in the affairs of the church at home and abroad and also in local, national, and international communities and issues
   - A confident posture toward building up the church and influencing societal life
   - An integrated view of mission that includes congregational ministry, evangelism, and international partnerships
2. An affirming approach to pluralism:
   - Practicing interreligious association and dialogue on the basis of mutual respect
   - Forming cross-cultural partnerships in local and international communities
   - Accepting cultural differences in the body of Christ and in our communities
   - Learning from other religious and differing manifestations of the church
   - Working toward national policies that preserve and celebrate ethnic, religious, and cultural difference
3. A confident evangelism:
   - Telling the story of Jesus
   - Describing how God's love and grace affects our lives
   - Demonstrating the effects of the good news by living the Christian faith
4. A concern that acts to address justice issues:
   - Poverty and affluence
   - Environmental preservation
   - Gender inequities
   - Ethnic/racial discrimination
   - Human rights and responsibilities
   - Peace among nations
5. A covenanted community of God's people:
   - As the source of all evangelism and mission
   - As a community of support of families and individuals, relating to one another in love and mutual respect
   - As a learning community, striving to understand how the Bible relates to us as the people of God
   - As a discerning community, seeking to hear the voice of God among us
   - As a worshiping community, giving praise and honor to the source of our life

munity that is established by this authority. "Go and make disciples of all nations" is a tall order. It involves more than itinerant evangelizing. It implies establishing communities of faith that can baptize and teach people to obey everything that Christ commanded (Matt. 28:20). The love that Jesus taught as the beginning and the end of the law is now to be embodied and taught in communities among all nations or groups of people.

"But some doubted." Here they were, seeing and hearing Christ on the mountain. "When they saw him, they worshiped him" (Matt. 28:17). Still there was doubt among some. How reassuring to modern Christians, influenced by the doubt of the Enlightenment, hesitant because of the overextension of the scientific method, convinced by arguments of the social construction of reality that we cannot know reality. Our doubt is part of our faith—we have partial knowledge. Even the disciples on the mountain had partial knowledge. Some doubted. But the church was established after Christ's resurrection, and it flourishes today.

The evangelism that springs from the Great Commission is not a narrow proclamation but a full-orbed work of mission through the church (see sidebar 2.2). We cannot even imagine the process of discipleship apart from the church. Moreover, we are promised the presence of Christ with us as we work: baptizing, teaching, worshiping, and witnessing to the resurrection. We use this model today—telling the good news through liturgy, teaching the gospel in Sunday school classes, patterning paths of discipleship for our young people, modeling the values of the kingdom of God in our communities. As we understand the ecclesial dimension of evangelism put forward in this great commission, we may realize that our congregation is doing more evangelism than we thought.

Examples of how the Great Commission model is used in evangelism can be taken from both mainline and evangelical branches of the contemporary church. William Abraham in *The Logic of Evangelism* demonstrates the ecclesiastical nature of this model. He encourages churches to strengthen their role in making disciples, from preaching the gospel, to baptism, to nurturing the life of faith, to telling the good news through liturgy. In Abraham's view, those activities of the church become a foretaste of the kingdom of God on earth (1989, 138–39). The ultimate goal of evangelism becomes building the kingdom, and the church plays a large role in that long-term effort.

The Billy Graham crusades also used the Great Commission model for evangelism. Those gatherings of thousands were backed by local churches that took on the task of discipling those who responded to the call. The first step, coming to Jesus "just as I am," cannot stand alone. Those who came forward in response to the call to a new life were counseled by local pastors, taken into their churches, and brought to a deeper knowledge of Christ through discipleship, fellowship, and worship (Muck and Adeney 2009, 201).

The Great Commission call to evangelism stresses both individual and community dimensions. Making disciples has to be done individually, one by one. That was the focus of the Billy Graham crusades. But baptizing, teaching, and "observing all that I have commanded you" are community activities. No one is baptized alone. Practicing the spiritual and ethical injunctions of Christian faith—"walking the walk"—is not done in isolation. William Abraham focuses on the community dimensions of the Great Commission (1989, 138–39). The community of the church functions as the witness to the life freely given by grace through faith. The Great Commission mandate is rich and full. It includes seeking individuals, discipling in communities, witnessing through the life of the church.

All of these instructions come with a promise from the risen Savior: "I am with you always, to the end of the age." The work of evangelism focused on individuals, the work of discipling Christians, and the work of witness through ministries of the church are each augmented by the presence and help of the Holy Spirit, Christ with us (Matt. 28:20; John 14:26).

Jesus as Model

The promise of the presence of Christ in our lives lends immediacy to the biblical injunction to follow Jesus as model. Through patterning our lives after the life of Jesus and by the grace of God working in our lives, we become a witnessing presence to those around us.

In the Gospel of John we read, "As you have sent me into the world, so I have sent them into the world. . . . The glory that you have given me I have given them, so that they may be one, as we are one, I in them and you in me, that they may become completely one, so that the world may know that you have sent me and have loved them even as you have loved me" (John 17:18, 22–23 NRSV).

Here the early church is reminded that the call to witness in the world is modeled after Jesus's call from God. The setting is a meal where the disciples gathered to begin the Jewish Passover celebration (John 13:1–2). Jesus washes the disciples' feet, showing a graceful love for those present (John 13:5). He knows who in that company will betray him, and yet he lovingly washes Judas's feet. He predicts his own betrayal and comforts the disciples (John 13:21; 14:1). He enjoins them to love one another, obey his teachings, abide in him, and expect the Holy Spirit to come to them (John 13–15). In the middle of the discourse, Judas dips the bread into the bowl with Jesus and then rushes out to betray him (John 13:26–30).

As the group is sundered by that horrendous act, Jesus prays for the disciples—that the unity he has with God will spread to them as a witness to the world (John 17:11, 22–23). From this prayer we learn that we are sent by Christ, as Christ was sent by God, to show God's love to others. Like the Matthew passage, the reader peers into a liminal space, feeling with the disciples both the incomprehensibility of Jesus's coming death and the incredible possibility of oneness with God. But the calling is clear—the disciples and believers to follow would be connected in love to Jesus and through him to the Father. Jesus was at one with God. And Jesus longs for his followers to be one with him. And because of that unity, the world would know of God's love.

This passage opens the Christian call to evangelism to all the methods used by Jesus himself to minister to others and convince others to follow the Christian way. Healing the sick, dispersing the money changers (those who would profit from the gospel), dialoging with outcasts like the woman at the well, dining with sinners and those despised by the proper folks—these radical habits of Jesus can be emulated as part of our agenda to display the love of God to all. The unity of Jesus and the Father now spreads to us.

Abiding in the vine, doing all that Jesus commanded us, embracing the Spirit of Truth—those forceful passages from the Gospel of John outline in more detail how we can model our lives after Jesus's example (John 13–17). As Christians we are called and sent to be the graceful presence of Jesus in the world.

Advocates of justice like Martin Luther King Jr., exhibitors of Christian love like Mother Teresa, and spiritual leaders who deeply connect with both God and society like Thomas Merton and Dorothy Day guide us in the use of this model today. Each spoke from within the church, declaring a unity with God that spilled out into the world. Their lives exhibited the love of God for people and society, a special care for the downtrodden, an anger at evil and injustice, and an overarching grace that allowed the presence of Christ to permeate their lives.

This incarnational model can also be seen in the lives of missionaries who gave everything for the cause of Christ. Hudson Taylor's China Inland Mission took Christians to China, where they adopted the customs, dress, and ways of the Chinese, and learned to speak and think in their language. They modeled the graceful attitudes of Jesus, showing the unity of Christ's body across cultures and distance. Many never returned to their homeland.

We find another example of that incarnational model in Ida Scudder, daughter of missionary parents in India. She vowed she would never become a missionary or practice medicine like her parents. Her intention was to never return to India at all. But to her surprise, the call of Christ took her back to India as the first medical doctor to work with women. Scudder founded a hospital that still reveres her memory today. She went to the hardest place of all for her, modeling her life after the life of Jesus (Anderson 1998, 609–10).

This view of evangelism as dedicated presence can protect Christians from narrow definitions of evangelism that limit us and are sometimes practiced ungracefully. Jesus's responses to others, while often surprising, always fit the situation. Sometimes he spoke. At other times he was silent. In every situation he showed compassion for the weak, anger at injustice, and a willingness to hear what others had to say. He not only taught but learned from others like the Canaanite/Phoenician woman who begged him to heal her daughter, even after he refused. Using Jesus as a model for evangelism can help us develop graceful responses to complex human and social situations.

Daily Living

As Jesus becomes our model, his life has an effect on our daily lives. The Epistles take up the task of showing Christians how our lives should be lived.

Paul admonished those in the church at Philippi to "work out your own salvation with fear and trembling; for it is God who is at work in you, enabling you both to will and to work for God's good pleasure. Do all things without murmuring and arguing, so that you may be blameless and innocent, children of God without blemish in the midst of a crooked and perverse generation, in which you shine like stars in the world" (Phil. 2:12–15 NRSV). Here Paul instructs Christians to live differently than those around them. It is a call to a life lived with honesty, patience, and grace. Paul reminds the Christians that God is working in them to help them do what they truly want to do: live a life that brings glory to God. And the result? A Christian witness that makes them "shine like stars in the world" (Phil. 2:15 NRSV).

As they traveled together, encouraging new churches, the apostles focused on the role of *Christian values* in spreading the gospel. The decadence of the failing Roman Empire placed Christians in an ethically challenging environment. Paul and Timothy encouraged the church at Philippi to live a life "worthy of the gospel of Christ" (Phil. 1:27). They claimed that as Christians lived out their faith, the good news would be proclaimed in the values that they practiced.

In other letters, Paul explains some of those values. He exhorts the rich to do good, to be rich in good deeds, liberal and generous, thus laying up for themselves a good foundation for the future, so that they may take hold of the life that is life indeed (1 Tim. 6:18–19). He encourages the Corinthians, whether rich or poor, to excel in the grace of giving (2 Cor. 8:7) and to work so that they can share with those in need (Eph. 4:28). He encourages the Corinthians to search for the best spiritual gifts (1 Cor. 12:31) and shows them how to restore Christians who need to overcome moral failures (2 Cor. 2:7–8). He outlines the best way to demonstrate Christ's power and presence in the world, the way of Christian love (1 Cor. 13).

The values of the kingdom of God, worked out through the lives of persons called to do the work of God, proclaim the gospel in powerful ways. Comforting the grieving, helping the sick, and inviting the poor to share our bread are acts that shine because they are different, and because they are good. Even simple things, practiced unselfconsciously, like avoiding profanity and being honest in small ways, become signals to others. Living the life we are called to live as Christians—walking in the way of faith, hope, and love—*is* evangelism.

Our knowledge of God spreads an odor that we are not even aware of. To some, it is a fragrant odor of life, to others its smells like death itself (2 Cor. 2:14–16). The fact that our lives exude an odor that attracts those who are seeking God and repels those who are running from God clinches the argument that daily living is, indeed, evangelism. Christ is a stumbling block for those who are doggedly going their own way, rejecting his claim of love upon their lives. And Christ is, on the other hand, attractive in graceful ways, like the odor of a delicate flower, to those who are seeking life. As Christians grow in grace and the knowledge of Christ, the good news is proclaimed through their daily lives. They become like an open letter of God's grace—a letter that all can read (2 Cor. 3:2–3).

Speaking of Hope

Carrying the odor of Christ through the witness of our daily lives doesn't mean that we never use words to tell how God through Jesus has given us new life. In the apostle Peter's first letter, he says "In your hearts sanctify Christ as Lord. Always be ready to make your defense to anyone who demands from you an accounting for the hope that is in you; yet do it with gentleness and reverence" (1 Pet. 3:15–16 NRSV).

The liminal experiences with the risen Christ strengthened the early Christians to believe and practice their faith in nearly impossible circumstances. In this letter, the apostle Peter writes to Christians persecuted and scattered by the fall of Jerusalem in AD 60. In his first letter, he describes the hope Christians have because of the resurrection of Jesus Christ (1 Pet. 1:3–12). He tells the Christian refugees, those who lost everything in the war, that they have a lasting inheritance (1:4). Although they have never seen Christ, they love him, they believe in him, and they experience joy and salvation. In their hearts they know that Christ is Lord. And that in itself is an inheritance to be grateful for.

Peter then enjoins them to prepare their minds for action, to practice self-control, to set their hope fully on the grace found in Jesus Christ (1 Pet. 1:13). Their salvation isn't instantaneous—they do not have wealth or security in the world. But their faith itself gives them hope, for the present as well as for the future. And they should be ready to tell others who ask about this hope the reasons for it (3:15). For others will see in them a different attitude toward life. Others were left homeless in the war and perhaps despaired, even of life itself. But Christians in the same situation experienced hope. They knew that Christ is Lord. And Peter tells them that they should be ready and willing to explain this hope to others. He also tells them how to do it—not with arrogance or triumphalism but with gentleness and respect (3:15–16). Gracefully, we might say.

This mild mandate encourages us to be alert to opportunities to tell others how God operates positively in our lives, to speak of ways that the redemption we know in Christ actually works itself out. We may find ourselves in difficult circumstances. There may be illness in our family, economic disaster looming on our horizon, political turmoil in our nation. But we have hope because, in our hearts, we know that Christ is Lord. How do we speak about this hope? The emphasis here is on compassion and humility, speaking only when the moment is right, and relying on God to use our words of hope in the lives of others. This way of approaching evangelism can empower those whose gifts center on empathy and support. It does not require assertive proclamation but focuses on listening and care.

In a pluralistic society, it is not always appropriate for national leaders to loudly assert their beliefs. Yet speaking of hope can be done "with gentleness and respect" even by national leaders. When Eleanor Roosevelt headed up the United Nations Commission on Human Rights, she encouraged the writing of a document that could be accepted by nations and individuals practicing many religions or no religion at all. Yet she was always ready to speak of the hope within her, praying nightly and letting others know that doing her best and trusting God would be her modus operandi (Glendon 2001, xi and 25). Desmond Tutu, moderator of the Truth and Reconciliation Commission in South Africa following the end of apartheid, also frequently spoke of the Christian hope within him. When asked by the president to serve on the commission, he immediately organized a spiritual retreat for the newly appointed members. He then called for prayer at the beginning and ending of their meetings, a public witness to God's presence in the process of reconciliation (Tutu 1999, 80–81).

As Christians we believe that our salvation is both now and yet to come. Our faith in God's sovereignty allows us to rest. Christ is Lord. We hope for that which is not seen and yet we have joy in the salvation of the present as well. Our hope in Christ makes us bold, giving us the freedom to behold the face of God and be changed by God's likeness and then the courage to speak of that hope within us (2 Cor. 3:12–18).

Relieving Oppression

"The Spirit of the Lord is on me, because God has anointed me to preach good news to the poor. God has sent me to proclaim freedom for the prisoners and recovery of sight to the blind, to release the oppressed, to proclaim the year of the Lord's favor" (Luke 4:18–19).

With this passage we come full circle back to the beginning of Jesus's earthly ministry. Here Jesus reaches into the Jewish tradition by doing a public reading of the Hebrew Scriptures in the synagogue. He recounts in the words of the prophet Isaiah a graphic description of what justice could look like (Isa. 58:6; 61:1–2). The prophet's words spoke of preaching good news to the poor, releasing captives, restoring sight to the blind, setting at liberty those who are oppressed—in short, proclaiming that it was God's time to do justice on the earth.

But Jesus did not just read the Scripture and sit down. Instead, he declared that *he* was the one who would do this work. In doing this, he followed a tradition of interpreting prophetic passages in layers of time. The prophecy may have been fulfilled in some way in Isaiah's day, yet it would also find fulfillment in some way in the future. Jesus declared, in effect, that the future was at hand, and that he was the one Israel was waiting for, the Savior and Redeemer of the Jewish people. The folks in his home synagogue in Galilee were just not ready to hear that.

We in the church today interpret those words in different ways. Some believe that the kingdom of God will be established after the promised return of Jesus to the world. Others, that the kingdom of God is gradually coming to be as God works through history and the church. In either case, the mandate to do justice speaks to Christians today. Those waiting for the imminent return of Christ want all to hear the good news of the gospel before that day comes. Without some partial justice in earthly affairs, that gospel is muted or goes unheard. Those wanting to do the work of God's kingdom now also understand the relevance of the life and death of Jesus to the work of the kingdom. Differences in eschatology do not necessarily lead to differences in action. We all know that just communities and societies are what God longs for on the earth.

From our vantage point, we can see further layers of Jesus's use of the prophetic voice. From Jesus's announcement, we can construe evangelism as proclaiming the gospel and bringing freedom, insight, and good news. We can construe evangelism as the work of bringing in the reign of God, announcing that the time of God's working justice in the world has come. We can also construe the declaration Jesus reinterprets here as a call to us to practice healing, to care for the weak, and to relieve oppression. The idea of the kingdom of God being present and "not yet" is crucial to each of those views of evangelism. Christians accept by faith the presence of God's kingdom on earth and work for its fulfillment, yet without seeing it fully operating in the world.

Sorting out the layers of prophetic texts needs to be done in each generation as the context and needs in the world change. Interpretations will differ from generation to generation and among different denominations, ecumenical bodies, churches, and cultures. Our task is to apply the justice focus of Jesus's public ministry to our time and place, interpreting how justice might be framed and heard in our contemporary world. But the call is clear—we are to work to free those who are oppressed, help the downtrodden, work for healing of persons and communities.

Timothy Richards, a Baptist missionary to China, shows us how evangelism strategies can change depending on the situation. He went to China as an evangelist, to preach the gospel. But cyclical famines in China prevented him from doing this effectively. He decided to return to the United States and study agriculture. He then returned to China as a journalist, spreading the word of better agricultural techniques that greatly reduced starvation in the area. People were starving, and relieving that oppression became a top priority in Richards's witness. It was the right thing to do. And it mirrored the wider missionary movement as it paved the way for a new generation of evangelists to spread the gospel (Walls 2002, 258).

Conclusion

Evangelism was done in many ways in the early church. We have looked at biblical models from Jesus's earthly ministry and his appearances after crucifixion. We have heard from the apostle Peter as well as Paul and Timothy. Although the models overlap, each one is distinctive enough to warrant examination and interpretation.

There are many ways to do evangelism in the church today as well. The five biblical models presented here can be used as we explore the possibilities for evangelism in our congregations and denominations. The models won't look the same in every time and place because each context cries out for a suitable model handled in culturally appropriate ways. Understanding the biblical models in their contexts is a first step. Using them in our own contexts is the task that lies ahead.

3

Patterns of Evangelism
through the Ages

When most of us think of evangelism today, we conjure up images of knocking on doors, handing out tracts, or preaching to natives in a far-off land. Those culturally stylized forms of evangelism certainly fit the definition. But most of them are of fairly recent origin. The nineteenth century saw a fervor for evangelism that followed two Great Awakenings in the United States. This movement sent Protestant missionaries all over the globe, taking with them not only the gospel but what they understood to be civilization itself.

But evangelism has taken many other forms down through the ages since the time of Christ. The church has witnessed to God's grace and Christ's power in multiple ways. Examining some of them will help us put Christian evangelism in historical context and broaden our understandings of what forms it can take in different settings.

Jesus's Ministry

A Prophet Arises

Prophets arose during Israel's history, especially at important junctures in its communal life. As in other religions, the prophets called the people back to their original vision. When it seemed that things were going wrong, or when the people ceased responding in justice and mercy toward their neighbors, a prophet would arise. Jesus's ministry began in this mode, following the examples of Miriam, Elijah, Isaiah, Jeremiah, Hosea, Amos, Anna, and others. When he stood up in the temple at the beginning of his public ministry, Jesus quoted Isaiah. He read the passage that proclaimed good news to the poor, the opening of the eyes of the blind, the curing of the lame, and that the day of the Lord was at hand (Isa. 61:1–2 quoted in Luke 4:18–19).

But Jesus did not just read the passage and sit down. He announced his prophetic ministry to the ears of all in the synagogue. "Today this scripture is fulfilled in your hearing" (Luke 4:21). Jesus became the first witness to the new work that God was doing in the world through him.

He continued this work of witness in his preaching and lifestyle. He called the religious leaders to account, exposing the hypocrisy of the Pharisees. He sought out people who needed and secretly longed to live more righteously, like the tax collector Zacchaeus (Luke 19:1–10). He showed a new way to recognize the full humanity of women, talking theology with the Samaritan woman at the well (John 4:7–25), praising Lazarus's sister Mary for pursuing spiritual wisdom (Luke 10:38–42), declaring that history would remember the woman who anointed his feet with oil (Matt. 26:6–13).

Jesus demonstrated the coming of a new day, and his words explained the characteristics of that new era. In the Sermon on the Mount, he blessed the meek, promised riches to the poor, and gave instructions for loving enemies that surely sounded unique to his hearers (Matt. 7:28–29). The kingdom of God would show a new way to live. And Jesus's ministry brought that kingdom to the earth gracefully.

The prophetic ministry of Jesus culminated in his death. He tried to prepare his disciples for this event; he attempted to help them understand that if he did not go away, the Holy Spirit could not continue the work of the kingdom into a new era (John 16:7). Of course they didn't understand. But Jesus's words were remembered when he appeared to them after the resurrection (Luke 24:8). They were written down, explained, and propagated. Jesus was the prophet and progenitor of the graceful evangelism that the church has been called to ever since.

The Inauguration of Graceful Evangelism

The word *grace* has many definitions and nuances. The theological use of the term indicates God's unmerited favor. An ethical use of the term connotes a willingness and openness toward others and a sense of what is right and proper. An aesthetic use of the term *grace* shows a beauty or winsomeness in actions or qualities, something that adorns and adds loveliness. The graceful evangelism practiced by Jesus was marked by each of these characteristics of grace (see table 3.1).

Table 3.1 Grace and Jesus's Ministry

Aspects of Grace	Jesus's Actions
God's unmerited favor	Grace of God upon him (Luke 2:40) Seeking God's grace through prayer (Matt. 14:23) Received grace to follow calling (John 1:14–17; Luke 22:27) Sought grace to escape cross (Matt. 26:39)
Disposition to grant something freely	Listened to needs of others (Luke 18:40–41; Mark 6:49–50) Fulfilled needs through healing, preaching (Mark 5)
Showing kindness, courtesy, charm	Listened to others' views (Mark 7:24–30) Responded to ideas of others appropriately (Luke 18:40–42) Willing to change point of view (John 4:46–50) Related to people with courtesy and compassion (Mark 8:2)
Qualities resulting from God's grace	Humility shown in donning human likeness (Phil. 2:6–8; Luke 9:48) Smoothness of adopting role of prophet (Luke 2:40; 4:14–22; 7:22) Ability to live in thankfulness to God (1 Thess. 5:18) Power to obey God (John 15:10; 1 Thess. 3:13) Strength to accept the way of the cross (John 14:30–31) Endurance through persecution and death (Matt. 27:45–50)

Jesus's life was characterized by God's unmerited love and favor, first toward Jesus himself and then through Jesus to others. We are told that as a child Jesus "grew and became strong; he was filled with wisdom, and the grace of God was upon him" (Luke 2:40). Jesus received gifts of grace from God that strengthened him in body and mind.

As he grew older and faced the challenges of his calling, Jesus sought grace from God. He frequently went to a solitary place to pray. He received grace to follow his calling—to preach and heal and tirelessly relate to disadvantaged people. He displayed that quality of grace that shows a disposition to grant something freely. He was able to listen to people's views, discern their needs, and fulfill them through God's unmerited favor, bestowed through him on those around him.

He healed the man who couldn't get into the pool quickly enough (John 5:1–8). He affirmed Mary's need to learn at his feet when her sister protested that Mary's role was in serving the guests (Luke 10:42). He healed Luke's mother when they arrived at her home and found her too ill to provide hospitality (Luke 4:38–39). He taught the people when they followed him to the shore because they were like sheep without a shepherd and needed his teaching (Matt. 9:35–36). He healed the woman who had hemorrhaged for twelve years as she boldly pushed through the crowd to touch his robe (Luke 8:43–48). He raised Lazarus from the dead because his family still needed him (John 11:32–44). In each of those actions, Jesus did what was asked of him. He didn't decide what each person needed. He listened to what people felt they needed. And he gifted them with what they needed—unmerited favor, the essence of grace.

Jesus listened respectfully and responded to the views of others. He didn't just explain how people should understand the kingdom, or family relations, or his own ministry—he listened. He was gracious, showing kindness, courtesy, and charm.

He listened to the theology of the Samaritan woman at the well (John 4). He met her on her own terms, dialoging with her about her theological views. Only after listening did he give his own theological perspective. And he kept it personal. It wasn't merely a theoretical theological discussion; it was a conversation that changed her life. But he listened first, with respect, and then he responded in a way that she could hear and understand.

When the Phoenician woman whose child was ill came to Jesus for help, he didn't seem so gracious. His response to her seemed rather harsh. He implied that his help was for the children of Israel, not for the gentiles. Yet Jesus allowed himself to be persuaded by the woman. She reminded him that outcasts could also benefit from the table of the rich. "Even the dogs under the table eat the children's crumbs," she said (Mark 7:28). And Jesus healed her child. It took a humble grace to "eat crow" in a public setting when confronted by someone of such low status. Jesus reversed his decision and went in a new direction because the woman confronted him. He let her argument sink in, and he changed his behavior. This interaction shows how deeply Jesus respected the views of others and how he could respond in a way that contradicted his earlier decisions. Grace and humility marked the interchanges between Jesus and these two women.

Humility is another aspect of grace. A graciousness that really listens, that doesn't insist on its own way, that honors the views of others—that kind of grace characterized Jesus's relationships with others. That humble graciousness was part of Jesus's calling. He was called by God into the world and into his ministry. Philippians 2 tells us how the Son of God became lower even than the angels, giving up his claim to equality with God, being born into a poor family, living as a servant to others on the earth. God's grace is evident in Jesus's calling and his willingness to accept it.

But Jesus's graceful evangelism contained more than the humble response to the needs of others. His prophetic ministry also called for transformation.

He said that his message would pit siblings against one another, children against parents (Matt. 10:34–39). People would be so changed by following him that other relationships would be affected, not always in positive ways. Jesus's good news demanded total allegiance. "Who is my mother, and who are my brothers?" he asked. "Whoever does the will of my Father in heaven is my brother and sister and mother" (Matt. 12:48–50). Jesus's message brought radical change to the lives of those who decided to follow him. Grace is apparent in this transformative process. Who would leave their parents, disagree with their siblings, and consider other followers of Jesus their primary family? It is only through God's grace that this radical reorientation occurs.

Paul explains this in Romans 1:5 when he says, "Through him and for his name's sake, we received grace and apostleship to call people from among all the Gentiles to the obedience that comes from faith." Both Jesus and his followers needed God's grace to reorient their lives to the way set before them.

That hard way also required many gifts of grace. The kind of grace that knows what is right and fitting lends a beauty to one's life. Jesus's life and ministry were characterized by that kind of adornment, the wisdom that will "set a garland of grace on your head and present you with a crown of splendor" (Prov. 4:9). Jesus's witness suited his context. He came into the world as a Hebrew baby and grew up within the religion of Judaism. He began his ministry as a prophet—a role common to his religion and familiar to his context. People knew what Jesus meant when he said, "Today this saying is fulfilled in your hearing" (Luke 4:21). Whether or not they accepted Jesus's prophetic ministry, they knew what he was talking about. Jesus didn't come into the world as an alien or an angel. He came as a participant who understood his setting and responded appropriately to it.

There is a certain gracefulness to coming in that way, a seamlessness between Jesus and his setting. Although Jesus's teachings and actions were radical and sometimes disturbing, he entered his ministry not with a jarring revolt but rather with a smooth entry into a role that was expected and appreciated.

Jesus also needed and received the gifts of God's grace required to be obedient to his calling and thankful for it. Many times he found himself tired, needing rest. He received the grace to be thankful, to persevere, to honestly meet each of those who sought his healing touch. And when his disciples couldn't pray with him, he forgave them, even as he forgave his persecutors. The gifts of God's grace were evident in Jesus's life until the last.

But Jesus did not receive every gift of grace that he sought. His prayer in the garden of Gethsemane hints at how difficult it was for him to fulfill God's ultimate claim on his life. "My Father, if it is possible, may this cup be taken from me," he prayed, "yet not as I will but as you will" (Matt. 26:39). Here Jesus was asking for the grace of a postponement or annulment of a required duty—a stay of execution. This grace he did not receive. Rather he found the strength of God's grace to take him through his final hours of trial. And in those hours Jesus himself displayed grace—the grace to do what is required, the grace to endure, the grace to forgive. How much grace was brought into Jesus's life during those hours we can never know.

But in a smaller way, God's grace is present with each Christian as all are called to bring the good news of God's salvation to the world. John records Jesus's prayer for his disciples: "As you sent me into the world, I have sent them into the world" (John 17:18). We can look back at Jesus's ministry of graceful evangelism and receive the grace to pattern our own efforts after his way.

Apostle Paul: Evangelist to God's Grace

Paul Encounters and Explains Grace

At first Paul, a zealous Jewish leader, was not happy with the impact that Jesus's life and death had on his community. Until accosted on the Damascus road, Paul used his rank and power to persecute the followers of Jesus (Acts 26:9–18). But that encounter changed his life direction. He found a new calling—to reach as many people as possible with the message of God's grace given through Jesus. He said that he was set apart for the gospel of God, receiving grace through Christ to call people to faith and to the obedience to God that comes through faith (Rom. 1:5).

Paul explains the way the grace of God works through Christ to bring people to that obedience, to the place where their lives are changed and they want to live differently. And through grace they find they are *able* to live differently (Rom. 5:20–21). Even before the law, God gave a promise to Abraham, a promise rooted in God's grace (Gal. 3:18). With the work of Christ, God's grace is offered universally to all (Rom. 3:23–24). It is God's grace that justifies humans through Christ's redemption (Rom. 5:15).

According to Paul, God's grace guarantees redemption to Abraham and Sarah and the many nations that came from them, unlike the law that is dependent on human actions (Rom. 4:14–17). So a Christian's standing is secured through grace. The gift of the gospel is given through grace, bringing a whole new

---

Sidebar 3.1 Paul and the Way of God's Grace

1. God's grace transformed Paul's life through the encounter on the Damascus road.
2. God's promise to Abraham was rooted in grace.
3. Jesus brings the way of God's grace to the world.
4. God's grace becomes available universally through Christ's work.
5. God's grace enables people to embrace God's promise of eternal life by faith.
6. A Christian's standing before God is guaranteed by grace.
7. God's grace brought through Christ saves us.
8. God's grace enables Christians to live in obedience to God.

way of living along with the promise of eternal life, because it is through grace that we are saved (Eph. 2:5, 8). Sidebar 3.1 sums up Paul's analysis of the prevalence of God's grace in his theology.

Paul was so excited about how God's grace can be received through Christ that he dedicated his whole life to explaining and sharing this message. He wanted to preach the gospel by all means to as many as possible, but especially where Christ was not known (Rom. 15:15–21). On his missionary journeys he went to synagogues, marketplaces, and shrines of other religions to appeal to all. He even acknowledged the usefulness of charlatans preaching from selfish ambition or rivalry because some might accept the good news even when it was preached with bad intentions (Phil. 1:15–18).

God's Grace in Action

Paul's letters are full of enthusiastic discourses and admonitions to Christians to continue in God's grace, to let it permeate their lives, to show it in actions. In 2 Corinthians 6, he told the Corinthians that they, having received God's grace through Christ, have a responsibility to live it out in their daily lives. He discussed how, because of God's grace, Christians were able to work and share their income with others (2 Cor. 8). He discussed the qualities that grace calls out in Christians' lives and their communities. Humility (Phil. 2) is a gift of grace. So is holiness and sincerity (2 Cor. 1:12). Grace engenders generosity toward others (2 Cor. 8:1–2) and gives strength for living (Gal. 2:21). Paul frequently referred to the influence of God's grace in his own life (Rom. 15:15–16; Eph. 3:8) and the lives of every Christian (Eph. 4:7; 1 Tim. 1:14; 2 Tim 1:9). The impact of God's grace continues after one accepts the gift of the gospel, becoming a source of new life for Christians.

Other New Testament writings add their voices to the chorus that shows grace as the source and an integral part of the gospel. Hebrews tells us that God's grace can help in times of need (4:16) and strengthen our hearts (13:9). In Acts, Luke shows how grace led to sharing possessions (Acts 4) and gave Stephen the fortitude to endure martyrdom (6:8). James stated that God gives grace to counter unhealthy human desires (4:6). Peter exhorted Christians to grow in grace and knowledge of Christ to avoid being carried away by the error of those who are lawless (2 Pet. 3:17–18). Jude warned against those who would change the grace of God into a license for immorality (Jude 4). Those sources confirm and explain the intricacies of the mysterious work of God's grace accomplished through the gift of the gospel.

Through his letters and missionary journeys, Paul articulated and spread the message of the gift of God's grace through Christ throughout Asia Minor in those early days. He gathered disciples, taught them, and sent them out to teach others about this new way that God was gathering the world together through Christ's work (Eph. 1). He traveled, sometimes taking disciples like

Barnabas and Timothy with him. He instructed new leaders, like Priscilla and Aquila, in the way and left them in cities to establish groups of disciples of Jesus. And so the church was born. We might call Paul the great evangelist of God's grace.

This turn of events did not sit well with the Roman Empire. The witness of the followers of Christ was too strong, too different, and too powerful. Here was a new sect that dared to defy *Romanitas*, the worship of the Roman emperor. Rumors began to be spread that Christians practiced despicable secret rites in their worship services. Nero blamed Christians for the burning of Rome in AD 70. Soon followers of the way were being arrested, jailed, and sometimes martyred. Crowds gathered in the Roman Colosseum to see Christians thrown to the lions. Sometimes the Christians went to their deaths singing. The two hundred years that followed Jesus's death were years of turmoil and persecution for the followers of Jesus's way. Evangelism during those centuries included not only spreading the good news of the gift of the gospel but sometimes facing martyrdom with courage.

Early Church Fathers: Defining and Institutionalizing of Christianity

By the second century the church had become a large movement. Institutional structures were formed, rituals were shaped, and leaders were assigned to carry out the rites of the church and to hold authority over members and congregations. Those leaders did not always agree on central ideas and doctrines. So councils were called to discuss Christian beliefs, define orthodoxy, and reject heresies. Many of the early church fathers participated in this solidifying of the church's forms so that its life could be orderly and vital.

This too was a witness. Without clearly defining the parameters of Christian belief and practice, Christian witness could not be perpetuated to future generations. During the first prophetic phase of a new religion, the dynamic presence of the leader, the oral transmission of ideas, and the energy of the community carry the teachings and practices forward. But once the leader and the first community are gone, structure is necessary to remember the tenets and rituals of the faith and pass them on to future generations (Weber 1946, 299). The process of institutionalization was a central part of the witness of the early church.

That process didn't always go smoothly. Theological debate was just that—debate. Debates over the humanity and deity of Jesus, the nature of the Trinity, and the use of icons were just a few of the crucial topics of the day. Those debates also had political import. The church at Rome focused on establishing the church and expanding its power.

Other leaders like Cyril (b. 826 or 827) and Methodius (b. 816) in Russia worked with the emperor of Byzantium to spread the gospel as well as the emperor's territories. They translated the Scriptures into the Slavic language and were accused of heresy for their trouble. Cyril also entered into many of the intellectual debates that solidified Christian theology at that time. Resisting the iconoclasts and the trilingual movement that wanted the Scriptures to be translated into only three languages also became some of Cyril's tasks (Muck and Adeney 2009, 105–6). The debates among churches became central in influencing how people of the day understood the world and how political powers were used.

Monastics: Witnessing through Community and Spirituality

The third and fourth centuries saw some Christians leaving the cities and forming monastic communities. They were places of study and contemplation, places in which one could develop spiritual insight and wisdom in the company of others. In most monastic communities a rule such as the rule of Ignatius set out patterns of prayer, Scripture reading, and devotion for the monks.

But those quiet monasteries turned out to be a great witness for Christ, both at that time and for later generations. St. Patrick formed one such community in Ireland after escaping from slavery in that strange land. Others were established on that model. Patrick welcomed all who were willing to follow the patterns set out in the community. He was convinced that belonging preceded believing (Muck and Adeney 2009, 94). After experiencing life in the community, individuals were drawn to Christ and became dedicated Christians.

Witness also occurred throughout Europe, Greece, and Asia Minor by the example of devotion and the ascetic practices of many monasteries. Witness to future generations also resulted as the monasteries preserved many intellectual works that were being destroyed by the failing Roman Empire. Witness to the power of Christ's way is still available to us through the writings of the monks themselves. Julia of Norwich, Hildegaard of Bingen, and St. Ignatius's rule all bring us wisdom today. The call to a deeper spirituality is as relevant to our own search for God as it was then.

Christendom: The Rule of Christ in This World and the Next

The Middle Ages brought another kind of Christian witness to the fore, the voice of the church in political affairs. Since Constantine had declared Christianity the state religion back in the fourth century, the church had exercised power and sometimes battled with kings over whose power should be held in higher regard.

Thomas Aquinas's rediscovery of Aristotle's works in the thirteenth century led him to articulate a lofty and powerful role for the church in societal life. Combining Aristotle's insights with Christian theology, Aquinas argued that the church had more knowledge of God's eternal law than human authorities. Those developments gave a strong voice to the church in matters of law and governance. Church order and rule applied not only to Christians but to whole societies. State churches were established in European countries where the powers of church and state worked hand in hand. Ensuing centuries brought out the problems of church and state convergence, but the idea that God longs for justice and uses governments to establish order still operates as a Christian principle in Orthodox, Catholic, and Protestant theologies.

Aquinas's style of rational argumentation also contributed to the development of Christian apologetics. In his work *Summa Contra Gentiles*, Aquinas argued for the veracity of Christian faith in a situation where strong convictions could be divisive (Muck and Adeney 2009, 117–18). He searched for agreement, using Muslim ideas and idioms to describe the beliefs of Christianity. He believed that reasonable argument would make the truth of the gospel plain. Aquinas's teachings on this matter make a huge contribution to developing a graceful evangelism for our own pluralistic age.

The witness of worship also played a part in evangelism in the Middle Ages. The great cathedrals of Europe were built by the common people, many of whom wanted to serve God in a tangible way. The church became the center of village life, declaring God's grace through worship and service. Corruption in the church of the Middle Ages damaged this witness but not irreparably. The witness of worship as a central form of evangelism still thrives in the Orthodox churches of Asia and the United States. The Reformation of the sixteenth century also worked to correct some of the problems that arose in the era of the centralization of power in the church.

Reformers: Rediscovering the Gospel Witness

During the sixteenth century, some Christians in Europe spoke out against excesses of church power that oppressed people and kept them from a deeper knowledge of God. Martin Luther reframed the gospel, recovering the theme of grace and forgiveness emphasized in the letters of the apostle Paul. John Calvin paved the way for a Christian witness through good governance and an emphasis on God's providence over all of life. Ulrich Zwingli focused on the special calling of the Christian community to proclaim the gospel. Certain high-ranking women in England risked their lives to persuade kings to understand the gospel in a new and personal way (Zahl 2001, 1). Theirs was an apologetics in action that changed the course of European history.

The reformulation of the gospel during the Reformation led to divisions in the church but at the same time reclaimed many of the gifts of the gospel that had been lost in the Western church over the previous centuries. Justification by faith for the individual, a focus on the importance of everyday life, an immediacy of contact with God, and an emphasis on God's overarching work through history are a few of those recovered gifts. The Reformation created whole new communities of Christians with new ways of understanding God's gracious work in Christ.

Christians in the Age of Reason: Cultural Interaction

The fermentation that occurred during the Reformation overlapped with the Enlightenment in Europe. The development of science, the rise of humanism, and the emphasis on reason, which had become prevalent with Aquinas in the thirteenth century, coalesced to define a new age. The Enlightenment's challenge to the authority of the church over all of life resulted in claims that through reason alone, human knowledge could be discovered and societies could be ordered. Philosophy and scientific inquiry began to be practiced without reference to the church.

Much was gained by this development as scientific and philosophical inquiry broke the bonds of church supervision. The physical sciences could proceed unhindered with investigations of physical matter, the human body, and nature. Resulting advances in medical and biological sciences, physics, and scientific theory are incalculable.

But there were losses as well. Christian theology now needed to defend its claims to God's work in the world and God's authority over all of life. Apologetics, the defense of the faith, came to the fore as Christians debated the veracity of Christian claims to truth. Christian communities that rejected some of the trends in society became a witness to a Christian way of life. Puritanism and Pietism became forms of witness that declared through their teachings and lifestyle that there was more to life than reason alone could discern. God acted through the witness of the church in society, and the Holy Spirit showed the way to a deeper understanding of the life God has for Christians.

Western Expansion: Spreading Christianity and Western Civilization across the Globe

The church and the state were closely intertwined during the centuries since Constantine. When European powers began explorations of the New World, Christianity was taken to the new colonies as part of those conquests. Spain, under King Ferdinand and Queen Isabella, saw conquest as part of the Christianizing process. Not until the natives were subdued and civilized could they begin to practice Christianity, they thought. Even under those harsh conditions, the proclamation of freedom in Christ was not silenced. The priest Bartolemé de Las Casas denounced the system of *encomienda*, which enslaved the natives of Central and South America. He spoke long and loudly of the full humanity of the natives and of God's gracious granting to all people the ability to understand and accept the gospel without the need for force (Muck and Adeney 2009, 129). This early argument for the freedom of religious choice later became a clarion call for freedom of religion as the American colonies transformed themselves into the United States.

Although the process was uneven, many Christian values became ideals in the new colonies and some were even enacted into law. The establishment of "the great experiment" of the British colonies, which became the United States, shows how Christian values of freedom and democracy were lived out in new ways. When John Winthrop gave his famous sermon on the ship the *Arabella* before arriving in the New World, he proclaimed that the community must become a "model of Christian charity" in which people extended care for one another even when it seemed beyond their ability (Bellah et al. 1988, 24). Winthrop still accepted class distinctions and did not want to do away with them and form a society of equals, but the Christian values of love for others and the good of the whole were dominant in his thinking. Winthrop longed for his new community to become like "a city set on a hill" showing to all that the ways of Christ were full of wisdom and grace (24).

Two Great Awakenings: Spreading the Good News in the United States

As the nation flourished, two waves of evangelical fervor spread the gospel in America. They were characterized by great consternation—a sense of sinfulness and lostness that overcame many. Jonathan Edwards, a teacher at what later became Princeton University, was called to the dormitory more than once to pray with students "under conviction." Preachers traveled, holding revival meetings that stressed the necessity of repentance and the dangerous consequences of the unrepentant heart.

During the Second Great Awakening, Charles Finney systematized that approach to preaching, and the modern-day evangelist was born. Many took up the call, including African American women like Jarena Lee, Zilpha Elaw, and Julia Foote. Their evangelistic messages included appeals to both personal salvation and social justice. Julia Foote officially became a missionary and the first woman deacon of the African Methodist Episcopal Church (Andrews 1986, 10). New sects grew up, and established churches flourished during those times of revival.

The Missionary Movement: Taking the Gospel to the Ends of the Earth

The marriage of economic and spiritual goals brought by colonialism to the New World resulted in confusion and complicity. Sometimes Christians stood for justice, practicing the values of the kingdom. Sometimes those values were compromised, either inadvertently or intentionally bringing harm to many.

That missionary movement was thoroughly evangelical in character. "The Evangelization of the World in This Generation" became the motto of the Student Volunteer Movement for Foreign Missions in the late nineteenth century (Piper 2000, 111). That vigorous movement focused on the importance of people everywhere hearing the good news of the grace of God given through Christ's work on the cross. Christian work for justice also gave a good witness to God's grace during the eighteenth and nineteenth centuries. Christians preached against slavery, Christian women led the temperance movement, and many Christians worked for improved conditions in mental institutions.

Because of the significance of the nineteenth-century missionary movement and its influence on our own understandings of evangelism, we will look at it in some depth in the next chapter.

Twentieth-Century Protestantism: Spreading the Gospel and Helping People

By the dawn of the twentieth century, evangelistic preaching, service, *and* work for justice characterized the outreach of the American churches.

The missionary movement of the nineteenth century influenced Christian outreach as the new century began. While missionary churches continued to send American missionaries and money overseas, work that was done in the United States became known as "home missions." Walter Rauschenbusch began a ministry to laborers in Detroit, helping them with their needs and working to overcome the injustices they faced in their daily lives. A movement of "women's work for women" stressed Christian evangelizing of women to bring them to salvation and foster Western-style social progress (Robert 1997, 130). In Chicago, the Pacific Garden Mission began sheltering destitute men, giving them food and clothing, and preaching the gospel to them. These and other home mission efforts played a vital role in shaping understandings of evangelism for the twentieth century.

Voluntaryism, the idea of freely joining a church or offering to work for a good cause, flourished in America. The concept of voluntaryism has much to do with freedom of religion as we understand it. Rather than establishing a national church in the United States, churches found members and support through opening their doors and receiving members who wanted to join. When applied to helping the poor, working with children in schools, nursing war veterans back to health, and other such humanitarian projects, voluntaryism takes on the qualities of grace. No one is forced to volunteer. Motives include a desire to grant something freely to another. Many times what is granted is undeserved. Dorothy Day's Houses of Hospitality show this kind of voluntaryism in action. Anyone could come to one of those houses and receive hospitality. Anyone could volunteer to work at one, serving soup, discussing theology, working on the farm (Day 1952, 185). This type of grace characterized many home missions in the twentieth century. Another method of graceful evangelism had been discovered.

Both proclamation and service became important methods of evangelism in the twentieth century. Unfortunately, the fundamentalist/modernist debate of the teens and twenties pitted those valuable theologies and methods of evangelism against each other. Because the conflict that was generated by that debate continues to plague the churches, we will look at the effects of that divergence in chapter 5.

Even a brief glance at Christian history reveals an array of theologies and methods of evangelism. Table 3.2 sums up some of them as they have been described here. Understanding our history as a church can give us new ideas about how evangelism can be practiced today.

Table 3.2 Evangelism through the Ages

Jesus	Inaugurates graceful evangelism
Paul	Explains and propagates the gospel of God's grace
Early Church Fathers	Formulate doctrines and institutionalize church
Monastics	Show God's love through community and spirituality
Christendom	Influences law and societal values through church power
Reformation	Rediscovers the gospel of grace and God's sovereignty
Enlightenment	Stresses apologetics and living in Christ's way
Colonialism	Christianity travels to the New World with economic exploitation
Great Awakenings	Revivals and personal repentance spread the good news
Nineteenth-Century Mission Movement	Message of Christ's salvation taken to ends of the earth
Twentieth-Century Home Missions	Proclamation and service evangelism both flourish

4

The Western Missionary Movement in the Nineteenth Century

An American Perspective

Since its inception in the Reformation, Protestant Christianity has influenced societies wherever it has taken root. The mission impulse of Protestantism reached its zenith in the nineteenth-century mission movement. The energy of this movement brought the churches together with an evangelistic purpose: to reach the world with the message of Christ.

One of the amazing facts about the nineteenth-century mission movement is that it happened. When Protestant Christianity was born, the focus was on reform of the church, the ordering of society on Christian principles, and the believer's responsibility in the world (Bosch 1991, 245). The Anabaptist reformers differed from this agenda, however, regarding all of Germany and the surrounding countries as mission fields (246). The Great Awakening in the United States and the second wave of revivalism that occurred in the eighteenth century followed that second model, directing religious fervor to the task of conversion. The growth of Pietism in Europe, particularly in England with the work of John and Charles Wesley, fueled that religious fervor with a passion for righteousness and self-sacrifice. As those powerful ideas met with conditions that allowed people to travel the globe, the missionary movement was born, drastically changing the face of Christian evangelism. Its influence is still with us in the twenty-first century.

During the nineteenth century hundreds of mission organizations were formed. By 1911, ninety of those organizations were centered in the United States. Overall, there were twenty-one thousand foreign missionaries, one third of whom were from the United States (Bevans and Schroeder 2004, 220). Thousands of individuals left their homes for destinations in Africa, Asia, and Latin America, knowing that they would never return to their native land and family. Many died on the long sea passage or in the early months of exposure to the harsh conditions of a new climate and strange cultural setting. "Don't be concerned for me" wrote a young woman missionary in Africa. "Although we have no wood to make floors, monthly applications of cow dung are making a smooth floor for us. Although I have no iron, we spread the linen sheets on the grass and after my son and Toko dance on them for awhile, they appear nearly pressed" (Davies and Shepherd 1954, 61). Thousands of letters to folks back in England or the United States show missionary courage in the face of domestic changes and worse—illnesses and deaths of children, spouses, and women in childbirth. That the missionary movement happened at all is amazing.

The uniting force among missionaries during this era was the importance of taking Christianity to the ends of the earth. Within the broad rubric of this mandate, several theological streams dominated the sending societies and the missionaries that joined them. The emphases varied among Reformed Protestants, enlightened Deists, radical Christians, and Pietists. Each of those streams took their particular theological distinctives, along with their church affiliations, to their mission posts. Consequently, the mission movement took diverse practices and theologies to these foreign lands.

Evangelical convictions tied those diverse mission efforts together. In fact, the mission movement bonded the church together, however temporarily. The agreement that the world needed Christ, and quickly, brought Protestants of every persuasion together. The missionary conference in Edinburgh in 1910 and the women's Jubilee mission conferences held across the United States in conjunction with the Edinburgh meetings convened those Christians to sum up the efforts of the nineteenth century and direct Christian mission efforts in the twentieth century (Robert 1997, 269). As a grassroots movement, the Jubilee of the Women's Missionary Movement had an immediate effect on American Missionary efforts (Robert 1997, 256). Edinburgh and the Jubilee Conferences became the precursors for both the ecumenical movement and evangelical missionary efforts of the twentieth century.

New Forms of Evangelism

During the great century of Christian mission, new forms of evangelism developed. The international and evangelical nature of the mission movement led to those new forms. As post-Enlightenment thinking increasingly separated political powers from religious institutions, outreach from Western countries changed. Colonial conquest did not equal Christian outreach. A spiritual focus for Christian witness grew as the church and state interests diverged.

The overarching rubric of evangelistic outreach became taking the gospel to the ends of the earth. Newly formed mission societies felt a sense of urgency about this task. Some believed that Christ would return imminently, so the time for spreading the message was short. Others believed that the world was entering the latter days when the kingdom of God would become more prominent and spreading the gospel was crucial to that task. All encouraged dedicated Christians to leave everything behind and put Christ first by taking up the call to overseas mission work.

Churches took up the call, raising money and sending their best leaders to the mission field. They were interested in conversion, stressing repentance and faith in Christ. The message of God's grace through Jesus Christ revived in the minds and actions of Christians across the United States and Europe.

Evangelistic Preaching

Preaching became a major form of evangelism during the nineteenth century. Revivals and itinerant preachers traversed the United States. Their work revitalized churches and brought new converts into the church, following the model of the apostle Paul, who preached to anyone who would listen, no matter what their ethnic identity, social status, or religious affiliation. Evangelistic preaching in the United States at this time took on a style that emphasized the hope of eternal life based on repentance. Personally experiencing the forgiveness of God became influential in some Christian revivals, while others stressed adult baptism as the way to open the gates of salvation. The itinerant evangelist became an appreciated visitor to small communities across the United States. Christians gathered from far-off farms to spend a few days in fellowship when the preacher came to town. New converts were added to the fold through their unique ministry.

Church Planting

Planting new churches was another form of evangelism that took hold in nineteenth-century America. Again, we find the roots of this practice in the work of the apostle Paul and those leaders whom he trained. New churches were founded in nearly every city where Paul preached. As America was pushing westward, Sheldon Jackson, a Presbyterian minister, traveled across the United States, planting churches as he went. He also collected records of existing Presbyterian congregations, thus preserving an important part of Presbyterian heritage in the United States. Jackson is affectionately known among Presbyterians as the only pastor ever to receive free lifetime passes on all the railroad lines of America (Presbyterian Church [USA] 2001).

A century earlier, in 1735, John Wesley, with his brother Charles, visited the United States. Although he did most of his work in England, he came as a missionary to the United States, where he worked for a few years with English settlers, Native Americans, African Americans, and Jews. He greatly influenced the growing Methodist Church in the United States. His well-known motto was "I look upon the world as my parish" (Anderson 1998, 723). There wasn't anyone anywhere who could not benefit from God's grace, and Christians were the bearers of that grace. Not only church planting but also work with the poor and outcast of society characterized Wesley's work. National, geographic, or economic boundaries were irrelevant to Wesley when it came to spreading the news of God's grace through Christ. His holistic approach to evangelism influenced the churches in the United States during the next century.

Evangelistic preaching and church planting grew uniquely in the soil of the evangelical fervor of the nineteenth century. When missionaries who were called overseas reached their "mission field," however, they found that other forms of evangelism were also needed.

Education

Education became one of those forms. People could not accept the gospel without understanding it. And that meant learning to study the Bible. The Reformation stressed the necessity of studying Scripture for knowledge and instruction in living. So Protestant missionaries translated the Bible into local languages, set up schools, formed Bible studies, and trained Bible teachers. Southern Baptists remember missionary Lottie Moon for her work training Bible women to go out as evangelists in China. Her work combined a sense of cultural appropriateness with an understanding that teaching was crucial to outreach. The grace of knowing how to interact with the Chinese people to produce effective outreach was one of Lottie Moon's gifts (Anderson 1998, 471).

Throughout Asia, Africa, Latin America, and the Pacific Islands, Bible translators worked to provide the Scriptures in the native tongues of the people. Other missionaries set up schools to teach reading so that people could study God's Word for themselves. Still others educated people in agriculture, geography, the humanities, and sciences. A good dose of Western civilization and values were incorporated into the education of those schools, something that has recently become a source of criticism of Western missions.

Medical Work

Most churches and mission organizations in the nineteenth century focused on proclamation and church-planting forms of outreach. Innovations for medical mission happened on the field because of need or because an individual sensed a strong calling to that work. Of course, Jesus set the precedent for healing that motivates Christians to do medical work. But the focus on saving the soul sometimes prevented sending agencies from recognizing the validity of healing the body. Albert Schweitzer experienced a roadblock with the Paris Mission Society when it rejected his candidacy to go to Africa and practice medicine. The society feared that his theology was not orthodox enough to ensure proper evangelizing of the natives. It could not understand his desire to heal rather than preach. After Schweitzer raised his own funds and offered his services to the society as a physician, it finally accepted his offer, causing much dissension among members of the society (Marshall and Poling 1971, 83–98).

Since then, many mission hospitals have been established throughout Africa and Asia. Medical work as a form of Christian outreach became more and more accepted as the twentieth century began, and it has flourished ever since.

Relieving Poverty

Sometimes missionaries encountered extreme poverty and oppression in their field assignments. God's special care for the poor led to numerous injunctions in the Old Testament. God's people were instructed to care for the poor, especially orphans and widows. Many Christians took those mandates to heart, attempting to relieve poverty wherever they went. Orphanages were built in China and supported by churches in the United States. Christians motivated by compassion sent money and goods to help relieve situations of desperate poverty. The nineteenth-century work set the stage for addressing structural issues of poverty, which has become a major focus of some twentieth-century mission efforts.

Looking back over this great century of mission, we can identify new forms of evangelism that were rooted in the Bible and traditions of the church and see how they were tailored to specific situations. Those nineteenth-century forms continued to flourish during the twentieth century. Yet both positive and negative effects resulted from this missionary surge from the United States and Europe to Africa, Latin America, Asia, and elsewhere. Identifying those effects can help us understand the situation for evangelism in the twenty-first century.

Positive Effects of Nineteenth-Century Mission Movement

Western colonialist expansion had been in full swing for two centuries when Christians in large numbers began to travel to far-off lands expressly for mission purposes. Missionaries brought back tales of strange cultures and pagan rituals. Artifacts and clothing became part of presentations by missionaries to home congregations. Tales of hunting wild game in Africa, fire walking in India, and Spirit dances in Southeast Asia came back to the West along with accounts of conversions and the establishment of churches.

Knowledge and Interest in Other Religions

Those tales of exotic cultures and strange religious practices piqued the interest of scholars in Europe and the United States. Emile Durkheim, a nineteenth-century sociologist of religion, studied Australian aboriginal religions through the lens of books written by people who had actually encountered the aborigines. Max Muller, founder of the modern discipline of religious studies, began studying religions with the intent of developing a science that would help missionaries in their work. Both sociology of religion and religious studies owe their origins to the expansive travel mentality and curiosity about other religions by those who pushed the boundaries of cultural exploration. Many of those people were missionaries.

The interest in religions other than Christianity grew in the mission-sending world, leading to international gatherings to share information and educate Westerners about mission efforts and other religions. The World Parliament of Religions, held in Chicago in 1893, was one such gathering. Although presentations by Christians about other religious faiths were elitist and sometimes demeaning, the presence of Hindus, Buddhists, and Muslims at the conference was a great step forward in the process of Western understanding of world religions.

Impact on Christian Theologies

Contact with people of indigenous and world religions influenced missionaries in the ways that they conceived of God and interacted with people different from themselves. Some of the attitudes developed were negative and harmful, but some of them were positive. Christians saw the power of the Holy Spirit working in African religions in the concept of a High God, in the belief that all life forms were animated by God's life and filled with purpose. Missionaries came to appreciate the depth of Chinese Confucian philosophy and ethics. Debates with Theravada Buddhists in Sri Lanka helped Christians to see their beliefs in a new and challenging context and showed the subtlety and completeness of the Buddha's teachings. Christian theologies became clearer, if not always more expansive, as they developed in conversation with the religious convictions and practices of others.

Worldwide Coordination of Protestant Mission Efforts

The proliferation of mission societies in the United States, the British Isles, and Europe also led to the realization that greater coordination of Protestant mission efforts was needed. Protestant denominations were united in the cause of evangelistic mission efforts but haphazard in their plans to carry Christianity to other lands. The need for communication and planning motivated the gathering at the Edinburgh Missionary Conference of 1910. Presentations by missionaries as well as denominational leaders brought together valuable information about societies and religions at this historic conference. Women's meetings across the United States during 1910–1911 gave women new vision for ecumenical mission and evangelism.

Given the chance to discuss their impressions of other religions and cultures, missionaries at that conference advanced their theologies of other religions in ways that were quite ahead of their time. Because of their interaction with those of other faiths in many countries, many missionaries had developed theologies of religion that were open and accepting (Cracknell 1995, x). Their work at Edinburgh 1910 resulted in "The Missionary Message in Relation to Non-Christian Religions," a great turning point in Christian theology of religions (xi).

Birth of the Ecumenical Movement

The Edinburgh conference marked the beginning of worldwide gatherings of Christians around mission concerns. Those periodic meetings brought Protestant leaders together to make missionary policy decisions about the expansion of the Christian church around the world. The history of Christian mission in the twentieth century can be told through the statements of those historic gatherings: Jerusalem 1928, Lausanne 1974, Nairobi 1975, Canberra 1989, and others are remembered for the policy statements about mission that the churches decided upon on those occasions.

As the twentieth century moved forward, the divisions among churches caused consternation among Christians both in the United States and in Europe. The missionary conferences presented the opportunity to work on issues of denominational divisions and gave Christians a chance to develop an organization that would work toward Christian unity. It was through those meetings that the ecumenical movement developed, leading in 1948 to the birth of the World Council of Churches.

Social Service Organizations

The mission movement of the nineteenth century focused on the salvation of souls and the proliferation of Christian churches. Those tasks could not be carried out without a focus on the value of persons and their welfare. Christian missionary efforts focused on alleviating hunger and poverty even if only as prerequisites to an ability to hear the gospel message. Timothy Richard, Ida Scudder, and Albert Schweitzer are only three of many examples of Christian missionaries who focused on social service as a major part of their Christian outreach on the mission field. Health care and agricultural cultivation techniques in two-thirds world countries were initiated by Christian missionaries.

Education

Through their focus on education, nineteenth-century missionaries developed the study of linguistics as they struggled to understand the languages of the peoples to whom they were sent. They translated the Bible into myriad dialects and developed schools so that people could read the Scriptures in their own language.

The right to education and a voice in governing their own affairs was also a by-product of the development of schools by Christian missionaries. Although the impact of those ideas has generated conflict in many countries, the value of persons and their ability to manage the affairs of their own communities has resulted in a valuing of democratic forms in many places.

Many Christians in countries that welcomed missionaries in the nineteenth century express appreciation for the advances in agriculture, health care, and technology that the missionaries brought to their lands. Today, as globalization changes societies in every part of the world, nations with modern technologies and systems of education and health care are better prepared to face the challenges of the world economic order.

Growth of the Worldwide Church

The missionary movement spread the gospel to every continent. The good news reached many for the first time. Lives were changed, Christian communities formed, the poor were cared for—God's grace reached millions through the work of Jesus Christ, carried to many lands by Christ's followers.

As the Christian message was translated into local languages, missionaries adopted indigenous cultural criteria for the gospel message (Sanneh 1989, 3). That radical indigenization meant in many instances that the gospel became part of their cultural history. The churches in Africa branched out into different paths during the twentieth century. Some are deeply connected to indigenous customs. Others have incorporated many Western elements of worship and lifestyle. In both cases, the churches have become African churches.

Christians in Asia often express gratefulness for the message of the Christian gospel itself. Dr. Lee Chong Kau at Trinity Theological College in Singapore, where I taught in 2002, told me that Singaporean Protestant leaders thought it strange that American Christians were apologetic about the nineteenth-century mission movement. "If it weren't for Christians from the West, risking everything to come to Asia, we would not have Christianity at all," he said (personal conversation). An Indonesian visitor to the PC(USA) dialogue meetings in Louisville in 2005 expressed consternation that American Presbyterians were decrying the mission efforts of their own denomination in Indonesia. "Why are they doing this?" she asked. "We needed the missionaries to bring the gospel to us. Now we want to take the message to others" (personal conversation with a participant who wished to remain anonymous). Asian Christians are grateful that American, Dutch, and British missionaries brought Christianity to their countries.

Negative Effects of the Nineteenth-Century Mission Movement

Presbyterians and others are aware, however, that those positive effects are mitigated by the negative impact of Christian missionary efforts of the nineteenth century. The efforts of missionaries must be considered as part of a larger picture that unfortunately also includes the influences of colonialism and its attendant economic exploitation, racism, and cultural imperialism.

Colonialism

From the vantage point of the twenty-first century, it is easy to see the intermeshing of Protestant missions and colonialist endeavors. European nations were colonizing Africa, Asia, and Latin America, exploiting those economies to a greater or lesser extent. Despite clear Christian injunctions to honor all humanity, Christians participated in those activities, even to the extent of justifying slavery with biblical interpretations (Cannon 2003, 43). Many missionaries who avoided involvement in economic exploitation benefited from the affluence and protection of their nation in foreign lands. Where missionary activity was supported by the colonizers, these connections ran deep. Even in locations where colonizers forbade Christian proselytizing, like Indonesia, Protestant Christians enjoyed the privileges of Dutch citizenship. Missionaries sometimes became complicit in severing the social and political bonds that held societies and cultures together (Grunder 2002, 25).

Moreover, the goals of mission activity were, to a great extent, compatible with the colonizing influences. Colonizers and missionaries believed that civilization was a Western commodity, and both groups thought that it would benefit the people of foreign lands to adopt Western mores and patterns of life. While European governments imposed legal and political forms on colonies, missionaries provided education in Western values. Although the United States held no colonial states, taking modern civilization to other peoples was seen by many as a moral obligation, resulting in a " 'moral equivalent' for imperialism" (Bevans and Schroeder 2004, 214).

Cultural Imperialism

As children of their era, most missionaries embraced the attitudes of Western superiority that underlay those civilizing efforts. The influence of the Enlightenment focus on rationality and individual autonomy led many missionaries to view indigenous cultures as inferior and barbaric. Western clothing and customs were imposed on Indonesians by the Dutch, for example. Missionary attempts to form churches consistent with Western customs and attitudes were understood to be part and parcel of the gospel of Jesus Christ.

There were missionaries whom we might consider more "enlightened" in today's terms—missionaries like Hudson Taylor, who insisted that the faith-based missionaries sent by China Inland Mission to China dress like the Chinese and learn from their culture and even their religions. People like Lottie Moon, who spent years training indigenous Bible women to carry the gospel to villages in China. Translators valued the customs of the people as aids to rendering the Scriptures in understandable terms. Women's missions often mirrored a holism that allowed cultural differences to be honored and interwoven with denominational approaches to Christian services such as health care and education. And there were missionaries who saw goodness in the religions of peoples to whom they were sent.

Manifest Destiny

Those exceptions were no match for the growing intermeshing of economic imperialism and the notion of Western superiority. The second half of the nineteenth century saw not only the expansion of economic imperialism but the explosion of an idea of manifest destiny that linked an optimistic view of human nature with notions of progress. Ideas of Anglo-Saxon racial superiority undergirded this notion, providing an impetus for imperialism and a climate for religious interpretations of manifest destiny.

According to the Reverend Josiah Strong, races of marked inferiority, like old religions, provided a wake-up call to Anglo-Christians to spread their civilization throughout the world. As a supporter of US "home missions," Strong wrote in 1885 that the English-speaking peoples were being prepared by Providence to spread the tenets of Protestant Christianity (Merk 1966, 240). Competition among the races would result in "the survival of the fittest" in the United States, in Mexico, and beyond. "The plan of God," he said, "is to weaken weaklings and supplant them with better and finer materials" (Strong, quoted in Merk 1966, 240).

The lethal cocktail of Western economic imperialism, the notion of a calling to spread Western civilization, and an idea of racial competition and the superiority of the Anglo-Saxon peoples had devastating consequences for Protestant missions. Protestant missionaries, on the whole, were children of their era. Most accepted the idea of Western superiority, believing that God was calling them to spread their ideas of civilization. Even missionaries who seemed to feel that the heathen should be strengthened by bringing them the gospel, not that they should be replaced with "finer materials" (Merk 1966, 246), embraced a vigorous program of Westernization in their mission outposts. Schools based on British standards and curriculum were established. Western health clinics and hospitals trained nurses and doctors. Although many positive benefits accrued with those developments, the basis of Western superiority also brought harm. Many missionaries looked down on indigenous people and sought to eliminate local customs and mores because in their minds Christianization went hand in hand with civilization.

This "benevolent colonialism" led, in some societies, to a sense of inferiority that has stayed with them. Strong saw Anglo-Saxon power in Asia as an open door for new fields in the "Orient" for Protestant missionaries (Merk 1966, 246). As missionary expansionism took hold, it went hand in hand with nationalist interests of Western powers. The Philippines, for example, has looked up to America and imitated all things American. This was due not solely to missionary efforts but to benevolent colonialism on economic, military, and political fronts as well. Indonesia, by contrast, has resisted identification with US or Dutch culture, maintaining its indigenous roots, Hindu heritage, and Islamic, as well as Christian, identities in various parts of the archipelago. This has resulted, in the twentieth century, in independent Reformed churches in Indonesia, some with strong women leaders (Adeney 2005, 18–19).

Impact on Twentieth-Century Evangelism and Mission

Both positive and negative effects of the nineteenth-century missionary movement affected Christian outreach in the twentieth century. On the positive side, the energy for overseas missionary work continued in some circles. Despite two world wars, American churches sent missionaries abroad. Young churches were nurtured and new churches planted. Regional organizations were formed and local leadership developed. The younger churches became partners in the worldwide church.

Types of outreach that had just begun in the nineteenth century became commonly accepted. Parachurch organizations focused on Christian mission proliferated during the twentieth century, sending linguists to translate the Bible, doctors and nurses to heal the sick and train others, and relief workers to lighten the burden of poverty. Hospitals trained local medical personnel, schools taught agricultural techniques and economics, and structural approaches to ending poverty were developed.

In the United States, missionary efforts also incorporated social service dimensions. "Women's work for women," outreach to the destitute, and health care for the poor became integral parts of Christian witness during the twentieth century. Many of those efforts were ecumenical, bringing together Christians from different churches around a common task. Community ministries also developed, linking Christians with civic organizations to enhance human flourishing in urban areas.

Churches also began providing space for ministries that cared for people not connected with the congregation. Self-help programs like Alcoholics Anonymous and Al-Anon began meeting in church facilities. Churches offered space and sometimes personnel for nursery schools and after-school programs, food cooperatives, and garden projects. Congregations reached out to immigrant Christians, sharing their sanctuaries with Korean, Chinese, or Hispanic congregations.

The impact of the missionary movement also led to greater appreciation for other religions among some Christians. Interreligious dialogue became an important form of outreach, not necessarily with the goal of conversion to Christianity, but for mutual understanding and fellowship.

Those positive effects were not achieved without tension. The fundamentalist/modernist debate, which we will look at in the next chapter, divided Christians on how to do evangelism and mission. A new division between social service and proclamation was created. Eschatological views lined up on both sides of this great divide. Those who believed that Christ's second coming was imminent stressed proclamation. Those who saw the kingdom coming stressed creating just societies and relieving oppression.

The negative assessment of postcolonialist critiques also caused dissension among Christians. Some Christians eschewed the idea of preaching with the intent that others would accept Christianity. In this view, introducing Christianity to other cultures created more harm than good. They focused instead on other forms of witness: political and economic efforts, and social service endeavors. Other Christian groups disagreed with that assessment, believing that the gospel message was crucial for all people to hear. Their missionary work became more focused on preaching the Word, planting churches, and translating the Bible to reach unreached peoples.

As the twentieth century progressed, some nations disallowed entry to Christian missionaries. In countries such as China and Pakistan, evangelistic efforts went underground or focused on educational and health service missions. Christians today disagree about the appropriateness of clandestine efforts to spread the gospel in those countries.

Despite those negative effects, much evangelistic work in the twentieth century remained holistic in practice. But the ambivalence around evangelism has led to tensions in congregations and denominations. Sometimes opposing factions claim that their strategies for evangelism are the best or only ways to do God's work of mission in the world. We will look at that "great divide," assessing the situation for evangelism in the twenty-first century, in the next chapter.

PART 2

Where Are We Now?

5

The Situation for Evangelism in the Twenty-first Century

Two Sides of a Coin

The impact of the nineteenth-century missionary movement and the development of forms of evangelism in the twentieth century that grew out of that movement contribute to the situation for evangelism in the United States in the twenty-first century. A host of other factors also helps us interpret our present-day understandings of Christian evangelism. Seeing where we have come from informs our understanding of where we are now and, at the same time, raises a number of questions.

A World of Diversity

As we enter a new millennium, there is nothing really new. Seed time and harvest, night and day, continue unceasingly as the rainbow's promise reminds us. Yet, in another sense, a whole new world surrounds us.

The sun rises every day on a world of diversity—different cultures and languages, new technologies and inventions, faster communication techniques and modes of travel. These changes bring us into closer contact with the diversity that surrounds us. More of us travel to foreign countries; video and Internet services bring a show-and-tell of diversity into our homes. Immigration spawns ethnic restaurants and neighborhoods. Mosques and temples spring up, and we hear strange languages on our street corners.

In my daughter's second-grade classroom in Berkeley, California, in the 1980s, there were six languages spoken by the pupils. In a class I taught at the Graduate Theological Union in 1994, twenty-five out of thirty-six students were non-Caucasians, coming from cultures as diverse as Fiji, Thailand, Ghana, and Haiti. At the University of Southern California in 1997, four of the students in my Introduction to Islam course were from the Middle East—Saudi Arabia, Iran, and Kuwait. The class visited a mosque on the corner just outside the campus on an LA street corner. On a visit to Hawaii in 2000, I visited Siva Monastery, a Hindu temple and retreat center on the island of Kauai. By the time I taught World Religions at Louisville Seminary in 2005, Islam was the fastest growing religion in the United States.

Those are my stories. I'm sure every reader has an incident or two that comes to mind as you think about how diversity has exploded in your own world. Globally, what comes to mind since 9/11 and the Iraq war is the confusion surrounding terrorist groups that claim religious connections.

The increasing diversity in our society demands Christians' attention. As our world changes, our call to share the good news of the gospel molds itself to our new situations. As religious pluralism increases and we find Muslims, Hindus, and Buddhists in our neighborhoods and our schools, we need to consider what our response will be. How will we, as individuals and communities, interact with our neighbors of other religions? As diversities of lifestyle increase, how will we reach out to people who live in forms of family or community different from our own? As mobility continues to increase, how will our churches relate to neighborhoods that change even if we stay in one place?

As we analyze our contexts of diversity, we also bring to that analysis differ-ent concepts of evangelism—concepts that have been shaped by our collective past and our personal experiences. How do we address the increasing diversity of our world with the gospel of Jesus Christ?

Is Evangelism Obsolete?

Many in the contemporary United States believe Christian evangelism—sharing the good news of the gospel of Jesus Christ in word and deed—to be obsolete or incompatible with religious tolerance. Reasons for this view among Christians and non-Christians are many and complex, but five stand out: religious pluralism, a relative notion of truth, a fundamentalist/mod-ernist controversy that divides the church, postcolonial critiques of Western Christian missions, and the mishandling of evangelism by charlatans. We will look at each in turn and ask what questions they raise for evangelism (outlined in sidebar 5.1).

Religious Pluralism

As Americans we think of ourselves as a tolerant and accepting people. But our diversity produces tensions among religions and among Christians with differing understandings of how they should relate to those who claim no faith or to people of other faiths. Despite holistic views of evangelism held by both conciliar and evangelical Protestant groups today, these tensions are fueled by persistent theological and sociological factors. What many people do not realize is that the tensions about religious tolerance result from the *achievement* of religious visions of Christians in our history.

Early American religion was characterized by religious visions, by pluralism, by religious creativity, and by a sense of mission in the churches. The vision of the Puritans who settled in Massachusetts was "a city set on a hill." They wanted to be an example to others of how Christian society should function. Puritans were not fostering free thinking. Massachusetts and other colonies had established religions that they transferred into state religions in the early republic. Those early settlers wanted to fashion a just society where political and religious affairs were modeled on biblical principles. They came to the New World because they had been persecuted for practicing those beliefs. In order to avoid that possibility in the future, Puritans—and later Baptists, Catholics, Quakers, and Presbyterians (the early version of today's religious pluralism)—had to reach a compromise as they formed a nation.

Separation of church and state and religious freedom for all is the compromise. To protect the particular visions of religious freedom of different groups, religious freedom for all was built into the system of *national* government. States still kept their established religions for a time. It wasn't until the 1830s that Massachusetts gave up Congregationalism as its state religion. This negative toleration, a live-and-let-live attitude, has grown into a positive American emphasis on tolerance of religious diversity. The foundational freedoms established by our religious forebears and the tolerance that grew from the establishment of those freedoms now result in a suspicion of religiosity.

Christian evangelism suffers from the ambivalence that has grown up around the established freedom to practice religion unhindered. Should Christians

> **Sidebar 5.1 Five Reasons for Questioning Christian Evangelism**
>
> 1. Religious pluralism
> 2. A relative notion of truth
> 3. A fundamentalist/modernist controversy that divides the church
> 4. Postcolonial critiques of Western Christian missions
> 5. A mishandling of evangelism by charlatans

try to influence others' religious beliefs? Does this go against the grain of religious tolerance?

Today's pluralism is broader than the pluralism that divided early settlers, partly because of their decision to support religious tolerance so that they could survive and practice their particular beliefs. In our contemporary world, people of many religions live in close proximity to one another. My neighbor was taken aback last summer when she saw a man in a turban in northern Wisconsin. She had never heard of Sikhism. When I taught at the University of Southern California in the 1990s, I was surprised to see Muslim men prostrate themselves in the stairwells of academic buildings five times a day on campus. Three different Muslim student groups held events and set up book tables on campus every day. A Hispanic-American guest speaker wearing traditional black Muslim dress told my Islam class about her journey from Catholicism to Islam. Buddhism and Hinduism in both Eastern and Westernized forms also flourish in the United States today, as do New Age movements. Visits to Hindu celebrations at the Kentucky Hindu Temple, the Islamic Center, or the Sokkai Gakkai Community Center in Louisville are now part of my course in World Religions at Louisville Seminary. A return to indigenous beliefs by Native American and African American citizens also characterizes American life today. The doctoral program at Asbury Seminary includes four Christian students practicing and exploring their Native American cultures. We are, in fact, seeing a renaissance of spiritual searching of all kinds in the United States. How should Christian communities advocate Christian faith in this free marketplace of religious ideas?

Relativism

The presence of diverse "paths to God" stimulates questions about the ultimacy of one's own beliefs. While 90 percent of Americans believe in God, those beliefs differ widely and questions about those beliefs abound. How can I know that the Christian way is true when so many other sincere believers follow other religious paths? These doubts are fueled by a growing apprehension among Americans that the beliefs we hold are determined by our context and perspectives. What seems "true for me" may be very different than what my Muslim or Hindu neighbor understands to be true. For example, a Hindu believes that the physical world is illusion, while the Christian insists that the world is created by God and has real substance.

Add to these problems the increasing privatization of religion. Since we want to respect the views of others, and since people voluntarily follow a particular religion, it almost seems confrontative just to discuss religion with others. How does one adjudicate between these truth claims in an intellectual climate that sees all truth as relative? How can we invite others to follow the Christian way if we are unsure of the universality of what we believe?

Fundamentalist/Modernist Controversy

A long-standing controversy among Christians leads some to think that evangelism is obsolete. Back at the turn of the twentieth century a disagreement erupted between Christians who wanted to affirm culture and embrace science as it pertained to faith and those who wanted to interpret Scripture more traditionally. That group called for a return to the fundamentals of the faith (Torrey et al. 1972, 5). Denominational tensions fueled the debate, augmented by status and class issues. The resulting split in Protestantism created two streams—fundamentalist and liberal. Liberals became embarrassed by verbal witness, focusing instead on social service. Fundamentalists stressed verbal witness, sometimes to the neglect of serving the poor. One sector of the Protestant church that has avoided this dichotomy is the African American church, which has held a traditional theology of evangelism alongside vigorous work for social change. The civil rights movement, centered in church communities, exemplifies this. But in other sectors of the church, an unnatural theological division has resulted in many tensions. Most Protestant denominations include congregations on both sides of the issue, and tensions within congregations also arise. Although most Christians today applaud an integrated approach to verbal witness and service, disagreements about appropriate forms of evangelism still cause conflict. Should verbal witness be part of Christian mission efforts? Is working for structural change in society evangelism? How should congregations approach witness to people of other religions? Where does work for justice enter evangelistic efforts? Those tensions have both historical and theological roots.

What is our mandate as Christians? To reach every person on the planet with an announcement of the work of Jesus Christ as Savior? To work for justice politically and personally as a witness to the power of the risen Christ? To heal the wounds and the suffering of people? To protect the environment, thereby honoring the integrity of the creation that God has made? To see that Christ's church is established throughout the world? How is evangelism related to these goals?

If our Christian mandate includes more than one of those goals, we need to ask if a *diversity* of theologies of evangelism can flourish in the churches of the United States.

Postcolonial Understandings of Christian Mission

Postcolonial critiques also lead to questions about what characterizes appropriate mission and evangelism. While in the past idealistic Christians tried to separate themselves from local political affairs, this is no longer possible. We cannot separate the presence of Christian missionaries in any country or region from the political and economic struggles of that place. Christians in the Northern Hemisphere have been accused, often rightly, of standing with political and economic oppressors in third world nations. In addition, along with the Christian message, European and American missionaries brought Western culture to those places. Christians often discouraged the practice of indigenous cultural forms or ways of dressing. A sense of inferiority developed in some cultures as Western forms were emulated. Sometimes diseases were transmitted from the West, even as hospitals were being constructed as centers of healing. Consciously or unwittingly, damage has been done. Some Christians have made postcolonial critiques the basis for asserting that attempts to spread Christianity are wrongheaded and should be stopped.

Mishandling Evangelism

While charlatans are nothing new, television and the Internet have amplified opportunities to exploit well-meaning or vulnerable persons in the name of Christ. Appeals for money in exchange for promises of healing, self-esteem, or wealth in the name of Christianity embarrass responsible Christians and the church at large. Stereotypes of Christianity arising from oversimplistic and economically motivated television evangelists give Christian witness a bad name. Those negative impressions have detrimentally affected views of Christian evangelism, making reaching out sometimes seem awkward and prone to misunderstanding. In my Evangelism and Modern Society class last term, two students expressed hurt at inappropriate evangelism targeted at them. Yet a third described a conversion experience sparked by a phone call from an acquaintance who said that, although he hardly knew him, he felt an urgency to tell him the gospel story. Every year I hear personal experiences of students on each side of this divide. It is not so easy to tell when the gospel is being preached inappropriately.

Religious pluralism, relativistic thinking, conflicting theologies of evangelism, postcolonial critiques of Christian mission, and the mishandling of evangelism all contribute to doubt about the relevance of evangelism in today's world. We need to take these issues seriously. Historical and cultural insights that change our understanding of the world and the role of Christianity in the world can be ignored only at our peril. When recognized, however, they become the basis for a more nuanced understanding of the challenges for Christian evangelism in the twenty-first century.

Turning Over the Coin

Let's turn the tables for a moment and look at each of these reasons for hesitation in evangelism from another perspective. "Turning over the coin" reveals positive effects from each of the problems discussed above.

Religious Pluralism

The tolerance of religions in the United States is a major achievement of our free nation. Our founders devised structures of toleration that allow human dignity and freedom of expression to flourish. As citizens, we are called upon to look with tolerance on all religions. As Christians, we have developed theologies of human rights that respect all peoples and their freedom to choose their religions (Adeney 2007). Christ's love allows us to embrace and respect those of other faiths. To the negative tolerance that our founders instituted to protect their own beliefs, contemporary Christians add a positive tolerance of acceptance and fellowship with practitioners of other religions. We recognize that our own understanding of God can be augmented by reflecting on the wisdom found in other walks of faith. God graces peoples and cultures in every part of the world with wisdom and beauty. We praise God's creativity exhibited in the diversity of human talents expressed in religious and cultural life of many shapes and forms. What kind of God creates a world that results in this amazing kaleidoscope?

Celebrating religious pluralism does not imply that sharing our faith in Christ as Savior, through both words and acts, is wrong. Sensitivity and respect for the values and beliefs of others does not negate the universality of Christian beliefs or the call to share the good news of the gospel. "I have come that they may have life," said Jesus, "and have it to the full" (John 10:10). Without denigrating the beliefs of others, Christians can model and talk about abundant life in Christ. Celebrating diversity reduces fear and confrontations without denying Christians the joy of sharing faith and service, worship and fellowship, with all who have ears to hear.

Relativism

What would it be like if, rather than resisting the proverbial "sea of relativism," we decided to swim in it! After all, we don't stand above or outside the world and pronounce all truth. We are influenced by our context, the teachings and values of our society. We do, as St. Paul reminds us, "see but a poor reflection as in a mirror" in our understanding of God (1 Cor. 13:12). Peter Berger argues that for people who live in the modern world, a certain acceptance of uncertainty comes along with faith (1993, 137–38). Our limited human perceptions spring from the perspectives we have inherited and experienced. Doesn't this amount to a relativizing of knowledge?

What we believe, that God in Christ is reconciling the world through Christ (2 Cor. 5:19), is secured in faith. We tell the story of Jesus as it has been told to us; we stand in traditions of theological interpretations of a set of texts we believe to be divinely inspired. We live and work and exist in God, whose Spirit is with us. Yet what we know is small and relative to our experience. H. Richard Niebuhr reminds us that the revelation of God that we embrace grows up within the Christian tradition and experience as we know it (1960, 72–73). It is in the internal history of the Christian community that we know God. And we see but a poor reflection as we try to understand.

The humility that the knowledge of our limitedness gives us can result in an appreciation for the insights of others and for the wisdom of other traditions. Rather than limiting our faith, such realism can bring us confidence. The apostle Paul reminds us that we hold the light of the gospel in imperfect ways. Just as jars of clay are weak and breakable, Christians hold the treasure of God's truth in imperfect minds and with limited language. According to Paul's analysis, this situation leads to glorifying God rather than giving credit to humans (2 Cor. 4:4–7). As we realize our finitude and the relativism of our knowledge, God's glory may appear larger and more mysterious. As I went through my own theological training, I remember feeling that as my questions grew, God seemed to become bigger. My convictions about God's gracious redemptive work in Christ deepened even as the limitations of my own knowledge became more apparent.

Fundamentalist/Modernist Controversy

Controversy is not new to the church. In some ways, Christianity seems to thrive on it, just as a climate of debate sharpens analysis. Understanding different theologies of evangelism can enrich the church rather than divide it. Liberals can remind themselves of the special calling evangelists have according to 1 Corinthians 14. Fundamentalists can remind themselves that Jesus announced his mission in Luke 4 as one of freeing captives and giving sight to the blind. Even when Christian communities seem diametrically opposed to one another or are internally divided on the issue of evangelism, mutual respect can allow for differences.

As a professor of evangelism and mission, one of my goals is to make *evangelism* a user-friendly word to students, faculty, and denominational representatives—Presbyterians of various stripes, as well as United Methodists and Wesleyans, African-American Episcopal Methodists, Progressive and American Baptists, Roman Catholics, Episcopalians, Pentecostals, and Free Church members. While the fundamentalist/modernist controversy splintered Christian approaches to evangelism, we can find unity in the larger arena of faith in God through Jesus Christ. Is it too much to suggest that we might actually learn to celebrate the diverse theologies of evangelism in the church?

Postcolonial Critiques of Christian Mission

Many Christians are embarrassed by historical interpretations that show connections between Christian missions, economic injustice, political exploitation, and the demise of localized cultures. We probably should be embarrassed, for although such readings are often exaggerated and one-sided, there is some truth to them. As the joke goes, "Many missionaries went overseas to do good, and ended up doing well." Often they did well because of their association with colonizers, because of their power to change economic conditions for the few, and because they reshaped social structures to suit Western customs and mores. Though often plagued by tropical diseases, cross-cultural misunderstandings, and alienation from political and social realities at home and abroad, missionaries also found themselves privileged by economic advantage and high social status.

Third world theologians have pointed out such anomalies in the work of the Western church. Is it any wonder that global mission from West and North to East and South have become suspect?

Two things can be said here. First, we need to recognize the truth in some of these accusations, repent, and devise new paths for evangelism. We can receive missionaries as well as send them, benefiting from the insights of Christians from other parts of the world. We can listen to third world voices of all persuasions, as well as talk to them about Christianity. We can work with institutions and communities to foster common human goals. Christians can begin to redress the economic and cultural dominance that Westerners have fostered. This process of redress, partnership, and equality is an integral aspect of evangelism for the twenty-first century.

Second, while not shirking the responsibility for the ills generated by colonialism and Western dominance, we do not want to forget the positive contributions that Christian missionaries have made in many parts of the world. Christians from East and West, North and South, can retell the accounts of mission success to balance the tales of failure so often seen in films, novels, and "historical" critiques. Education, health care, agricultural advances, and the benefits of modernization have been positive side effects of Western Christian mission efforts. The hope and healing carried by God's Spirit through the story of Jesus have also been the fruits of Western missionary work. We can celebrate those accomplishments, affirming the relationships between God and God's people that have extended God's grace through Christ to so many.

Because of those successes, peoples in Africa and Asia are practicing the Christian gospel in their vernacular languages and indigenous cultures, expanding their churches, developing local theologies, and sending missionaries to Europe and the United States. God's Spirit is not limited by human failings, but God works over, under, around, and sometimes through those failings. The growth of Christianity in the two-thirds world informs approaches to evangelism today. As contexts shift, past failings can be addressed as new theologies and forms of evangelism arise.

Mishandling the Gospel

Some televangelists will handle God's Word badly; some will preach the gospel for personal gain; some will embarrass us with bad theologies and simplistic views. But we are family with all in the church. Every family has its characters, its failures, its embarrassing moments. What can we do? Rather than disparage the efforts of others, we can get into the business and do it better. There are needy people out there who will turn on their televisions to hear the story of Jesus. We can tell it well.

Religious pluralism, relativism, controversy between fundamentalist and modernist approaches, postcolonial assessments of missions, and mishandling the gospel each influence current understandings of evangelism. Both positive and negative assessments of those trends can enable Christian churches to develop new and relevant approaches to living and proclaiming the good news of God's love for the world, shown by grace through Jesus Christ.

Why Evangelize?

Assessing the situation for evangelism in the twenty-first century leads us to a key question. Why evangelize at all? There are a number of convincing answers to this question (outlined in sidebar 5.2).

Christianity Shines Like a Jewel

This is one of those things that has not changed, even as our fast-paced culture reforms itself in so many ways. The way of Christianity brings life and hope to the lost and suffering—which is, as always, most of us. When we know in our beings and experience in our communities the light of Christ in our life, it becomes axiomatic to let that light shine. For, as the gospel puts it, "You are the light of the world. A city on a hill cannot be hidden. Neither do people light a lamp and put it under a bowl. Instead, they put it on its stand, and it gives light to everyone in the house" (Matt. 5:14–15). The good news is its own advertisement, its own motivation. Having received grace, we share its source and meaning with others—by our lives and by our words.

This Is a Message the World Needs to Hear

The awareness of religious pluralism has led to a kind of relativism that makes putting one's faith in the death and resurrection of Jesus especially difficult for modern people. If vast portions of the world accept other religions, how can we know that Christianity is true? Even as Christians become more tolerant of other religious paths, they can become uncertain of their own. People seeking peace or spiritual aid turn to numerous other paths—Hinduism, Buddhism, New Age religions. Many deny their spiritual longings altogether, focusing on work, money, or leisure activities. Wherever these seekers turn, it is often away from the familiarity and values of their Christian roots.

Ironically, it is precisely in those Christian traditions that life can be renewed and values that are universal can be reformulated. The cacophony of voices purporting to be about human rights, environmental concerns, and the goodness of human growth and development can find a harmonious and centered focus in Christian tradition. We will explore ways to connect the gospel to contemporary concerns in a later chapter.

Church Decline

For contemporary people to recognize the relevance of the gospel to their lives and communities, Christians must modulate their witness into forms and language that are understandable in twenty-first-century global contexts. Statistics on the decline of mainline Protestantism in the United States indicate that people are not turning to the churches for spiritual nurture. The high status that Protestant clergy enjoyed a century ago has declined drastically. Even as recently as fifty years ago, the *New York Times* published sermons in its Sunday edition, a practice that sounds quaint if not offensive to twenty-first-century ears. Christianity cannot count on support from the wider culture to perpetuate its views and support its values. As a result, mainline Protestant denominations have aging congregations as young people follow cultural trends, leaving their communities of memory for secular pursuits or novel spiritual paths. We need to practice evangelism to woo people back to the church.

Some of this decline is offset by the growth of Pentecostalism, evangelical churches, and megachurches. Cooperation among denominations around evangelism could also help balance the decline by teaching mainline churches some of the forms of evangelism that seem relevant in today's society.

Religious Pluralism Comes Home

Because of increased travel, immigration, and sophisticated communication techniques, the religions of the world have come to our neighborhoods and into our schools and homes. We need to understand our Christian faith and be ready to give an account of the hope that Christian faith inspires. In order to do this, we need to understand what we believe and be able to dialogue with those who hold other convictions.

Christianity relates both competitively and cooperatively with other religions (Muck and Adeney 2009, 28). As Christians we believe that Jesus is the way to fully appropriate God's grace and that Christian practices and values are life giving. We want people to embrace Christianity, to get to know God's grace, to live life to the full. Yet Christians are also called to cooperate with people and communities that practice other religions. That cooperation is based on love as the central focus of Christian practice. Understanding the reasons for Muslim women covering their hair, accepting Hindu vegetarianism, or exploring Buddhist meditation techniques can foster goodwill and reduce prejudice toward those who are different from ourselves. Cooperation also fosters the common good. Working together on neighborhood, educational, or health concerns solves problems, fosters solidarity, and builds community. Cooperation does not require agreement on theological issues but builds on a mutual respect for one another's humanity. Such cooperation can foster the values that all religions agree on—peace, love of life, and the significance of nonmaterial realities and values.

Evangelism can be as broad as we and the congregations and denominations we serve want to make it. We can reach out in words or actions, locally or globally, personally or through a community. God welcomes us with wide-open arms. So welcomed and embraced, we can open our arms to the world.

6

Today's Mission Trends

Much has changed in the understanding and practice of evangelism during the last one hundred years in the United States. Not only do cultural and philosophical shifts, geographical mobility, and technological advances influence the situation for evangelism in the twenty-first century, but trends in Christian mission itself complicate the context for evangelism, presenting unique problems and opportunities.

Let's explore some of those trends: diffusion of the locus of authority for evangelism, shifts in the global makeup of the church, growth in mission efforts from the two-thirds world, decline in mainline church membership alongside the growth of the charismatic church, decline in missionary spending and sending by denominations together with an expansion of congregation-based mission efforts, growth of parachurch organizations and social service work unrelated to the church, and a growing contingent of women leaders. Each of these trends influences concepts and strategies of evangelism. They affect funding, mission personnel, approaches to evangelism, and the responses of others—Christians and non-Christians, churches and governments, people in the United States and in other countries—to evangelistic efforts.

To effectively chart the way forward into graceful evangelism for the twenty-first century, we must consider how these trends influence the whole picture for evangelism and the church today (see sidebar 6.1).

A Shift in Authority for Evangelism

The missionary movement of the late nineteenth century was a high-water mark for the Protestant church in the United States. Historians of religion often refer to the nineteenth century as the "Christian century." Christian leaders were highly respected, their views sought after by presidents and populace alike. After World War I the situation changed drastically. The authority of church leaders in society at large sharply declined and continued to decline throughout the twentieth century. Reverend Billy Graham was the last prominent Christian to be called upon by US presidents to give his studied opinion of international relations and national problems. Although a vague religiosity still enhances the image of political leaders, the influence of Protestant church leaders in national affairs no longer holds the prominence it once had.

The same may be said for the influence of church leaders on the general population. Martin Luther King Jr.'s call for civil rights for African Americans appealed to the conscience of the nation. It was a call rooted in Christian values of the equality and dignity of all people. Many lament the silencing of his and other voices coming from the church and advocating positive social change. Pat Robertson's bid for political office in the 1980s marks this decline. One may see this trend as part of a "privatization of religion" or understand it as a lack of Protestant leaders today. In either case, it is part of a shift of authority away from the church.

That shift affects Christian evangelism. Where do Christians look for the encouragement to witness to the power of our faith? Are there "American idols" we look up to for inspiration and instruction about how to go about the business of the Great Commission? Of course there are such sources of authority, but their configuration has changed. Authority no longer resides mainly in the church and its leaders. Rather, we see a diversified authority for Christian witness in the United States. The authority of the Bible, congregational leaders, parachurch organizations, denominational leaders, umbrella organizations, family, and an individual sense of calling all still figure into the equation. But they figure in differently, without strong connections to national Christian leaders or a worldwide mission movement.

Shifting Patterns in the Growth of the Church

The worldwide church itself has shifted its growth patterns across the globe. No longer does Christian authority and activity emanate only from Europe and the United States. Christianity grows quickly in Africa, Latin America, and parts of Asia as church membership declines in the West. At the beginning of the twentieth century, there were 20 million Christians in Africa. Today there are 350 million. China began the twentieth century with 800,000 Christians and ended with 50 million. Estimates vary in China, but the trend is obvious. In Latin America, evangelicals numbered 900,000 at the turn of the twentieth century and now number 20 million. Most of this growth has occurred in the charismatic church. Overall, in the less-developed world Christians numbered 823 million in 1900, surging to 1.1 billion by AD 2000 (Barrett, Kurian, and Johnson 2001, 1:3).

That shift from developed to developing countries in the growth of the church has implications for American mission activities. Worldwide denominational fellowships need to listen to the voices of their growing constituencies outside the United States and Europe. Newer theological voices as well as viewpoints on economic development may run contrary to traditional Western theologies or economic strategies. Taking those voices into account and making changes accordingly becomes necessary for graceful evangelism to flourish in our day.

Missionary Activities of Two-Thirds World Churches

Those growing churches in many parts of the globe now influence views of evangelism. For example, South Korea's Protestant population has grown tremendously in the past century, doubling in size every decade since 1940 (Barrett, Kurian, and Johnson 2001, 1:684). Korean missionaries to Indonesia, Thailand, and other Asian countries now take the gospel from Asia to Asia. The growth of the charismatic movement, projected to reach one billion by 2040, has changed the face of evangelism, especially in Latin America (Barrett and Johnson 2001, 451). Eighty percent of Latin American Christians are evangelical Protestants, and the Protestant and postdenominational churches are expected to experience a resurgence in Brazil (Barrett, Kurian, and Johnson 2001, 1:134). There is also a growing interest among Latin American Christians to reach out in evangelistic efforts to North Africa. A growing independent church movement in Africa now reaches out to neighbors and those in other countries. The diaspora churches of Ghana and other African countries have established many congregations in the United States. In China, teachers of English from North America have replaced traditional missionaries but still influence Chinese people to consider Christian faith. And Chinese missions to Chinese people worldwide are growing as well.

Those trends have now become part of how Christians in the United States understand and practice evangelism. Chinese Christians, Ghanaian Christians, and Latino Christians are part of who we are as an American church. Voices of missionaries from other countries to the United States influence how we understand evangelism. Sometimes those voices produce tensions around theologies and strategies of evangelism. What some Western churches see as culturally oppressive forms of evangelism may be vigorously practiced by non-Western missionaries. Although those evangelism strategies were learned from Western missionaries, they may be opposed by Christians in the United States today. Missionary efforts from the two-thirds world churches to countries that have traditionally received missionaries from the West can also produce tensions with long-entrenched Western missionaries. Openness and patience need to characterize American evangelistic efforts as evangelistic theologies and strategies of two-thirds world churches now affect the worldwide church.

Presence of Other Religions

Another key element of the situation for evangelism in the twenty-first century is the assertive presence of other religions in the United States. During the late nineteenth and early twentieth century, immigrants settled into the United States, bringing their religions with them. The New Age movement of the 1960s and 1970s brought Eastern religious ideas to mainstream America. Today, Islam is the fastest growing religion in the United States. Soka Gakkai Buddhists have established a university in Colorado. Hindu temples dot the landscape in Texas, Hawaii, and other states. Adapting to the cultural styles of Americans, some religions hold Sunday services and social gatherings for inquirers. Migration, travel, and Internet communication bring Islam, Hinduism, and Buddhism into our neighborhoods and our living rooms.

Those trends have led to a focus on interreligious dialogue and cooperation with other religions as part of Christian mission. Christian seminaries are including courses in world religions in their curriculums, and guides to studying those religions help students with research and facilitate contact with adherents. The awareness of other religions on our doorstep also increases competition with them for adherents. A focus on evangelizing Muslims is one result of that trend in the United States. Whether here in the United States or in Islamic nations like Pakistan, Indonesia, and Morocco, mission to Muslims has increased. Both cooperation and competition must now characterize Protestant Christian interaction with other religions (Muck and Adeney 2009, 29).

Growth of Nondenominational Missions

The growth of parachurch mission organizations during the last century has shifted the focus of mission efforts from denominational structures to parachurch organizations. World Vision, Habitat for Humanity, Wycliff, and other Christian organizations do the work of mission and evangelism in many countries. Ecumenical organizations like the World Council of Churches and the World Evangelical Fellowship provide guidance for evangelism through conferences and official documents. Community ministries bring churches together with like-minded people from other religions or secular groups to work on community projects. Many Christians work with nongovernmental organizations (NGOs) to do health care, community development, and poverty relief in numerous countries.

The presence of other religions and the shift in authority for evangelism affects not only churches but also parachurch organizations. The presence of other religions leads to questions about the focus of mission efforts. Should social-service aid stand alone when provided for people with other religious beliefs, or should Christian statements of belief be part of the package? Should Christian organizations provide relief and development aid only to churches in other countries? To what authority should parachurch organizations be responsible in their efforts to evangelize? Should funds from denominational missions be shifted to parachurch organizations?

Decline in Support for US-Based Denominational Missions

The growth in parachurch organizations does correspond with a decline in support for denominational missions from the United States. One denomination, known for its commitment to mission, drastically reduced its giving in recent decades. In 1990, over 50 percent of its mission giving was spent for support within the Christian world (Barrett and Johnson 2001, 57). Christians in this denomination may be giving as much to missions but are shifting that giving to a single-focus organization or one of four thousand foreign mission agencies (62). The rising costs of supporting long-term missionaries may be another factor in the decline of denominational missions. The cost of supporting an overseas missionary today has risen to eighty to ninety thousand dollars per year. Many congregations find it difficult to support their denominational missionaries at this level.

Not only do rising costs influence the decline of denominational missions, but postcolonial critiques of Christian missionary efforts lead some churches to the conclusion that the era for sending missionaries from the United States to other countries is over. They are convinced that a cultural imperialism combined with economic dominance in two-thirds world countries has resulted in harm for indigenous peoples. As a result, mission efforts shift to social service activities without an evangelistic component. Often those mission efforts are parachurch efforts. According to David Barrett and Todd Johnson's analysis, "Christians, in fact, consume over 99% of the whole range of Christian resources, leaving under 1% for all forms of outreach to non-Christians" (2001, 62).

Furthermore, conflicts around the world have increased the number of dangerous areas for Americans during the past twenty years. Living in Palestine, Indonesia, Peru, Colombia, Cote d'Ivoire, former Zaire, Laos, China, Philippines, and Sudan has become more difficult. In addition, the Islamization of countries like Malaysia and Indonesia has led to visa restrictions in those countries. Missionaries are not welcome in many areas, and changing one's religion may be forbidden, as it is in Pakistan. These issues influence denominational decisions on sending missionaries overseas.

Growth of National Church Leadership

Those negative influences are compounded by positive reasons for a decline in denominational sending. The national church leadership in some countries has grown strong. The indigenous churches themselves have taken on the tasks of church management and missionary activity. Rather then depend on Western missionaries, those churches are utilizing missionaries for special tasks. The Presbyterian Church (USA) sends mission coworkers only to countries where the national church requests certain types of workers. Health workers or educators may be requested. Aid for specific projects may be required. In both cases, the partnership model practiced by the PC(USA) regulates mission sending according to the needs and requests of the overseas churches. Denominational mission workers from the United States go where they are invited. They do not lead but work alongside the national church. The mission workers do not make a lifetime commitment to a single location but train nationals to take over their area of expertise. The focus is on strengthening and supporting local and national leadership in the mission field. The overall result is fewer Presbyterian missionaries in other countries.

The decline of denominational missions need not be considered solely a liability but can also be seen as an asset. As long-term denominational missions decline and national churches grow, the places and purposes for mission activity from the United States to other countries change. More short-term mission projects develop. In 2000, four hundred thousand short-term missionaries did projects around the globe (Barrett and Johnson 2001, 62). Mission exchanges are set up. Lay people participate in sending and receiving missionaries from other countries. Young people participate in vacation Bible schools in Mexico. Youth mission exchanges send Americans to churches overseas and welcome young visitors from those churches to US churches. Such short-term mission exchanges educate US churches about cultural forms of Christianity in other parts of the world. Visitors learn American theologies and styles of worship. Short-term disaster relief projects educate Americans about pressing economic and social conditions in other countries. Sometimes the insights gained help develop relationships between churches in the United States and those in other parts of the world. Funds from US churches provide economic sustenance to poorer churches, and social and cultural gifts are given by national churches to churches in the United States.

But changes need to be appraised and evaluated in an ongoing way. In some cases, the support of national leadership and economic development may be a more effective use of US denominational funds than the support of long-term American missionaries in those places. Mission trend analysts Barrett and Johnson don't think that shift is being made. They claim that 90 percent of monies for mission are used by the 131 *mission-sending countries*, with only 10 percent reaching the four billion non-Christians of the world (2001, 63). In certain cases, a lifetime missionary committed to a particular place can support churches in their outreach efforts in ways that funding neither nationals nor short-term mission work can. American churches can also receive wonderful gifts from overseas churches as people learn of the grace of God through building relationships with those in other countries, both missionaries and nationals. And overseas churches can grow through partnerships that honor their autonomy and address the needs that they consider important.

Rise of Congregation-Based Mission Efforts

One of the side effects of the decline of denominational mission efforts has been the growth of congregation-based missions. Many Americans have both curiosity about other places and peoples and the economic ability to travel to those places. That energy combines in many congregations with a longing to spread the gospel of Christ and to get to know Christians around the world. Rather than sit on the sidelines, many congregations have gotten involved with churches in other parts of the world. This has a revitalizing effect on the congregation and also creates goodwill overseas.

For example, a Presbyterian congregation on the outskirts of Minneapolis set up a partner church arrangement with a congregation in Slovakia. They sent congregants over to visit the church. As they formed relationships with that congregation, they were renewed by the faith of the Slovakians. They also learned that they could contribute to their livelihood by helping them set up a cottage-industry tailoring enterprise. Repeated exchanges took sewing machines over and brought back renewed hope to the US congregation. God's grace in many forms was given and received. My sister and her family began attending this church. After a trip to Slovakia with a church member, she told me that although the interim pastor was leaving the congregation soon, she would never leave. "Our sister church needs me," she declared. And she needed them.

There are pros and cons to congregation-based missions. On the pro side, they are flexible and creative, adapting more easily to new situations than denominational bureaucracies. They are immediate and relevant, presenting hands-on opportunities to ordinary people who love God and want to serve the kingdom. They are manageable financially because congregations can gauge their level of giving, changing it according to their own needs and their dedication to a particular project. On the con side, congregational ministries can be like the proverbial "flash in the pan"—here today and gone tomorrow. That can leave a sister congregation stranded in the middle of a project that takes time and effort on its part and depends on long-term financial support from the US church. In addition, the US congregation may not be aware of the cultural and theological commitments of the church it is partnering with. The danger of alienating its sister congregation from its own denomination or endangering it in some way through unawareness of political situations in its country is very real. A lone-ranger congregation can do more harm than good in mission efforts without the denominational wisdom gained through years of interaction with the overseas situation.

As a mission trend, congregation-based mission efforts are here to stay. Those who participate in them need to do so with their eyes open, taking advantage of the pros and minimizing the cons by staying in touch with the denominations both here in the United States and overseas.

Growing Recognition of Women in Mission Leadership

Women were very active in the nineteenth-century mission movement. In fact, by 1890 they comprised 60 percent of US missionaries despite the restrictions they faced (Robert 1997, 130). Some mission-sending agencies would not send single women overseas. Other women faced physical problems related to pregnancy and childbirth that restricted their activities. Most did not have theological training. Yet despite these limitations, women worked effectively as missionaries. Many worked ecumenically, not allowing denominational differences to interfere with their work for the gospel.

Scholars are now working to recover information about women in mission. Dana Robert documents historical accounts of American women's missionary activity in *American Women in Mission*. Rosemary Radford Reuther and Rosemary Skinner Kellers' *Women and Religion in America* and Mary Bednarowski's *Religious Imagination of American Women* portray broader pictures of women's work in religion. *Sisters of the Spirit*, by William Andrews, offers three autobiographical accounts of nineteenth-century African American evangelists. A dissertation currently in progress charts the development of the Assemblies of God three-point mission plan in the 1920s—a plan created by a woman. And Susan Smith's *Women in Mission* highlights efforts of Catholic women. Women called to Christian mission today can find mentors and models in the history of mission as it is being recovered by these and other scholars.

During the last century, the development of national leaders in Christian mission has included many women. The Ecumenical Association of Third World Theologians (EATWOT) in Asia, the Fellowship of Theologically Educated Women (PERUATI, Persekutuan Perempuan Berpendidikan Teology) in Indonesia, and the Evangelical and Ecumenical Women's Caucus in the United States are a few examples. My research on gender ideology and social change in Indonesia shows that Christian women are following their callings and developing their leadership capabilities in Indonesian church and society (Adeney 2003). In 2000, over five hundred organizations worldwide were serving lay women and girls, many developing leaders, and two hundred were working with ordained women (Barret, Kurian, and Johnson 2001, 2:677). These changes put women at the cusp of positive change in mission in the global church today.

Challenges to the Church Arising from Mission Trends

The mission trends described above present major challenges to the church in the United States today. No longer can we ignore the implications of these trends—theologically, financially, socially, or culturally. Although each trend needs to be evaluated and tailored to the current situation, some general implications can be drawn from this brief study (see also sidebar 6.2).

First, there is no one method for Christian evangelism and mission. With increased religious pluralism affecting so many contexts, evangelistic efforts must pay close attention to the beliefs, lifestyles, and cultural contexts of our

---

Sidebar 6.2 Challenges for Christian Mission Today

1. No single method characterizes all Christian mission.
   - There is no single way to do missionary work.
   - No single group of people become missionaries.
   - No single church or parachurch method is best in all situations.
   - No single theory of mission suits every context.
2. Evangelism is multidirectional.
   - Missionaries listen as well as talk.
   - Missionaries learn as well as teach.
   - Missionaries receive as well as give.
   - Mission moves from East to West as well as from West to East.
   - Mission from South to North as well as from North to South.

neighbors from different religions. As globalization draws more and more communities together through international travel, Internet communication, and migrations of cultural groups, we need to develop approaches that do not offend but attract diverse peoples to the gospel.

That means there is no single way to do missionary work. A Christian mission in Bangladesh may focus on basic health care for villagers. An outreach in Thailand may center on teaching English. A Christian community in France may focus on creating employment opportunities for immigrants. And a ministry in Israel may primarily address the conflicts between Israelis and Palestinians.

No single group of people will become missionaries. As a diverse range of activities are included in evangelistic outreach, persons with a variety of talents will be called to different aspects of the work. Medical work, agricultural efforts, education, and youth work will be augmented by finding jobs for displaced persons, caring for the homeless, organizing peace efforts, and establishing cottage industries in poor areas. Christians from different countries will become missionaries to new places. South Korea now sends missionaries to Indonesia; Christians from Ghana plant churches in the United States; Americans go to China to teach English; and Christians from Mexico establish ministries of outreach and service in California. Today, mission is from everywhere to everywhere.

Consequently, no single church or parachurch organization has a corner on the best method. Graceful evangelism is practiced in many and diverse ways as missionaries from different places cross the globe, adapting their methods to different situations. Bangkok pastor Ubolwan Mejudhon and her husband developed the concept of "meekness evangelism" to reach out to villagers in the poor eastern sectors of Thailand. Muslims hear the gospel from converts who have not left Islam but practice their faith within the Islamic religion. Chinese women travel within their country teaching the Bible to other women. And Palestinian Christians sponsor art contests to bring Muslims and Christians together around evangelistic themes like the resurrection.

Neither does one theory of evangelism suit every context. Different biblical models frame evangelistic efforts. Contextually oriented theories and theologies from churches around the world focus and direct those efforts. Incarnational models work best in places where Christianity is not welcomed by governments. Proclamation theories of evangelism take precedence in areas where the church is growing quickly. Discipleship theologies are utilized in countries where the church is established and growing toward maturity. Needs-based evangelism thrives where people are poor and need not only words of peace but basic health care, food, and shelter. Justice theologies of evangelism flourish in wealthy nations, helping people to share their time and money with others who have much less. A theology of gratefulness motivates Christians from many areas of the globe to go out, leaving the comfort of their homes and communities and taking risks to bring the gospel to those who have not yet heard the Word of Life.

Just as no one method holds sway, one-directional evangelism is also a thing of the past. To understand today's complex situations and respond appropriately, evangelists must listen as well as talk. Missionaries need to learn as well as teach. As we learn to receive as well as give gifts, evangelism becomes multidirectional. Those who are sent hear the good news just as much as those they are sent to.

Traditionally Christian mission efforts went from West to East, from North to South. But mission trends show us that increasingly evangelistic efforts are moving from East to West as well as from West to East, from South to North as well as from North to South. The church is growing exponentially in Latin America and Africa. Filled with energy and a sense of God's call, churches in those areas are sending missionaries to Europe and planting churches in the United States. The South Korean Protestant church is also sending missionaries to the West. Mission is multidirectional. Gifts are given and received, and Christians are crisscrossing the globe with the good news of the gospel.

Mission trends in the last century have given us a new template on which to create, with the help of God, new theologies and approaches to graceful evangelism.

7

Contemporary Theologies
of Evangelism

Christians define evangelism, present the task of evangelism, and envision the good news of the gospel reaching people and communities in many ways (chap. 1). The Bible outlines several approaches to evangelism (chap. 2), and the history of the church displays a number of different modes of evangelism (chap. 3). The nineteenth-century missionary movement worked out of a strong evangelical theology of evangelism (chap. 4). In the twentieth century, councils on evangelism in evangelical, Reformed, Orthodox, Catholic, and ecumenical circles brought out diversities among perspectives on evangelism. Those diverse perspectives, along with societal changes, bring us to our current situation for evangelism (chap. 5). In the twenty-first century Christian theologies of evangelism are being analyzed and applied in new ways (chap. 6).

This chapter will appraise seven contemporary theologies of evangelism. Those theologies each have a strong focus and find their place in the *missio Dei* (mission of God). We will analyze each, show their links with some of the biblical and historical models, and explain their relevance today. Confluences and compatibilities will be stressed as well as the suitability of a theology to a particular context. As theologies of evangelism take shape in various settings, they take on cultural forms. Where one approach becomes obsolete, others become meaningful. Where one style offends, another is embraced.

Theologies of evangelism in the twenty-first century can differ in significant ways. Theologians presenting their theology emphasize a major area, which sometimes accentuates those differences. For example, William Abraham in *Logic of Evangelism* emphasizes the goal of evangelism as building God's kingdom through the church. Robert Coleman's *Master Plan of Evangelism* puts the focus on fulfilling the Great Commission through developing leaders. Both, however, focus on spiritual practices, modeling one's life after Jesus's example, and working through the church community. Abraham says that we need to focus less on proclamation (1989, 171), while Coleman wants to train leaders to "win the multitudes" (1993, 95). But for both, modeling one's life after Jesus's example activates outreach in the lives of leaders and ordinary people in the church.

Similarly, certain theological themes recur in the seven contemporary theologies of evangelism in this chapter. Although each theology focuses on a major theme, one finds something about proclamation, liberation, spiritual practices, the church, and the kingdom of God in nearly every one. A stress on the Christian values of love, the importance of relationships, witness, and serving others occurs repeatedly. Although springing from different historical traditions and theological perspectives, those themes recur, giving these contemporary theologies of evangelism a compatibility that is often overlooked.

Consequently, contemporary theologies of evangelism need not compete but can complement each other. Overlapping theological themes of the seven contemporary theologies of evangelism highlighted in this chapter are shown in table 7.1. Each theology springs from a specific tradition and fits a particular context. Each can become a powerful agent of change as the Holy Spirit uses the fullness of the gospel in gracious ways in different settings today.

Table 7.1 Seven Contemporary Theologies of Evangelism

Theologians	Focus	Overlapping Themes
Scott Jones	Discipleship in Context	Love, Kingdom, Church
Robert Pierson	Fulfilling Needs	Service, Acceptance, Proclamation, Church
Bryan Stone, John R. Adams	Community Practices	Community, Acceptance, Practices, Witness
Paul Hiebert, H. Richard Niebuhr, George Lindbeck	Transforming Worldview	Apologetics, Proclamation, Liberation, Church
J. Alfred Smith	Prophetic Preaching	Proclamation, Liberation, Community
Martha Reese, Becky Pippert	Faith Sharing	Church, Lifestyle, Proclamation
Vincent Donovan, Bob Roberts Jr.	Church Planting	Church, Apologetics, Proclamation

Discipleship in Context (Love, Kingdom, Church)

Scott J. Jones, writing in 2003, laments the dearth of theologies of evangelism in systematic theology. To rectify that perceived lacuna, he situates his theology of evangelism in the broadest possible biblical theme, God's love for humanity. Building on the work of William Abraham and other missiologists who use an eschatological framework of the kingdom of God to situate a theology of evangelism, Jones expands Abraham's theology by asserting that love for God and neighbor is an essential attitude without which evangelism cannot operate.

Focusing on God's love for the world and Christian love for God and neighbor illuminates a central message of the Bible: God is for us (Jones 2003, 32). The Wesleyan tradition stresses that love is God's most basic attribute. It is the gracious, saving love of God that motivates Christians to love one another. First John 4 claims that the one who does not love does not know God and that God's love is revealed by sending Jesus into the world so that we might live through him. God's love is evangelistic because God's actions are good news as God actively works in history to solve humanity's problems. God's love is also invitational, encouraging persons to participate in the reign of God (43).

Building on this strong theological foundation, Jones goes on to show how God's efforts to love and restore persons to their full humanity builds the reign of God. Jesus's mission was to announce God's reign and fulfill it through his death and resurrection (2003, 39–40). God's reign now continues to be built through God's work within and beyond the church. God's grace, a grace that is often costly, now becomes the mode of outreach for Christians (47). The church becomes a visible witness of God's reign when it acts in accordance with God's will, which doesn't always happen (53–54). But at its best, the church, as part of the *missio Dei* shows the way to reconciliation and judgment. The worship of the church is the main task in this endeavor and shows our love for God (56). Spiritual formation helps Christians develop their ability to love and shows love for ourselves. And bearing witness to God's love through loving others shows God's love for others through the loving witness of God's people "By worship we love God. By formation we love ourselves. By witness we love others" (55). Another part of the ministry of evangelism becomes announcing to the world that the forces that destroy life are wrong and have, in an ultimate sense, already lost (47).

When people respond to God's love, their faith in God involves a radical trust. They trust God with their whole life and commit themselves to loving all whom God loves (Jones 2003, 49). They go on in their life of discipleship, learning to obey all of God's commands. The gospel, as described in Matthew, calls Christians to radical, costly discipleship (49).

In Jones's all-inclusive theology of evangelism, the mission of the church ties in with God's overall mission of bringing in the reign of God. All the church's activities become part of that mission as they are done in love. Evangelism is not a separate piece of the mission of the church but is interwoven with the larger project of God bringing grace to the world through God's reign. This most broad of theologies of evangelism resists compartmentalization and understands the mission of the church as part of the broader work of God in the world. That view coincides with my own understanding of the mission of the church as described in the sidebar "The Mission of the Church" in chapter 2. In this view, evangelism is not a separate project of the church or a committee of the church but rather includes all the ways the church works, in love, to bring about the reign of God. God also works in realms beyond the church in God's evangelistic love of the world.

Fulfilling Needs (Service, Acceptance, Proclamation, Church)

Robert D. Pierson picks up the theme of loving God and neighbor as a core source for a theology of evangelism in his book *Needs-Based Evangelism*. Speaking as a Methodist pastor to a mainline denomination that is losing members, Pierson calls the church away from an effectiveness-based view of evangelism to a focus on following Christ in meeting people's needs. He takes Luke 10:25–37 as his starting point—in order to find life, one must love God and neighbor. Jesus follows this discussion with a story—the story of the Good Samaritan. So, who is our neighbor? The person in need. Pierson wants the church to "decide to do whatever is necessary to lead people to Jesus Christ" (2006, 8). What that entails is discovering what people need, getting the word out that the church can fill those needs, and proceeding to go about doing it. This is love in action.

The mission statement of Pierson's church in Tulsa, Oklahoma, is "We have been called to meet needs" (2006, 9). The story of the sheep and goats in Matthew 25 makes it clear that it is those who help others who become part of the kingdom of God. Pierson sees this approach as one that has brought people to Christ throughout the history of the church. But he also insists that ministries of service must be combined with an energetic proclamation of the gospel of Christ. Whether we are feeding the homeless, organizing a basketball team, or offering a parenting class, the gospel needs to be proclaimed in each setting (11).

Pierson goes on to discuss the ways and means of meeting people's needs and proclaiming the gospel along with those ministries. First on his list of priorities is a nonjudgmental attitude toward those served by the church. "Needs-based evangelism is built first on grace," he declares (2006, 12). There is no room for judgment or condemnation of those who come needy to the church. Genuine acceptance and nonmanipulative care mark this approach to evangelism. As people experience God's love through having their needs met nonjudgmentally, they will also be invited into the church.

Presenting the gospel with grace does not imply that beliefs are unimportant in Pierson's needs-based evangelism approach. The local church, as the basic unit of evangelism, understands its role in making disciples, in preaching the Word, in following the mandate of the Great Commission (2006, 18). The church goes about feeding and clothing people because it is the right thing to do. It invites those it serves to become part of the community of faith, accepting the beliefs and making behavioral changes in their lives on the basis of Christian values.

This holistic theology of evangelism begins with service to others but doesn't end there. "Hurting people are desperate for the message of grace," Pierson insists (2006, 20). Our most basic needs are fulfilled in the atonement of Christ, who gave his life for our salvation. Pierson lists those most basic needs as forgiveness, truth, salvation, and purpose (20). He makes a point of linking service with proclamation, seeing both as integral parts of the message of the good news of the gospel.

After laying this foundation, Pierson goes on to give practical advice to local churches so that they might find their way into a vital ministry of service linked to evangelistic outreach. He covers topics such as filling needs in the church community, finding ways to market the services the church offers, refreshing a church's thinking about meeting needs, and organizing ministries. Meeting personal needs and developing a personal witness style also get attention in Pierson's approach. He shows how authentic worship and preaching are also part of the evangelistic witness of the church that focuses on meeting needs. Worship that suits the indigenous people, preaching that is based on the needs of the listener, and different styles of music and praise that suit the needs of different constituencies all become part of Pierson's needs-based evangelism approach (2006, 80–83). Like many of the approaches we discuss in this chapter, needs-based evangelism becomes deeper and broader as the multiple levels of needs of congregants and community are explored.

Community Practices (Community, Acceptance, Practices, Witness)

A number of differing theologies of evangelism focus pointedly on the practices of church communities touched upon by Pierson. In these theologies community practices become the focal point of a theology of evangelism.

So You Can't Stand Evangelism, by James R. Adams, an Episcopal priest, suggests that people be brought into the community and accepted before being asked to make a commitment to Christ or the church. Not only will an influx of new people bring energy and funds, it will also open conversations about doubt and provide an infusion of hope (1994, 42–43). The acceptance Adams advocates mirrors Pierson's theology of grace and nonjudgmental attitudes toward those being served. The process of discipleship happens as new people are exposed to liturgies, learn about the Bible and church traditions in Sunday school classes, and, most importantly, feel the acceptance and love of God through the people of the embracing community.

St. Patrick took a similar approach in the fifth century as he gathered people together in monastic communities in Ireland. Rather than preach to them, explain the Christian worldview to them, serve their needs, or proclaim liberation, Patrick's communities embraced people as they came to the community (Muck and Adeney 2009, 97–98). The "community" referred to in the theologies of Adams and Patrick looks much like the church referred to by Jones and Pierson.

Another community practices approach is worked out in Eastern Orthodox churches. Evangelism, in Orthodox theology, is *being the church*. The church itself is witness to the world. Its presence in society, its liturgies, its sacraments, its teachings—all display the gospel to the world.

The Roman Catholic Cathedral in Louisville, Kentucky, practices a somewhat similar theology of evangelism called an "Evangelism of the Threshold." This community does not seek people to join its church. However, once a person crosses the threshold of the sanctuary, the church community welcomes and disciples them. That is its form of evangelism.

Bryan Stone in *Evangelism after Christendom* develops a theology of evangelism as community practice from another perspective. Following the Anabaptist tradition that understands the work of God in history to be creating a particular people, Stone sees the community practices of the church as evangelism. Rather than calling people to a personal relationship with God or trying to serve felt needs of individuals in a market-oriented society, Stone sees the countercultural message of the cross as a basis for the life of the church. It is the community itself that calls people out of the world to an obedient and sacrificial following of Christ (2007, 16–17). The end (*telos*) of evangelism becomes the character of the church itself. A church announces peace and bears "faithful public and embodied witness to God's reign in its own context" (10).

That general view of evangelism is complemented by a more specific understanding of evangelism as a virtuous practice. In contrast to evangelistic strategies that seek numerical results, Stone's adaptation of Alasdair MacIntyre's notion of practice sets the goal of evangelism as faithful witness. He outlines the practice of evangelism as one that establishes goals that are internal to the practice itself. In other words, Christians practice evangelism as faithful witness and in so doing faithful witness is accomplished. In the community-based theologies we are discussing here, the faithful witness of the community that embraces others becomes the central mode of outreach.

Furthermore, the criteria of this model for excellence are internal to the practice itself. To assess the success of the practice of evangelism, one need look not to numbers of new church members but rather to the character of the church community. The practice of evangelism in this model is socially established and cooperative. This places evangelism squarely in the arena of the witness of the church, certainly a biblically informed position. Finally, the practice is systematically extended through self-discipline and community evaluation.

Stone contrasts the application of that model of practice with a current instrumental view of evangelism as a practice, asserting that a technique-oriented model that seeks results cannot accomplish the biblical goal of evangelism as faithful witness for a number of reasons (see sidebar 7.1). First, the ends or goals of the "evangelize to get converts" model are external to the practice itself. That is, one may succeed or fail at producing more Christians or church members. Second, the means to the goal originate outside the practice itself. That is, strategies or techniques of evangelism are developed according to their effectiveness in producing converts rather than from the demands of faithful witness itself. Third, effectiveness of the practice of evangelism is assessed by the achievement of the goal of producing more Christians. Finally, those ends

Sidebar 7.1 What Is Excellence?
Two Models of Practice

Contemporary Western Society

Characteristics:
- Ends are external to means.
- Means are instrumental relative to external ends (evangelism reduced to set of techniques) (Stone 2007, 50).
- Effectiveness is determined by achievement or production of ends.
- Ends are not informed by substantive goods.

Evangelism in this model becomes an autonomous creative act of "making" on the part of the evangelist (50). The goal is making converts.

Alasdair MacIntyre's Aristotelian Model

Characteristics:
- Goods that are realized are internal to the practice (30).
- Criteria for excellence are determined by the practice itself.
- Practice is a socially established and cooperative human activity (35).
- Practice is systematically extended through discipline and community evaluation (36).

Evangelism in this model becomes a virtuous practice lodged in a narrative and tradition that evaluates the internal goods and external ends of the practice itself. The goal is faithful witness (49).

(producing more Christians) are not informed by substantive goods. By this Stone means that the goals of quantitative growth, power, and influence of the church are not substantive goods that determine faithful witness (2007, 34). In fact, they may ultimately undermine faithful witness if the desired influence, power, and numbers are achieved, for what then remains as a motivation for the practice of evangelism (35)?

Stone's critique of growth-oriented theologies of evangelism can certainly be countered. Bob Roberts Jr.'s church-planting theology of evangelism focuses on numbers but contends that the quality of witness itself is a crucial part of an effective evangelism.

A theology of evangelism that focuses on community practices can be seen in the World Council of Churches' focus on interreligious dialogue. In this view, God's work in the world goes beyond the church to bringing all things together under the reign of Christ (Eph. 1). Practicing loving our neighbors of other faiths, engaging in a dialogue of life with them, and building peace among religions all become evangelistic practices in this theology.

Community practices as a theology of evangelism, then, can be articulated from a number of points of view: the church as a welcoming place for all comers (Patrick), the church as a visible sign of God's grace in the world (Orthodox), the church as the place to come to find out about God's love (threshold evangelism), the church as a witness to God's creating a people of God's own (Anabaptist), the church as a community of reconciliation of people of all faiths (World Council of Churches).

Transforming Worldview (Apologetics, Proclamation, Liberation, Church)

As Christians, we believe that we have an accurate (although not complete) view of how the universe operates. The material world is real, created by God. Humans, created good by God, are also sinful. Jesus Christ was sent by God to redeem the world and will ultimately renew creation and restore the relationship between humans and God that was marred by the fall. Through the work of the Holy Spirit in the world, we can already see signs of restoration: in our personal lives, in our social worlds, and in creation.

This knowledge comes to us through the Holy Spirit and through God's revelation in the Bible and is appropriated by Christians through faith. After explaining God's work in history in the first ten chapters of Hebrews, the author explains that the surety of that knowledge comes through faith. "Now faith is being sure of what we hope for and certain of what we do not see. This is what the ancients were commended for. By faith we understand that the universe was formed at God's command, so that what is seen was not made out of what was visible" (Heb. 11:1–3).

Even though we are confident in that knowledge, we also realize that our understanding is partial and limited by our perspective. Our society, our historical heritage, our scientific understanding, our family, and our church experience all influence our understanding of how the universe operates. Paul in 1 Corinthians 13 reminded us that our knowledge is partial and our teaching is therefore partial as well (v. 9). It is as if we are trying to see clearly in a darkened mirror. Consequently, Paul declared, "Now, I know in part" (v. 12), but despite that partial knowledge, faith remains (v. 13). It is through faith that we know with certainty that the Christian worldview is true.

In philosophical terms, we might say that our knowledge of *what is* (*ontology*) comes to us through faith. We are secure in that knowledge because of God's revelation and God's promises to us. *How we know* (*epistemology*) is much trickier, influenced by our particular experiences and educational resources. As Christians, we need ontological confidence and epistemological humility (Coleman 1985). We boldly assert that the general worldview we hold is true, but we humbly admit that our knowledge of it is partial and limited. As we confess our faith in Jesus Christ, we do so boldly, but as we explain our understanding of the mysteries of God and the universe, we do so humbly.

H. Richard Niebuhr explained this dynamic by asserting that revelation comes through the community of faith (1960, 81). It is in and with the church that we understand that God created all things through Christ and that the universe is held together by his power (Col. 1:16–17). Situated in history, in the community of faith, and influenced by the understandings of our time as well as the voice of God through the Scriptures and the Holy Spirit, we know the truth of the gospel. *How we know*, then, is through this rich context of Christianity, a particular tradition. *What we know* through that context is universal. We can confess the truths that we know through this community with confidence. But it is, nonetheless, a confession—informed by our faith.

George Lindbeck describes this dynamic by speaking of knowledge as *situated* culturally and linguistically. There is no knowledge without a context. Lindbeck stresses the epistemological side of the equation—*how we know*—through our situated context. Abstract, universal knowing is impossible—all our knowledge is limited by experience and context. *What we know*, according to Lindbeck, cannot be universal but is always culturally and linguistically situated (1984, 18). We cannot know about *ontology* (*what is*). We only have limited culturally situated knowledge because that is *how we know*. Without confessional faith, belief in an *ontology*, universal knowledge recedes and ultimately disappears.

The Christian doing evangelism through worldview transformation, or apologetics, as it is traditionally named, needs to understand the difference between confessional knowledge, which comes through revelation by faith, and contextual knowledge, which comes through our limited understandings of the world. Through discussing the Christian view of God, the world, human salvation, and the creation, Christians influence others to accept the

Christian faith. As we engage in this process, a confident faith that the Christian worldview is true combines with a humble attitude toward the ways we understand and explicate that amazing knowledge.

This kind of evangelism is not new. The apostle Paul in Acts 17 showed the Romans who were seeking to hear something new that Jesus was actually the unknown God they were worshiping. Paul affirmed their epistemology but showed that their knowledge was incomplete. Knowledge of Jesus, Son of God and Judge of the world, could complete their worldview. Augustine in his work *The City of God* outlined a new dimension of political life—the idea that there is another realm of reality altogether, one that he called the City of God. That ontology came to Augustine not through the study of Plato or Cicero but through the revelation of God in Scripture and through the church. Thomas Aquinas in his treatise *Summa Contra Gentiles* worked with worldview transformation evangelism. He addressed the Muslim ideals and ideas about the world from a position of Christian faith. Using epistemological tools to outline how people can know the truth, he asserted an ontological vision that sees God's hand in history at every turn (Muck and Adeney 2009, 118).

During the middle of the twentieth century, a worldview-transforming approach became widely used among young people in the West. The countercultural movement questioned the given worldview of materialism, militarism, and judgmental religion. The Beatles, Joan Baez, Bob Dylan, and others critiqued the current order through songs of protest and hope. Intervarsity Christian Fellowship groups arranged for Christian speakers to lecture on college campuses about the veracity of the Christian worldview. Coffee house discussions were organized by Christian campus groups, providing a place where serious reflection about life's questions, both personal and political, could happen. Books such as Frank Morison's *Who Moved the Stone?* arguing for the resurrection, and *How to Give Away Your Faith*, by Paul Little, fueled the worldview transformation movement among Christian young people. Francis and Edith Schaeffer, a conservative Reformed couple, began L'Abri Fellowship in Switzerland. At this mountain retreat they held lectures and discussions about Christianity and philosophy, art, and current topics of global concern. The basic premise of all that activity was that the Christian worldview was the best, most relevant, and true understanding of the universe. Many people came to accept Christ through those worldview-transforming efforts.

A contemporary text on this topic is the late Paul Hiebert's book *Transforming Worldviews: An Anthropological Understanding of How People Change*. Hiebert outlined characteristics of worldviews and showed how context informs them. He contrasted a number of worldviews including peasant, modern, and postmodern views, using anthropological tools to analyze them. He proceeded to outline a biblical worldview and show how people, in shifting their worldview understanding, change in dramatic ways. According to Hiebert, the biblical worldview asserts the oneness of all humanity. The church, then, becomes part of that unity, the new people of God. In the church there are no "others"—there is only one body (2008, 290).

A worldview transformed by the gospel includes more than a different way of thinking about the world (see sidebar 7.2). Hiebert outlined the affective changes individuals experience when they embrace the gospel: encountering the mystery of God, experiencing joy, developing the fruit of the Spirit (Gal. 5:22), and understanding love in a new way (2008, 291–92). That affective knowing is informed by an evaluative form of knowledge that includes the biblical moral themes derived from the character of God (295). Finally, a transformed worldview includes a cosmic dimension—a new *ontology*. World history, for the Christian, becomes part of God's bigger story. "This cosmic story has a *telos*, an end, and that end determines its meaning," Hiebert declared. "The problem is that we live in the middle of the story and don't know its end" (302).

Prophetic Preaching (Proclamation, Liberation, Community)

Although Christians don't know the end of the story, we believe that we have some insights into the broad shape of the world God longs for. Prophetic preaching brings the vision of a just society and a world of peace to the attention of Christians and society at large.

Sidebar 7.2 Characteristics of a Biblical Worldview

Transformed Knowledge

1. Changes to our cognitive knowledge as a result of a biblical worldview:
   - Believing in the oneness of all humanity
   - Viewing the church as part of that unity, the new people of God, so that in the church there are no "others" (Hiebert 2008, 290)
2. Changes to our affective knowledge as a result of a biblical worldview:
   - Encountering the mystery of God
   - Developing the fruit of the Spirit (Gal. 5:22)
   - Experiencing joy and peace
   - Understanding love in a new way (291–92)
3. Changes to our evaluative knowledge as a result of a biblical worldview:
   - Deriving ethics from the character of God (295)—e.g., good and evil, grace and restoration, etc.
4. Changes to our cosmic knowledge as a result of a biblical worldview:
   - Ontological understanding of cosmic story and God's role in history
   - Perceiving Christians as part of God's bigger story
   - Knowing that the *telos*, or end of the story, is yet to come (unknown by humans now) (302)

In the early days of life in the United States, slaves from Africa were presented with Christianity by their white slave owners. Slaves combined that religion of submission with African beliefs from their former life. They discovered portions of the Bible—the exodus story in particular—that became an overarching theological paradigm for their life and worship. Prophetic preaching became part of this American liberation theology. Groups of slaves met secretly, listened to sermons about freedom, and took action to release many of their numbers from bondage. Spiritual songs often had double meanings—"Swing Low, Sweet Chariot," for example, was fervently sung to bring hope of a future with God to many, but it also sometimes signaled that an escape was planned for that night. Prophetic preaching of slave religion and documents of appeals for freedom spoke out against the evils of slavery and insisted that God's people deserved freedom and not servitude (Wilmore 1984, 34–35).

The theology of evangelism embedded in religion among slaves was a theology of liberation not just for a future life in heaven, although that was vital to the Christian faith of African American slaves. It was a call to liberation in this present life, for freedom from inhumane treatment, the breaking apart of families, the use of women and men as chattel, and the degradation of children. The community of faith played a central role in working toward that liberation as slaves worshiped together, proclaimed the truth of their liberation, and conspired to achieve it.

South/Central American liberation theologians developed a similar type of prophetic preaching. They struggled for freedom from political domination by oppressive governments. Catholic theologians confronted the institutional church and the powers of secular government to teach liberation within and outside the church. Oscar Romero became a martyr in that cause. The theology of evangelism of these prophetic preachers was not the same in every case. But the emphasis on taking action toward making the world reflect God's justice is common to them all.

Missionaries sometimes took up prophetic preaching as a way of denouncing evil in their contexts. William Sheppard, the first African American missionary from the Presbyterian church, spoke out against King Leopold's atrocities against Africans on the rubber plantations of the Belgian Congo. His spoken theology of evangelism was a soul-saving theology, but his practice took him into prophetic witness against the degradation of native peoples. He appeared before both the British Parliament and the president of the United States to plead the cause of the oppressed Congolese (Sheppard 2006, 26).

Feminist and womanist theologies also proclaim the gospel in prophetic ways. The emphasis on a fully human life for women and the struggle for equality in church and society marks the prophetic teaching of theologians Rosemary Radford Ruether, Jacqueline Grant, Letty Russell, Maria Isasi-Diaz, and Nyambura Njoroge. While they hold different theologies of evangelism, each finds motivation in Jesus's model of relating to women and his insistence on releasing the captives in their work of prophetic preaching.

J. Alfred Smith, retired pastor, professor, and teacher in the National Baptist and Progressive Baptist conventions, provides a contemporary example of prophetic preaching as evangelistic witness. A basic theme of his prophetic preaching is seeking justice. His theological entry point is Luke 4:18–21, Jesus's inaugural sermon. On that basis he encourages Christians to "speak truth to power" (2006, 4). Smith bases his call for faithful discipleship in the preaching of the cross (30–31). He insists that the witness of the church is crucial to God's work in the world and that witness centers on preaching Jesus Christ, crucified (35). He also speaks prophetic words to the nation, for example, after 9/11 and Hurricane Katrina (3). He calls the nation to avoid doing evil and to take on a spirit of humility (22–23).

A distinguishing mark of J. Alfred Smith's prophetic preaching is that he includes everyone: all are prone to temptation; all are in need of the good news of the gospel. Rather than separate Christians and unbelievers, Smith calls all to the cross through his faithful witness of prophetic preaching. And he insists that those who practice prophetic preaching be ethically consistent in their private lives and their public policy and practice (2006, 15). Smith's holistic approach links justice with proclaiming the gospel, ties personal lifestyle with public witness, and gives strength for the journey to individuals and to the church.

Faith Sharing (Church, Lifestyle, Proclamation)

The thought of sharing one's Christian faith in words produces a number of reactions. In many mainline churches, the reaction can be one of fear or distaste. Evangelism in those circles has become the "E word," a word that evokes instant discomfort and sometimes feelings of guilt (Reese 2006, 3–4). For those in evangelical churches, sharing one's faith is part of the Christian life. A person may feel confident or timid, successful or a failure at sharing the gospel. Either way, talking about Jesus's life and its meaning is an expected part of becoming a disciple of Christ.

Martha Grace Reese in *Unbinding the Gospel* explores the first attitude toward faith sharing. She outlines the necessity of sharing the gospel and drawing people into Christian community as part of the faithful witness of the church. On the basis of her five-year study of evangelism, a study that included over a thousand interviews, she gives an account for the lacuna in faith sharing among mainline Protestant denominations in the United States. She gives numerous suggestions for how churches might develop their ability to share their faith with persons inside and outside the congregation. Helping congregants learn to articulate the meaning Christ has in their lives is one prong of her method. Identifying societal groups that can be targeted—our children and their friends, uncommitted church attenders, transfers into the church, those who have drifted from church, those hurt by the church, and non-Christians—forms a beginning point for faith sharing (Reese 2006, 89).

Reese points out that faith sharing already happens in the church and beyond its walls, sometimes without awareness. But the focus on self-aware sharing of the faith is a major part of Reese's approach.

She explores with mainline Christians the reasons that Jesus has meaning for their lives. She comes up with a list of six reasons that motivate them to share the gospel among people who do not want to focus on life after death as the main meaning of Jesus for them: the joy of seeing people's lives change, seeing people who have had it tough get a new start in life, people becoming Christians and joining their church, seeing the power of God healing people's lives through the church community, seeing a relationship with Jesus change the lives of prisoners and the lives of those reaching out to prisoners, and feeling the work of the Spirit while in prayer for someone (outlined in sidebar 7.3). Those miraculous events motivated the Christians Reese interviewed to share their faith. Then she asks the reader, "So, what motivates you?" (2006, 21).

Becky Pippert's classic book *Out of the Salt Shaker* takes a similar approach for a different constituency. Aimed at evangelical Christians, Pippert's approach focuses on building relationships with non-Christians as an entrée to sharing the good news of the gospel. By forming a friendship, the Christian models Jesus's love, a preparation for sharing the news of Christ's love for the world. Pippert stresses a personal relationship with Christ, using the human friendship component as a base.

These examples show that a theology of faith sharing crosses the lines of theological thinking from liberal to conservative. The practice of sharing one's faith can be done in a congregational setting, a workplace, a travel situation, or a family devotional hour. Although more comfortable for Christians in some denominations, this approach can find meaning in many.

> **Sidebar 7.3 Six Reasons for Faith Sharing**
>
> 1. The joy of seeing people's lives change
> 2. Seeing people who have had it tough get a new start in life
> 3. People becoming Christians and joining their church
> 4. Seeing the power of God healing people's lives through the church community
> 5. Seeing a relationship with Jesus change the lives of prisoners and the lives of those involved in faith sharing
> 6. Feeling the work of the Spirit while in prayer for someone
>
> adapted from Reese 2006

Church Planting (Church, Apologetics, Proclamation)

When we think of church planting, our minds immediately leap to the missionary church-planting movement. Christians who long to see the gospel preached to all people everywhere go to great lengths to take the gospel to places where people have never heard it. Jim Elliot, martyred missionary to the Aucas in South America, typifies the zeal and sacrifice that many missionaries in this movement have shown in their work for the kingdom. His wife, Elisabeth Elliot, tells of the five missionaries who decide to fly into Auca territory and attempt to communicate with the head-hunting villagers. In her book *Shadow of the Almighty*, she speaks of the prayers and initial attempts at communication that the missionaries use. And she recounts the terrible consequences of the missionary venture when the deaths of the five missionaries are discovered. In later works, Elliot brings the story up to date, showing how the martyrdom of those early missionaries has resulted in the conversions of many Aucas and the ending of the head-hunting practices in those remote regions.

Usually we associate church planting with this kind of missionary work—a vigorous attempt to reach unreached people groups. Actually, church planting occurs across a spectrum of approaches used by various denominational groups. Independent churches commission small groups to start new churches that become independent entities. Jesus movements in Asia grow out of maturing church members and disciples, not church planters (Roberts 2008, 34). The Roman Catholic Church has taken the gospel all over the world by establishing Catholic churches in every place it has gone. It also builds schools and health clinics, works with the poor, and seeks justice for the communities it serves. Mainline Protestants also plant new churches. The Presbyterian Church (USA) planted 284 new churches between 1992 and 2002. The Christian Church (Disciples of Christ) has a national goal to plant one thousand new churches between 2000 and 2020 (Reese 2006, 33–34). The Orthodox Church in America actively seeks to establish new congregations and has grown considerably in the last thirty years.

Church planting is not a theology of evangelism that is limited denominationally. Let's look at two examples.

Vincent Donovan, a Catholic missionary who worked in Africa in the 1960s and 1970s tells of his experiences in his book *Christianity Rediscovered*. What Donovan found when he reached Tanzania was a well-established Catholic community living comfortably in walled compounds. Despite seven years of work, including the establishment of a hospital and a school that provided religious instruction, there were no adult practicing Christians among the people (2002, 15). Donovan's vision was for the tribes of the outlying villages. But he couldn't connect with them while living in the city, sequestered behind mission-compound walls. He appealed to the authorities to allow him to live among the people, to travel as an evangelist to small villages, to plant churches if the village chiefs accepted the Christian message.

Donovan tells about his visits to the tribal villages, about preaching the gospel, then rehearing it through the responses of the villagers. He recounts his experiences of reframing the gospel in culturally adept forms, of watching whole villages accept Christianity, of churches planted in those villages. He shares his disappointment as some villages reject Christianity and he has to walk away. His reliance on the Spirit of God and on God's grace in moving the hearts of whole villages to embrace the gospel inspires those who read his story. The gospel is "rediscovered" together by Catholic missionaries and African tribes (see sidebar 7.4).

Bob Roberts Jr. in *The Multiplying Church* talks about "the new math for starting new churches." He uses his experience as the founding pastor of the twenty-five-hundred-member NorthWood Church near Fort Worth, Texas, to set forth his model of church multiplication. Roberts takes his cue from the Asian Jesus movements and their focus on small groups that go out to form new churches. The focus is not on revival or church growth but rather on indigenous multiplication. Local churches start new churches in their locale. Unpredictable patterns of rapid growth characterize the church multiplication that Roberts describes. That multiplication is fueled by the churches themselves. Not individuals but groups of Christians catch the vision and spontaneously multiply (Roberts 2008, 44–45).

Roberts tells the story of Abba Love Church in Jakarta, Indonesia. Eddy Leo, an Indonesian college student, found Jesus and, along with two friends, sparked the growth of this twenty-five-thousand-member church. The key to this explosive growth did not lie in charismatic leaders; it was not orchestrated or driven from the outside; it was a movement, not a program (Roberts 2008, 46).

From such a start, it is not surprising to hear that the church itself gets into the act. Roberts insists that although church planters may begin the action, it is churches themselves that spark and sustain a movement of church multiplication (2008, 46).

Roberts further contends that "a global church planting movement is the natural progression from where we have come" (2008, 46) (see sidebar 7.5). The explosive growth of church-planting movements like the one in Jakarta are

---

Sidebar 7.4 How to Reach Tribal Peoples with the Gospel of Christ

Donovan's Method

1. Live outside of the Catholic compound.
2. Travel from village to village.
3. Seek permission from the village authorities to preach the gospel.
4. After preaching, ask for responses from villagers.
5. Preach the gospel again using their cultural forms.
6. Continue this dialogue of the gospel for two weeks.
7. After two weeks ask the village chiefs to decide if the village should become Christian.
8. Respect their answer and leave the village, whether they decide to accept Christianity or not.
9. Resist the temptation to stay and form a church; the indigenous people with the help of the Holy Spirit will do that.

Donovan 2002, 31–33; see also Muck and Adeney 2009, 273, 297–98

easier to find in Asia than in the West. But Roberts points to the NorthWood Church in Texas as a possible starting point. He claims that there are more people interested in church planting than there were twenty years ago. Young pastors want to plant churches; churches in nations want to plant churches in other nations. And Revelation 5:9–10 speaks of a new song that people will sing from every tribe and nation. Theologically, Roberts believes that "a global church planting movement will be necessary for the bride of Christ to be prepared for the coming of Christ" (47).

Common Themes

In outlining the seven theologies of evangelism above, it is easy to see that much overlap and confluence of themes occur among them. Each focuses on a major theme but includes other themes for support. Much like a musical symphony, each theology presents a unique composition but utilizes similar themes. Themes of proclamation/apologetics, love/acceptance, church/community, liberation, and practices/lifestyle recur in most of the theologies presented.

There are also real differences among them—interpretations of eschatology, views of women in leadership, ideas about church authority, conceptions about how God works in the world. But those differences need not produce conflict. In fact, usually conflict arises when proponents of a particular theology attempt to "claim the turf" by separating their view from others. Theologians who wish to distance themselves from the evangelistic fervor of the Protestant churches in Europe and the United States in the eighteenth and nineteenth century sometimes assert that their interpretations are correct and all-inclusive

---

Sidebar 7.5 Why a Global Church-Planting Movement Makes Sense

A global church-planting movement:

- Is the natural progression from where we are
- Is the natural response of the emerging global church (Rev. 5:9–10)
- Will be necessary for the bride of Christ to be prepared for the coming of Christ (John 3:29–30; Rev. 21:2–3)
- Is possible in a world with an emerging third culture
- Is possible like never before because of the technology that exists in the world today
- Will happen only when we learn to treat each other with respect and have a classless and raceless church (Gal. 3:26–29)
- Will happen when we recognize there is only one church (Eph. 4:2–6)

Roberts 2008, 46–49

while the interpretations of others are narrow and imperialistic. Theologians who wish to perpetuate the evangelistic efforts of the eighteenth and nineteenth century into the future life of the church claim that their traditional theologies are the only viable ones and that shifting the focus from proclaiming the gospel in traditional ways is wrongheaded and dilutes the power of the gospel. As the church learns to accept our history as belonging to all of us, perhaps those turf wars will become less virulent and we will learn to live more graciously with one another.

The theologies in this chapter are all helpful as we move forward in evangelism. The overlap among them instructs us to expand rather than exclude as we develop our own theology of evangelism. The next chapter describes what it is that all of us are seeking as we share the gospel with others. We seek abundant life, a life that exhibits the qualities outlined in the theologies of evangelism of this chapter—love and relationships, service and community, practices and lifestyle, proclamation and apologetics, discipleship and justice—an abundant grace-filled life.

PART 3

Where Are We Going?

8

Abundant Life

"Keep your eyes on the prize" is an African American saying that helped keep civil rights advocates on track during the 1960s. In a similar way, Christians need to stay focused on the goal of evangelism. What is the good end that we are after when we share and serve for the sake of the gospel? Let's examine the prize so that we can keep our eyes on it.

What is it we are after for ourselves? For others? For the world? I think if we are honest, most of us would admit that we want to flourish. We want life in abundance. We want meaningful relationships and safety for those we love. We want our world to be at peace. We want food and shelter, clean water and clean air. We want nature to flourish around us. We want to be free of guilt and fear in our lives, now and after death. We want spiritual nurture and insights into the meaning of our lives. We want to know God. We want discipline and achievements to characterize our lives. We want laughter in good times and consolation when we are sick or grieving, or when our world seems to be descending into chaos. We want abundant life.

Seeking Abundant Life

How do we find the path to abundant life and share it with others? Even the characteristics of abundant life listed here can be disputed. And obviously human flourishing, however described, is not automatic or guaranteed in this life. We sometimes worry about the life to come as well. It is precisely in those ambiguities that the good news of the gospel fits into the picture.

In order to flourish, we first need to know how this world works. If we all want the same thing, why doesn't it happen? Understanding human longings for goodness and peace along with the human capacity for greed and destruction is imperative if we are to move ourselves, our communities, and our world in the direction of human flourishing. We need to understand the balances of power that can lead to war or peace, the environmental tipping point between rejuvenation and debilitation of the ecosystem, the economic balances that must be achieved so that humans and all creation can flourish. We flourish only if we all flourish together—persons and nations, lenders and borrowers, plant life and animal life and human life.

No one person can grasp all those aspects of life on our planet. We each work and play among people in our community and in larger spheres of public life. Working together in relationships can enable us to be part of the struggle for balance that leads to flourishing in the world. And relationships are not incidental or less important than knowledge of our world—analyzing good and evil and achieving necessary balances.

Scholars from different communities have argued for the centrality of relationships for abundant life. Christian theologian Emil Brunner claimed that humans are *created* for relationships. For Brunner, the basis of the Good is found in creation, and the calling of the Christian is to serve the neighbor (1947, 208–9). The neighbor is not distant, but definite and near. "Your neighbor is the person who meets you" (208). Without relationships with our neighbors, humans cannot flourish. American philosopher George Herbert Mead argued that we only come to know ourselves through seeing how others respond to us. That process of action and response gives us our social bearings and helps us to form our attitudes and values (Mead 1934, 158). In *The Relational Self*, psychologist Archie Smith argues that working with this relational quality is crucial for the life of the African American church. Even self-knowledge is connected to relationships with others in this view.

Theologian H. Richard Niebuhr asserts that the self has a social character (1989, 46–47). Niebuhr further suggests that relationships are more than a two-way street; instead, they are triadic. Building on Josiah Royce's concept of a common loyalty called upon in any relationship, Niebuhr identifies our common loyalty as God (1989, 60–61). God is in our relationships, the third party who helps us trust one another. God longs for human relationships to flourish and bring good within and beyond them.

The apostle Paul describes this three-way partnership in his work with the gentiles (Rom. 15–16). His call to the gentiles is from God, and he is empowered by God's Spirit and supported by the church in Rome in that endeavor. Paul makes it clear that God is always present in relationships with people—be it the non-Christian gentiles or the Roman Christians. Our common loyalty (God) is part of the relationship. That is how the world works. Understand-

Sidebar 8.1 Partnership in Mission

Paul's Triadic Approach

Romans 15 and 16 describe Paul's approach to reaching unreached gentiles. Triad of ministry:

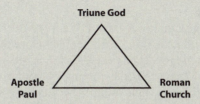

1. Triune God (God and Christ, 15:5–6, 17–19; Holy Spirit, 15:13)
   • The relational God works with us in ministry.
2. Paul's work (15:15–17, 30–32)
   • Paul serves God by becoming a minister of Christ to the gentiles.
3. Roman church's work (15:1–2, 7, 22–24, 32; chap. 16)
   • The church builds up the neighbor, accepting one another, and praying for Paul. They offer hospitality, do the work of apostles, and work hard serving the church.

ing that triadic dimension of relationships helps us do evangelism that yields abundant life rather than dissension and division (see sidebar 8.1).

In these chapters Paul illustrates mission in partnership, linking his call to the gentiles, the support of the Roman church, and the work of God in Christ through the Holy Spirit. And lest we think that the work of evangelism is for church leaders only, historian Peter Lampe concluded that most mentioned in Romans 16 were gentiles, freed slaves, or descendants of freed slaves (Muck 2005, 1872n).

Josiah Royce, an early American philosopher, argued that every relationship includes self, other, and a common loyalty. H. Richard Niebuhr applied that notion to Christian fellowship. The self relates to the other, in this case Paul to the church at Rome. But the common loyalty (God) is central to that relationship.

Reading Romans 15–16 as a narrative clearly shows how the Triune God works with Paul and the Romans to bring the gospel to the gentiles. Paul highlights a number of important facets of this triadic view of partnership. First, God is always present in the relationship—the third party in the partnership. Paul repeatedly mentions that God is working in the relationship between himself and the gentiles (15:15–19). And God is working in the relationship between Paul and the church at Rome (15:28–32). So God is present in relationships between ourselves and the other. Second, through God's call to Paul (15:18–19) we infer that God can work through Christians today in this same relational way. Third, God's work in relationship can be applied to the church, the Roman gentiles in this case (15:5, 13–14 and chap. 16 commendations). This pattern of triadic partnership in outreach can be seen to be God's work in Rome. We can apply that model to mission in partnership with God and God's people today.

Focus on our common loyalty (God) is part of the relationship of partnership in mission. God is working with people before the evangelist gets there. Paul's vision to reach unreached peoples is furthered by their longing for God (15:21). Isaiah 52:15 says that the coming Messiah will "sprinkle many nations, and kings will shut their mouths because of him. For what they were not told, they will see, and what they have not heard, they will understand." God goes ahead of us, already there when we arrive. God's work, Paul's effort, and the partnership of the Roman church bring new people whom God has prepared into the church.

Trying to understand the world in its stark contrasts between goodness and baseness, along with the need for human action to achieve balance, leads us to relationships. And trying to understand and make relationships work in a way that results in flourishing leads us to trying to understand the third partner in relationships—that is, God.

In our search to understand God, God reaches out to us with the good news of the gospel of Jesus Christ. That God, who is always with us and goes before us in every relationship and action, sent Jesus into the world to help us find human flourishing is good news indeed. Jesus modeled for all of us the path to human flourishing. He gave his life to mend the world, to break down walls of hostility, to bring forgiveness and peace to the confused relationships of people with one another and balance to the chaos created by sinful people and the social structures we create.

To find abundant life, we try to understand the world, thrive in our relationships, and know God. Evangelism is at the heart of this endeavor because God sent Jesus into the world to reveal God's self and to bring all things together in Christ (Eph. 1:9–10). Through relationship with God, persons and communities can learn to pursue peace, to share God's goodness with one another, to change oppressive social structures, to show compassion for the poor. It is through the gospel that Christians leave aside their fear and walk forward into the unknown, seeking change in themselves and in society. We walk in the way, bringing good tidings, announcing that the kingdom of God is at hand.

Christians don't have all the answers about how to achieve human flourishing and the flourishing of all creation. Christians disagree about ways to go about changing the world, the nature of the afterlife, the role of the church in the world, even the qualities of good and evil. We may stress different aspects of abundant life in our theologies. But Christians *do know* that abundant life is the goal and that Jesus came into the world to save us and point the way toward that goal.

So, we need to keep our eyes on the prize. So much of what we focus on is peripheral to the good news—even detrimental to it. The times we live in are not simple, and the answers to how to achieve abundant life in the world are not simple either. But Jesus Christ has come. He has atoned for the sins of the whole world. God has sent this light into the world and has given us the grace to follow the way. Paul counted on that grace in reaching out to gentiles (Rom. 15:15). We can count on God's grace too. We have good news to share. And we can learn to share it gracefully in our contemporary world.

Evangelism Brings Abundant Life

In the last chapter we outlined seven theologies of evangelism. Each of them called the church to develop a particular area of abundant life—building the kingdom of God, faithfully serving the needs of others, worshiping and welcoming others into community, transforming worldviews, seeking justice in society, sharing our faith, and growing the church (see sidebar 8.2). In building the kingdom, Christians embody a vision that leads to making disciples. In serving others, Christians model the love of Christ for the world. In accepting those who come to our communities, we practice the welcome that God has shown to us. In understanding and explaining a Christian worldview, we

---

Sidebar 8.2 Evangelism Brings Abundant Life

1. **Building the Kingdom of God**. A vision of the church making disciples for the kingdom; discipleship in context.
2. **Faithful Service**. God's people orienting their lives to meet the needs of others; fulfilling needs.
3. **Worshiping and Welcoming Communities**. Communities of the faithful worshiping together, welcoming others, and leading Christ-like lives.
4. **Transforming Worldviews**. Bringing people to a biblical understanding of God and the world that transforms lives.
5. **Prophetic Preaching**. Speaking truth to power until justice is realized in society.
6. **Sharing Our Faith**. Building vital relationships with God and sharing the wonders of those relationships with others.
7. **Growing the Church**. Multiplying churches so that lives are changed and the gospel is proclaimed in congregations.

participate in God's transformation of lives. In prophetic preaching, we show the liberating influence that God wants to have on the world. In faith sharing, we tell others about the life-changing experience of knowing God through Christ. And in growing the church, we work with God to expand God's influence in lives and communities around the world.

Taken together these theologies of evangelism show a picture of what Christians long for in the church and in society and how we work toward those ends. They show how abundant life can result from working together with God in evangelism.

Let's take one of those theologies as an example, to show how evangelism reaches toward and proclaims abundant life.

Central to a Christian understanding of abundant life is the idea of the kingdom of God. Christians have a vision of God's reign that goes beyond the church but sees the church as a major agent of change in society. Christians want to grow in faith so that they might have a positive effect on the world, helping to realize the values of the kingdom. Jesus announced his purpose in life in terms of bringing in the reign of God—preaching good news to the poor, releasing captives, giving sight to the blind, healing the lame—and Christians are called to take up that work of Jesus in the world today.

Consequently, Christianity is intrinsically mission oriented. Jones, in his book *The Evangelistic Love of God and Neighbor*, outlines two prongs to that missionary endeavor: first, the church exists to worship God and serve God's mission by bearing witness to what God has done, is doing, and will do (2003, 54). This vision of abundant life includes a community of worshipers whose worship focuses on God. A vision of all of life lived in awareness of God's presence becomes part of abundant life for Christians (56). Jones's second prong includes bearing witness to God's work in the world. Abundant life includes both speaking and acting on behalf of the kingdom (58). Fulfilling this vision of abundant life requires spiritual formation. Jones stresses growth in discipleship as a way of increasing our ability to love as God loves. He envisions a choreography of Holy Spirit action in human spirits. Abundant life includes the dance of God through persons and communities as Christians imagine and live into the kingdom of God.

Since the vision of abundant life is larger than the church, the church is seen as a unique people that offers hospitality to the stranger. The abundant life that Christians imagine is not limited by the walls of the church itself. The church, as God's agent of kingdom building, reaches out to the stranger. It seeks justice in the world, proclaiming the truth of Jesus and working to see the world learn the ways of peace (Jones 2003, 58).

It is easy to see how an evangelism focused on the kingdom of God affirms God's mission partnerships in the world and includes a broad vision of abundant life for all. Each of the other theologies can be explicated in a similar way. Communities involved in faithfully serving the sick and needy send a clear message about abundant life and its center in Christ. Worshiping communities proclaim the gospel by their very presence in our pluralistic world. Worldview seminars and God and Science courses as well as liberation theologies and lifestyle evangelism point to a biblical worldview that continues to change lives and communities. Seeking justice in society as Christians work to change oppressive social structures includes the public witness of speaking truth to power and showing Christ's concern for all of life. Building vital relationships in our own corner of the world provides opportunities for sharing our faith in Christ. Church planting changes people's lives and reforms communities around Christian values. Together those theologies of evangelism form a tremendously broad and rich view of abundant life in Christ.

Focusing on Essentials

Since the concept of abundant life is so broad and full, diverse theologies and outreach emphases show a corresponding breadth. Not all Christian communities work at all the methods of evangelism outlined above. But all of them do focus on three essential themes, both in theology and in practice: our relationship with God, the necessity of serving the poor, and a vibrant fellowship surrounding worship. These are essential features of any community that is doing evangelism.

Relationship with God

So many of Jesus's comments reflect his dependence on his relationship with God. He would go off to the mountains to spend time alone with God. He longed for his disciples to be one with the Father as he himself felt that oneness (John 17:20–21). That relationship energized and nurtured him. It was always present in his relationships with others. Jesus described the person living close to God as one full of springs of water—living water that wells up inside and flows out into life-giving patterns of living (John 4:14). As those springs of water well up and overflow, others are drawn to the life in Christ that Christians experience.

St. Augustine, who discovered relationship with God after searching for meaning in many ways, surmised that there is a God-shaped vacuum in every person. Finding our way into relationship with God is part of abundant life. Finding forgiveness and new life in a relationship with God through Christ leads to a desire to share that life with others. In fact, our very way of living changes, allowing us to become a witness to those around us.

A contemporary example from villages that I visited in Indonesia in the 1990s makes the point. The indigenous religion of the people on the island of Sumba, Indonesia, emphasizes relationship, not with the living, but with the dead. Women spend their days weaving intricate cloths. These valuable weavings are not used or sold. They are stored in the peaked roofs of the house and saved until the elders die. The bodies are then wrapped and buried in these beautiful cloths. Showing respect for the dead in this religion consumes nearly the whole livelihood of the living. The reason for this attention to the dead is that the people believe that the spirits of the ancestors will retaliate if these rituals are not carried out. The result would be disaster.

Villages that practice the traditional religion in Sumba are poor. Children with extended bellies stare out from drab porticos of simple wood houses. By contrast, brightly painted fences and playful children greeted me in the Christian villages I visited. Women brought out their lovely woven clothes to sell. The rooftop rooms were empty, but the children's bellies were full. Relationship with God had dispelled fears of disaster, and the villagers lived a more abundant life.

Good News to the Poor

The Sumbanese Christians were released from abject poverty because their fear of spirit attacks was replaced with trust in God. But there are other reasons for poverty. And while God does not promise us unending health and wealth, the abundant life does require freedom from hunger and want. Jesus felt compassion for the crowds who followed him—people searching for direction, wandering like sheep without a shepherd. Jesus not only told them the good news of the gospel; he sat them down in groups and shared fish and bread with them (Matt. 14:13–21).

As Christians continue Christ's mission, we strive to relieve physical suffering. Large-scale poverty from global economic imbalances or natural disasters and small-scale suffering from unexpected illness or loss of income are all concerns of Christian mission. We participate in the church's long-standing tradition of bringing education, health care, and famine-relief services to those in need. Those mission efforts proclaim that God wants abundant life for all people. As we follow Jesus's example of relieving suffering and want, we point the way to Christ; we proclaim the gospel.

When my sister's church in Minnesota established ties with a congregation in Slovakia, the fellowship between the two churches resulted in a sharing of both faith and physical resources. A "giftive mission" was established (Muck and Adeney 2009, 354). Rather than a one-way mission, gifts were given and received between the two congregations. The American Christians were inspired by the dedicated dependence on God shown by this little, poor community in Slovakia. The Christians there benefited in their turn by receiving sewing machines and other income-producing resources from the church in the United States. By showing that physical well-being is part of the abundant life, the outreach program proclaimed the gospel. For as James reminds us, telling a person to be warm and filled without giving them what they need simply does not show the love of Christ (2:14–17).

Joyful Fellowship

By seeking the welfare of Christians around the world, my sister Catherine also participated in a joyful fellowship of believers. Working and worshiping together in Christ and sharing our lives with one another helps Christian communities to develop a sense of the love of Christ in our lives. Jesus showed the disciples that as we love one another we experience joy. The result of following the new commandment to love, Jesus promised, would be a fullness of our own joy as Christ's joy fills us (John 15:9–11).

Joyful worshiping communities show the love of God for the world through Christ. Consider the many ways people can spend a Sunday morning. The witness of those who choose to worship God with a community stands out in our pluralistic world. At a small church in northern Wisconsin, where snowmobiling in winter and fishing in summer are major attractions, we always end the service by saying, "Thank you for coming to church." People come because there is life there. The vibrancy of the worship draws others to the community. People are attracted to life and tend to go where they see it happening.

There are many ways to intentionally bring people into the circle of companionship that we feel in our churches. Taking a loaf of home-baked bread to visitors who leave their address on the visitor's card at the morning service is one simple way to welcome them. That effort shows a real commitment on the part of the congregation to welcome the stranger.

One pastor told me that if a visitor returns a second time, he or she is asked to usher, to read a Bible passage, to bring coffee, or to do some other small task that contributes to the life of the community. "We try so hard to fill people's needs," he told me, "but we forget that everyone has a need to be needed" (Adeney 2000). The need to be needed and the need to feel included are both met by the bold and creative actions of these congregations.

Receiving fresh bread, taking on a task, building Christian friendships across cultures—these are a few ways that churches are nurturing the joy of Christian fellowship and finding abundant life in their congregations. There are many others. Ways of welcome spring out of communities that experience joy in their life with God and in their fellowship together.

Finding and sharing our relationship with God, faithfully serving the poor among us and in the world, and building a community that shares joyfully in worship and service are essential features of Christian evangelism that proclaims abundant life in Christ. We don't all do it the same way—our theologies and ministries vary. But these three essential features mark the evangelism of all our communities of faith.

9

A Mission Statement for Evangelism

When I returned to the United States in 1996, after living in Indonesia for five years, I noticed something new in many businesses, hospitals, and educational institutions. Prominently displayed on their reception-area walls were mission statements: "St. John's Hospital exists to enable patients in the healing process." "The Kleen Carpet Company transforms the carpets in homes and businesses in a thorough and efficient manner."

Most of our congregations have mission statements. Our mission statement at the seminary states: "The purpose of Louisville Presbyterian Theological Seminary is to serve the church and the world by educating men and women for participation in the continuing redemptive ministry of Jesus Christ." That sums up, in the most general terms, our educational goals at the seminary.

Congregational mission statements attempt to summarize a church's central calling as a community of God's people. Evangelism fits into that calling. Differences in theologies of evangelism can make some churches' missions seem incompatible with the callings of other churches, but perhaps understanding the mission statements of others can lead to a broader theology of evangelism. How does evangelism fit into the mission of the church?

What Is Our Mission?

Jesus made it clear that everyone has a purpose in life. In John 10:10, for example, he told his disciples that thieves exist to steal. Jesus then goes on to state, in contrast, what his mission here on earth was: "I came that [people]

108

may have life, and have it abundantly" (John 10:10 NRSV). The reason for Jesus's existence on earth—his mission statement—was to bring abundant life to the world.

That goal, abundant life, can become the basis for a mission statement for evangelism. When Jesus left this world, he passed the torch on to the church. The church exists to bring life to the world—abundant life.

But not all congregations focus on every area of abundant life described in the last chapter as part of evangelism. Different denominations develop distinctive theologies of evangelism and focus on these as they prepare their mission statement for evangelism. Some focus on growing the congregation through warm fellowship, others stress discipleship, and still others plant new churches or serve the poor of their community. Not every mission statement for evangelism is alike. Do they need to be alike?

Tensions in Evangelism among Denominations

Tensions arise among denominations because one focuses on proclamation through revival meetings or prison ministry, another on church planting, another on serving the poor, while another stresses social justice as a way to witness. As we saw in the last chapter, the different theologies of evangelism all fit into a broader concept of abundant life. But people disagree on what part of abundant life should be considered evangelism.

Sometimes there are good reasons for hesitation about certain types of evangelism. If people are hurting others through their witness, if witness serves merely to stock the coffers of an organization, if Christians deceive others as they witness, if unorthodox theologies are at the center of witness—those are good reasons for rejecting certain forms of evangelism.

Jesus's words in John 10:10 recognize those dangers. He makes the statement about abundant life using an analogy of himself as a shepherd who cares for the sheep and hired hands who abandon the sheep when danger strikes (John 10:11–14). Not all evangelistic efforts spring from Christian love or care for God's people. Sometimes a stereotype about evangelism; a painful memory of an experience of evangelism; or a theological difference about the nature of God, eschatology, or mission methods can lead Christians to categorically reject the mission of evangelism as others see it.

When I moved from a university setting and began teaching evangelism and mission at Louisville Seminary, there were two kinds of students who drew for me the outer limits of the theological framework for Christian mission and evangelism. One was the gung-ho evangelist. This student felt that most of us at Louisville Seminary, students and faculty alike, were not mission-minded enough. Repeated references to the necessity of reaching the world for Christ were combined with strong admonitions to others to get with the program. I remember one student announcing to my evangelism class a prayer time for the evangelization of the world, to be held at 7:00 a.m. the next morning around the flagpole. Later that day, an e-mail arrived saying that the demonstration would be convened "where the flagpole would be if we had one." The student was so anxious to get a prayer meeting scheduled that he neglected to organize a concrete location for it.

In contrast to this unbridled enthusiasm was the student on the other end of the theological spectrum—the evangelist to the evangelists. This student usually said little during the first few weeks of class. But the impatience behind her or his surface stoicism eventually burst out with a vengeance. This student was convinced that evangelism was a bad thing and should be stopped immediately. Evangelism perpetuated the injustice of colonial imperialism. Those students evangelized students and faculty alike to quit the notion of evangelism and limit Christian mission to good deeds.

How can we move beyond those narrow stereotypes to a graceful evangelism? One group had a constricted view of Christian mission, limited to a particular and culturally determined interpretation of the Great Commission. The other group, with similar evangelistic zeal, insisted that actually talking about the good news of Jesus's way was detrimental to the church and to the world. Of course, neither ideological framework fits the facts. And both can be destructive to Christian unity and human flourishing.

Beyond the Great Divide: Perspective and Location

I decided to approach the problem of this theological chasm in my classes in two ways. The first was a theoretical approach. With the help of social theorists Max Weber, Peter Berger, Cornel West, and Robert Bellah, we uncovered ways that our perceptions about evangelism are formed and how those perceptions affect the world. Our theologies do not find their sources only in the Bible or in church tradition; they are also shaped by our historical location, our social/economic situation, and our cultural setting. A wholesome recognition of the limitedness of our own perspectives, along with a broadening of what might be considered acceptable theologies of evangelism resulted. Different ideas of evangelism for different settings, varied but not incompatible, entered the realm of possibility for the students.

My second approach was a narrative one. The complexities and dilemmas of a particular person in his or her context became the vehicle for a richer understanding of the function of evangelism and mission in the world. Real-life stories defy the categorizations imposed by limited theologies of evangelism and mission. Hearing real evangelism stories not only broadens our own theologies, if we have ears to hear, but also changes our theory of mission. We begin to see Christian mission operating in the world in ways we had not perceived. We see a myriad of effects that evangelization and mission have in real-life settings. Our thinking about Christian mission and its role in society changes as we study the lives of particular people (Adeney 2009).

Combining those two approaches can heal the divide on evangelism that Christians experience in the church today, bringing us to a more graceful evangelism. Understanding our context, which the topic of the next chapter, and the social location of those with whom we disagree can go a long way in aiding understanding and acceptance of types of evangelism that differ from our own. Getting to know people who practice evangelism differently can bring us to a better understanding of what they are doing and why. Telling someone about Jesus in different ways, or showing Christ's love in different ways, can be better understood if we know the person who is committed to that type of evangelism.

An open mind toward other styles of evangelism doesn't mean we have to practice all forms of evangelism in our own setting. We can, however, develop a more gracious attitude to others' approaches in theological and social settings different from our own.

Beyond the Great Divide: History and Theology

Tensions among churches throughout the world have sometimes focused on how the church has grown and changed. The negative implications of Western colonialist expansion hurt the church today. The growth of some sectors of the churches in Latin America, Africa, and Asia causes distress to founding churches and new churches in the regions. The decline of Christianity in the West produces anxiety. A historical explanation of these changes can help heal the wounds.

Missiologist and historian Dana Robert speaks of the movement of the global church from North to South, pointing to the massive changes in the global composition of the church that occurred during the twentieth century. Africa, Asia, and Latin America all experienced growth while the European churches declined numerically. By the end of the twentieth century, the typical Christian was not a European man but an African or Latin American woman. There were more Anglicans in Africa than in the United States. Both liberation theologies and Pentecostal-like movements have prospered in Latin America since World War II (2008, 118).

The differences are not only numerical. Robert claims that "Christianity throughout the non-Western world has in common an indigenous, grassroots leadership; embeddedness in local cultures; and reliance on a vernacular Bible. Christianity is growing in the South; it supports stable family and community life for peoples suffering political uncertainty and economic hardships" (2008, 129). Such changes indicate that the tensions between a liberation emphasis and more traditional evangelistic approaches can be overcome in practice if not in the theological perspectives of different groups. Understanding the growth of the church in the settings Robert describes can help us, as twenty-first-century Christians, appreciate a variety of theological emphases in evangelization.

Theological divisions between a social justice emphasis in evangelism and a traditional approach need not perpetuate tensions among and within denominations. New theological approaches to that tension can bring healing to traditional divides.

Theologian Mercy Oduyoye works from a church practices approach, reaching out from Christian practices of baptism, Eucharist, and mission to heal divisions between traditional and more contextual African approaches. First, she argues for a complementarity between the World Council of Churches' statements *Baptism, Eucharist and Ministry* and *Mission and Evangelism: An Ecumenical Statement*. Moving beyond the divisions caused by diverse theologies of Christian rituals, she shows the link between unity and mission (2008, 331). Whereas *Baptism, Eucharist and Ministry* challenges the churches to take the causes of their division seriously, *Mission and Evangelism: An Ecumenical Statement* challenges them to "announce the reign of God which alone is the ground of hope in this world" (332).

Oduyoye understands evangelism as both conversion to Christ and the enculturation of human culture, the building up of "cells" of Christian believers in the midst of human communities (336). Her methodology combines both a liberation approach, bringing action and reflection together, and an ecclesiology bringing baptism, Eucharist, and ministry to the center of the church's attention (332).

Finally, she argues that unity itself is mission. Without visible unity, the credibility of the Christian message weakens (Oduyoye 2008, 338). By working with the two documents, Oduyoye explores ways to develop and strengthen the mission of the people of God. It is all the members of the body of Christ, not only theologians, pastors, and evangelists, "who care for the united mission of the church and its effectiveness in this world for which Christ died" (339).

Letty Russell came at ecumenical unity from a liberation approach. In her essay "Liberation and Evangelization: A Feminist Perspective," she argues that "liberation and evangelization are interrelated because of the *freedom of God*" (2008, 416, emphasis original). She supports this notion by arguing for a view of salvation that includes both *shalom* (peace) and *soteria* (salvation). It is God who introduces humans to both, giving the gifts of God to humanity and all creation. Struggling to represent the wholeness of the biblical perspective has led Russell to encourage the church to share the whole gospel with the whole world. That sharing includes not only liberation but *kerygma* (word), *koinonia* (fellowship), and *diakonia* (service) (418). Although ecumenical unity around theologies of evangelization and salvation has failed to materialize in recent decades, a global dialogue is beginning to emerge (419). It is through that dialogue that both feminist perspectives and ecumenical perspectives can join together to share the good news about God's liberating and blessing action in the world (419).

Russell does not argue that such an approach will ameliorate the theological divisions in the church around evangelism. But she argues against a one-sided approach—either from a liberation perspective or from an evangelical perspective. She states that "the church's role is to point to Christ in the world and not to itself. . . . Remember that evangelization includes the totality of God's concern for liberation and blessing in all aspects of human life. . . . The gospel is contextual and situation-variable" (420). Remembering those complex factors in our twenty-first-century approaches to evangelism can help heal the great divide on evangelism that the twentieth century left us with.

Even as we broaden our acceptance of others' approaches to evangelism, we must face the question of how our churches will go about bringing abundant life to the world. Those approaches may be based on complex theologies, but they must become short and simple enough to put on a plaque or print in a church bulletin. Stated in clear terms, they then need to become part of the action of an ecumenical organization, a denomination, a congregation, an individual.

Developing a Mission Statement for Evangelism

Mission statements on plaques in businesses, hospitals, and educational institutions address the need for a clear statement of purpose. Most of them are backed up with lists of specific goals and objectives that those working in the establishment strive to fulfill in order to actualize the mission statement. The ways in which St. John's Hospital brings healing to the sick are many: radiology takes x-rays, the lab does blood work, the doctors diagnose, and the nurses give bedside care. Louisville Seminary fulfills its purpose by educating pastors and Christian counselors, educators, and other church leaders. Specific goals outline tasks that, when fulfilled, bring the mission of the group into being in the world.

How do we as communities of Christ's followers make specific our mission of bringing abundant life to the world? Not all tasks in evangelism are suitable for all churches, and different groups decide to practice mission in varied ways. There are four tasks that can help a particular congregation or denomination to assess its specific calling to evangelism (outlined in sidebar 9.1).

1. *Look around*. Before we can delineate specific steps to bring abundant life to others, we need to see what the situation around us presents. What does our congregation lack? What are the needs in our surrounding community?

Sidebar 9.1 How to Develop a Mission Statement for Evangelism

1. Look around
2. Assess needs
3. Cooperate with others
4. Act together on their concerns

When Jesus met the woman at the well, the presenting need was water (John 4:6–7). He and the woman came together because they shared this common need. Are there needs that a church shares with other congregations and/or the wider community?

Perhaps reconstruction of a road in front of a church building makes access difficult. Could church leaders meet with other businesses on the street to devise cooperative access, advertising, or parking schemes? Maybe the public schools in a particular area are cutting arts and music programs. Could a congregation cooperate with the PTA to find creative funding or even establish after-school art classes at the church? Maybe a new correctional institution or hospital is being built in the region. Could a church cooperate with other denominations in the area to set up a chaplaincy program or provide worship opportunities in that place?

These are just a few of many community service opportunities congregations can explore. David Bos's book *Bound Together* develops a theology for community ministries that encourages congregations to get involved with their communities. Those activities in turn lead to abundant life and witness to the gospel.

2. *Assess needs.* Seeing one's surroundings with new eyes includes interpreting the needs of the community and evaluating a congregation's ability to meet those needs. Do the talents and successes of the congregation line up with the needs of the community? Will the projects that are engaged connect with core theologies of the denomination and be a stimulator for abundant life in the community?

A number of years ago I visited a small, struggling Presbyterian church near a school for the blind. I greeted a blind couple who attended Sunday worship that day. What could this church do as it recognized the presence of blind people in its community? It could print the order of worship in braille, provide braille pew Bibles, inquire about doing a service at the school, invite a blind person to speak to the congregation about the special needs and capabilities of the blind. It could add braille books to the church library and send special invitations to church events to the school for the blind. It could offer evening sessions on music appreciation and encourage sung or spoken contributions from the blind visitors, drawing them into the community. It could inquire about the school's needs for sighted readers.

That is just a short list. The church needs to begin by recognizing the unique facets of its surroundings, assessing both the needs of the community and the talents of the congregation.

3. *Cooperate with others.* A mission statement for evangelism includes listening to others in the community—especially those we intend to serve. The process of assessing how to respond to specific community needs occurs in conversation.

Jesus listened to the woman at the well as she described her beliefs and expressed opinions. He entered into conversation with her about her concerns

(John 4:9–26). Listening to others and cooperating with their agenda is a crucial dimension of mission. We can't simply "give" abundant life to others. We must find our way together. Jesus didn't tell the woman what to do about her lifestyle. He simply told her that he was the source of living water (John 4:14).

The Presbyterian church near the school for the blind couldn't tell the school that the school needed oral readers or an in-house Christian worship service. Listening to others and hearing what *they feel they need* to make life more abundant is a crucial part of fostering abundant life. The Presbyterian church mentioned above *did listen* and took on many of those challenges. Today its congregation thrives.

4. *Act together on their concerns.* Sometimes the way a person or group assesses their own need is different from the way we might assess their needs. Listening and cooperating with them on *their concerns* may open the door to abundant life.

In Seram, an undeveloped, sparsely populated, and poor island of Indonesia, an old tribal chief explained his dilemma to me. "The Muslims want us to become Muslim; the Christians want us to become Christian. We don't want either religion. But our culture is dying" (1993, personal conversation). Only the week before, someone from his tribe had murdered a member of a neighboring tribe. Local police were investigating the crime. The tribal chief explained that a young man needed to bring a head from another tribe before the chief could sanction his marriage. This centuries-old cultural custom was now outlawed by the Indonesian government.

While the chief described the dying of his culture in terms of religious rivalries, it is evident that new laws and morals and the power to enforce them were encroaching on the chief's society as the national government of Indonesia reached into this outlying island. Cultures inevitably change. New political forces assert themselves; economic powers rise and fall; values shift. This Seramese chief attributed the changes in his village to the influx of new religions. But modern political forms, values, and economic structures also brought change to the village.

How could Christians cooperate with this chief? Could his lament of cultural loss be heard? What could be done? Through education the villagers could learn to recognize the complexities of the changes influencing their society. They could respond by interacting positively with democratic reforms and values. They could select ways to change their customs to conform with new political realities without losing their cultural distinctiveness.

If the church engaged in this process *with the chief and his people*, it is likely that Christian values would influence them. Some of their religious practices and rites of passage might change to reflect Christian values. For example, before marriage a young man might be required to bring an economic prize or an opportunity from a rival village rather than the head of a rival villager.

In addition, as the Seramese villagers learned to understand the Indonesian governmental system that was imposed upon them, they would gain power in that system, electing officials and influencing public policy.

As the church brought abundant life to the village by listening across difference and cooperating with the villagers in their assessment of their own needs, people would turn to the source of that abundant life. Rather than perceiving Christianity as a religion that pressured their village, they might begin to see Christianity as the source of a better life. The good news could then be heard. Tribal customs could be infused with Christian meaning. A dying culture could be transformed into a lively Christian society, contributing to the good of the village as well as the Indonesian nation.

In-Reach as Evangelism

We can't give away what we don't have. So evangelism actually begins with *in*-reach rather than *out*-reach. Cooperating with people's felt needs isn't only important to mission efforts across the globe. We need to listen to the needs of those in our own community because nurturing abundant life begins at home, sending a strong message to those around us.

Abundant life can be nurtured at home by quality in-reach to our children. Margaret Alter, a psychologist and member at Montclair Presbyterian Church in California, implemented the use of *Godly Play*, a Sunday school curriculum for young children that combines Bible stories and church practices of prayer and communion. Each child is greeted personally at the classroom door by an adult who stoops down to the child's level, helps her take off her shoes, and inquires about her readiness to come into the worship setting. This caring in-reach to the children is revitalizing the church, as Sunday school teachers gain confidence that they are communicating the faith to their children and children respond by developing habits of Christian faith in their abundant lives.

Sometimes the picture is less clear. We may see conflicts between nurturing a congregant and effective outreach. Will reaching in to a member of the congregation embarrass us or create discomfort for those we are reaching out to? A middle-aged and mildly retarded man who was a faithful member of a Presbyterian church in California provides an example. Our university church was filled with well-educated, well-dressed, and articulate people. It attracted visitors from the University of California community. Michael came to worship each Sunday in a very worn and soiled navy blue suit. His personal hygiene was somewhat lacking. Although his gaze was sometimes empty, he carried a large black leather briefcase stuffed with papers. He told everyone that he was a lawyer. Sometimes he passed out typed sheets filled with an incoherent theology of nuclear war and the end times.

Our adult Sunday school group welcomed Michael, took him seriously, and listened to him. While not intellectually capable or socially attractive, Michael faithfully attended church services. It became clear that he wanted to be respected and somehow recognized by the community. Recognizing this need to feel important, the Sunday school class arranged for Michael to become an usher at one of the morning services.

By responding to Michael's felt need for recognition, the church showed compassion by giving him a public task to perform. Michael responded with faithful service. Rather than worry about its public image, the church cooperated with Michael's felt needs, bringing abundant life to both Michael and the congregation. I was never more proud of our Sunday school class than I was on the first day a smiling Michael led me to a seat for morning worship. Did his public role in worship cause some people to turn away? We don't know. But this in-reach was too important to neglect.

Showing grace as Christ's disciples is an important part of in-reach. Learning that practices of inclusion, such as the example of Michael's ushering ministry, have a role to play in the church doesn't happen automatically. Adult classes that show patterns of discipleship, explain how to reach out to others, and develop the importance of spiritual practices in family settings as well as in the congregation contribute ultimately to evangelism. Learning to speak to others about the gospel begins in the church itself. Telling the story of how Jesus's life and death have made an impact on our own lives prepares us for speaking to colleagues at work, or strangers on an airplane, or people in another cultural context.

Ronald Crandall developed a discipleship program for the Methodist Church that focuses on growth in spirituality titled *Witness: Exploring and Sharing Your Christian Faith*. He uses the metaphor of a backpacking trip to illustrate how growing in Christ can become a personal journey that is shared with others. Using this six-week study guide gives Christians a chance to analyze their own spiritual path, discover areas from which to grow, and explore ways to share the gospel. In significant ways, the program helps individual Christians to develop their own mission statement.

Jesus explained his mission statement in the synagogue in Nazareth. He was preparing to free people from bondage, to announce that God is active in the world, to proclaim that God's time has come to us on earth (Luke 4:16–21). Those goals amazed people, since he was just a young man from town. The church can amaze people too, when we pursue the goals of finding freedom from oppressions of bondage of all sorts—the pride of status, the distortions of anger, the thoughtlessness of greed, the inequities of wealth and poverty, the loneliness of life without God's love. The potential for healing and happiness through God's grace springs out of the gospel. It is the good news of God's love for the world. It spills out from our communities as we follow Christ's way. We discover abundant life. Christianity shines like a jewel in our communities and in our world.

10

Changing Context

Transforming Mission

When I was a child, I often heard the phrase, "Jesus Christ, the same, yesterday, today, and forever." When our family had to move suddenly from New Jersey to Illinois, I found special comfort in this thought.

The gospel message doesn't change. Jesus came to earth to let us in on a mystery hidden throughout the ages—that is, God wants to bring unity to all things in heaven and earth under Christ (Eph. 1:9–10). The apostle Paul explained it like this: "In him all the fullness of God was pleased to dwell, and through him God was pleased to reconcile to God all things, whether on earth or in heaven, by making peace through the blood of his cross" (Col. 1:19–20 NRSV). Certainly this is a reason to be glad, to be comforted. And the gospel hasn't changed in the last two thousand years. "Jesus Christ is the same, yesterday, today, and forever."

What Has Changed?

But something *has* changed. We no longer live in the Roman Empire. We travel not on stone streets but through the air or in cyberspace. It is *we* who have changed, not the gospel.

Those changes demand something of us. First of all, we need to recognize with H. Richard Niebuhr that "we are in history as a fish is in water" (1960, 48). We cannot escape our age or the advantages or mistakes in perception that are a part of our societal understandings. We cannot, for example, revert to an understanding that slavery is supported by Scripture. That's an advantage. On the other hand, we collectively make errors in perception and judgment that we are blind to—errors that will be revealed by future generations. How could they have thought that it was all right to _____, they will ask. We cannot fill in the blank, though. Our understanding is limited by our location. We are in history as a fish is in water.

Another implication of this fact is that the ways that the gospel was presented in past ages do not suit us today. In the fourth century, monastic communities living apart from the degradation of life in the decaying Roman Empire presented the gospel to the people. This evangelism of presence not only proclaimed the good news; it preserved much knowledge that was being destroyed by the empire. The church's mission in that time included copying the Bible and preserving the works of Greek thinkers in their libraries. The works of Aristotle, for instance, rediscovered in the twelfth century, had a huge impact on the development of the church in the Middle Ages.

The practices of evangelism of the fourth century seem strange to us. And although we can learn from them, they are unnecessary today. The *gospel* is the same, but how we go about proclaiming that gospel changes with each generation.

The nineteenth-century missionary movement presents another example. During that time, Christianity spread with Western civilization. The gospel was taken by missionaries to China, Asia, and Africa. Many Christians gave up everything to become part of the greatest wave of Christianity the world has ever seen. Along with the gospel, hospitals, educational institutions, and Western culture were taken to foreign lands.

In the last fifty years, much criticism has been focused on the nineteenth-century missionary movement. Along with the good news, economic and cultural imperialism brought oppression to many lands. Native cultures were seen as destructive; American and British laws and mores were imposed on other nations. The gospel was preached, but harm was done as well.

As we cannot simply adopt fourth-century methods of evangelization, neither can we mimic the methods of the nineteenth century. The twentieth century has brought many changes to the church. At the beginning of that century, the typical Christian was a European or American man. But as Dana Robert reminded us, at the close of the twentieth century, the typical Christian is a Latin American or African woman. The church has shifted from North to South. More and more women are participating in the church. The global context for Christianity has changed.

The third implication of recognizing our immersion in our own history is that we must forge methods of evangelism that are relevant today. Contemporary Christians are asking questions about methods of spreading Christianity without spreading Western culture. Can it be done? What does our moment of history demand of us?

Context Determines Method of Evangelism: An Excursion into Magic

A common saying among real-estate agents is that there are three things that determine the selling price of a house: location, location, location. As we recognize our own deep ties to culture and modern society, there are three things that determine our methods of evangelism—yes, location, location, location.

Perhaps I can explain with an analogy to a fascinating British novel, *Jonathan Strange and Mr. Norrell*, by Susanna Clarke. The protagonist, Mr. Norrell, claims that he wants to revive the practice of magic in England. He has thoroughly studied the history and arts of magic, amassing a huge library of books of spells, historical incidents, and theories of magic.

Mr. Norrell has a vague idea that magic could help the British win the war over Napoleon Bonaparte, so he sets off to London to influence the British government and win the war. He gets connected with London high society, eventually meeting the high officials who determine war policy. He proceeds to do some outmoded but simple magic that should help the British—*old* tricks like creating an illusion of a vast naval fleet to scare the French away from British warships. But the war drags on, and nothing seems to help.

Theory versus Practice

About a quarter of the way into this eight-hundred-plus-page tome, a young man by the name of Jonathan Strange decides on a whim to study magic. Becoming Mr. Norrell's student, he studies the theory and history of magic. But the *practice* of magic seems more important to Jonathan than getting the history and theory right. And he doesn't see much of that with Norrell, who spends all day every day in his study exploring the ancient art of magic. So Strange does tricks for the people, and soon he too gains favor with the high officials.

The intrigues of the story are too intricate to detail here. Suffice it to say there are those who would like to see Jonathan Strange disappear from London. Perhaps moving magic off of the theoretical shelf and into the streets has made some people nervous. (Could it be the best and only other magician in England, Norrell himself?) Whoever it is arranges to have Strange sent to the front, ostensibly to help the generals in the war. Strange finds himself in Portugal, but try as he might, he makes no progress influencing General Wellington. In fact, every proposal he suggests, by letter from the capital to the front lines, where Wellington lives with his men, comes back with bold red letters scrawled across it—DENIED.

Some of his ideas have seemed so good to him too. Creating a plague of frogs on the French, for instance, is not only biblical, but has proved quite effective in deterring the enemy in the war with the Egyptians. Why has Wellington rejected it? (What Strange doesn't know is that Wellington is starving out the French and, well, you know, the French consider frogs a delectable delicacy.) In any case, that suggestion, and every other suggested magic stroke Strange proposes, Wellington rejects, much to Strange's chagrin.

Experiencing Another Context: Participation, Empathy, Understanding

One day Jonathan meets a medic who gives him some wise advice. It boils down to something like this: Why don't you go to the front lines yourself, live with the men, hear their stories, and commiserate with the miseries of life in the mountains on the borders of France? They are a great bunch, the medic insists, and I think they would like you as well.

So Jonathan Strange sets off from Lisbon, marches up and down mountains, wades through rivers, and tumbles over rocks until he comes to a British camp. There he discovers that the front lines are miles and miles long. Wellington is nowhere in sight, but Jonathan settles in, offers some good champagne to the men, and in a few weeks finds himself both admired and respected.

He begins to ask the soldiers what they want most. Let me repeat that: he begins to ask the soldiers what *they want most*. The most frequent reply is, "new boots." New boots. Now why, wonders Jonathan, do they want new boots? The soldiers explain that the roads are terrible, rocky at best, full of holes at worst. Those roads wear out the soldiers' boots at an amazing rate, and on the front lines there is no possibility of getting new ones.

Particular Needs Require Particular Methods

This deplorable situation gives Jonathan an idea. He immediately writes another letter to General Wellington offering to build magic roads wherever the army has need of them, roads that will disappear after the British go through and before the French can make use of them. What kind of roads would the general want? Jonathan asks. Brick, gravel, wood planking? The reply comes back quite quickly. The general gives detailed reasons why none of those will work and suggests that large stones, as in the old Roman roads, some of which still exist in the region, would be far superior to anything Jonathan had suggested.

And so it is that magic returns to Britain and is used to help defeat Napoleon. Jonathan Strange must stay on the front lines during the duration of the war. He works closely with each military unit, magically creating Roman roads just where they need them, and having them disappear just when they don't need them any more. There are a few fiascos, such as the time the road isn't built in time, slowing the army down to a snail's pace as they trudge through the stormy night. And there is the time that Jonathan forgets to take the road spell off and the French catch up with British troops. But on the whole the plan works beautifully. Jonathan stays on location with the troops, making a great many good friends, listening to the needs of the soldiers, and doing his level best to provide what is needed. And that is good news for all of England. Napoleon Bonaparte eventually meets his Waterloo and the nation enjoys peace again for a while.

Postwar Difficulties with Methods of Magic

But wait a minute. It seems that a number of years after the war has ended, complaints about how magic had been used begin to arise. Magical changes in the course of rivers have left towns stranded far from the trade routes. People living in villages that had been moved for the convenience of the British army—some moved as far away as North America—aren't happy with their new environs. Now as hard as that may be for West Virginians to imagine, this really was a legitimate complaint.

Besides wreaking havoc on landscapes and cultures in the war, magic in Britain is experiencing other problems. Conflict arises between *theoretical magicians* who have sole access to the texts but are actually against the contemporary *practice* of magic, and the *practical magicians* like Strange who want desperately to do something helpful but sometimes bring on more harm than good. Then there are the *uneducated magicians* who have grown up around Strange and Norrell. After learning a trick or two, they take to the road, impressing audiences with their magical skills but never looking back to see what kind of long-term results their actions engender. Magic in England is in a muddle.

The Dilemma for Evangelism in the Twenty-first Century

I won't pretend to know enough about British magic to sort out those problems. But I will say this: the problems have a familiar ring. They sound to me a lot like the problems facing Christian evangelism today. Like British magic in the novel, evangelism has fallen into disrepair. Use of simplistic or outmoded patterns and ideological debates lend confusion to the whole subject. Let me explain.

We have the texts. Theologians sort them out, develop models of evangelism, and if they are responsible in their work, show how those models fit the contexts of the times and places in which they were written. Those theologians may or may not *practice* evangelism of any sort. Like Norrell, some *theoretical theologians* have become distant and bookish. They find the study of the texts themselves sufficient.

Then we have what we might call the *practical theologians* who want desperately to help the world, who want people to receive the good news and be changed by it. They often pick up a text, or even a model of evangelism developed from the text, and apply it everywhere possible. Like Strange, they forget to live with the people and listen to their cares and needs. The *text* becomes a clarion call to do evangelism in a certain way, and *only in that way*. The Great Commission becomes a mandate to "evangelize the world in one generation." The cry of "peace with justice" becomes a rallying point for political action as the basic model for evangelism. An "evangelism of presence" becomes a strident critique of those who feel called to speak. An ecclesial model of evangelism becomes a lever for staking out a "canonical territory" that keeps other Christians out.

Applying Models of Evangelism

Herein lies our dilemma. How do we apply the textual models of evangelism to twenty-first-century contexts? That task includes stepping back from oversimplifications of the models that prevent us from seeing them in their fullness as well as distinguishing differences in contexts and adapting the biblical models to suit those contexts (see sidebar 10.1). The project is a big one: reformulating the craft of evangelism for the diversity of contexts in our pluralistic world.

We need to understand the texts in the first-century situations: the decadence of the Roman Empire and the persecution of Christians, the Greek philosophical world leaning in on the church, and the practitioners of paganism with their economic and psychological advantages resisting the gospel. We need to understand evangelism *in the situations* in which the texts were written. And we need to understand *for whom* those texts were written.

But that is not nearly enough. Remaining theoretical theologians won't spread the good news of the gospel story. We need to *adapt those models* winsomely to the situations we face today. We need to avoid becoming simplistic practical theologians who insist that evangelism be done only in one way. Particular needs require particular methods. The gospel is the same but the magic needs to be different. The good news must come packaged for the culture's relevant needs—felt needs.

Sidebar 10.1 Applying Models of Evangelism to Our Context

Nine Steps

1. Study the model in its original context.
2. Study the group to whom the model was addressed.
3. Explore the biblical roots of the model.
4. Examine the contemporary context.
5. Examine who we are.
6. Study our context.
7. Adapt the model to fit the current context.
8. At every step, avoid polarizing simplifications.
9. Apply the model without attacking other ways of doing evangelism.

Sidebar 10.2 From Present to Future

Moving into Change

This exercise invites individuals to jot down their thoughts, then discuss the questions in that section in groups of five to six persons. After completing the entire exercise, all participants can come together for discussion of insights from the small groups. The entire exercise will take about one hour.

What about the Present?

Each person should take about five minutes to jot down answers to the following questions. Then discuss in small groups.

- Am I happy with the position of the congregation in its neighborhood, in the denomination, and in the broader community? Why or why not?
- How does our congregation's outreach and in-reach (growth in relationships, spirituality, and energy) compare with the way we did things five and/or ten years ago? Which is better?

Nostalgia and Change

Each person should take about five minutes to jot down answers to the following questions. Then discuss in small groups.

- Is there something you love about our church that is disappearing or already gone? What is it? Why do you wish it were still here?
- Identify the "nostalgic places" of the discussion of the present (see above).
- How might these nostalgic impulses prevent us from moving into creative change around evangelism—both outreach and in-reach?

Moving into the Future

Each person should take about five minutes to jot down answers to the following questions. Then discuss in the small group.

- Make two lists, pros and cons, of the way you see the congregation doing evangelism in the present.
- Imagine ways that the pros can be strengthened. How might the cons be turned from problems into possibilities?
- Identify some developing potentials from your two lists, steering away from ideas that take the congregation back into the past, focusing on attitudes and programs that might suit the present situation as it is.

Do you feel uncomfortable? If so, celebrate! Creative change doesn't feel like an old shoe!

The Context Determines the Form of Evangelism

But this work of contextualizing the gospel cannot be done once and for all. And it cannot be done alone. We need to understand *who we are* and *where we are*—what our identity is and what our own context is—to determine which models of evangelism to use in our attempts to reformulate the good news here and now. That is the task before us in the church today because it is the context that determines the form of evangelism. Identity as a community of believers in a particular tradition, in a specific location, with a history and particular gifts and a calling experienced together—these are the components that will guide us toward an evangelism that fits, that becomes relevant to the broader community and the world—an evangelism done with grace that brings joy to people and glory to God. Use sidebar 10.2 to explore your identity with others as you begin the adventure of moving into change.

Exploring our location as individuals in a congregation, as a congregation in a changing local context, and as a part of a denomination in a twenty-first-century global environment will help focus our sense of identity in history and geography. For example, a congregation may be considering making needed renovations on a historic building. That topic opens the congregation up to explorations of its history, how the building fit the congregation at the beginning, and how it suits it now.

A church might continue the process by asking how the building itself influences the congregation and its worship style. Other considerations might be the impressions the church gives to the surrounding neighborhood. Who feels welcome here and why? These and other issues will come out of discussing how the building, as part of the congregation's context, shapes and limits identity and outreach. Such a study might result in new ways to use the building or reveal ways to move beyond the building into other neighborhood gathering places for some activities.

We are shaped by our context, but we, in turn, shape and reform the context. Demographic studies, for instance, can reveal how communities are changing around the church. Economic shifts, new populations entering the community, neighborhood changes and needs, once recognized, can give rise to ideas for serving and reaching out to the surrounding community. Who lives in the community, apart from members of the church? And what do they want? Like Jonathan Strange, we may be assuming that we know what others need without ever spending time with them and asking them what it is they want.

Finding out about our neighbors who aren't part of the congregation requires more than demographic studies though. Getting out into the area takes time and effort. It also requires a strong sense of identity as a congregation. Getting advice from congregations that are already actively serving and reaching out to the surrounding community is a good place to start. Discussing ways to focus more energy on evangelism might be another. In order to do that, discussions of identity and outreach are crucial. Who are we as a congregation, and how have we done outreach in the past? Exploring those issues leads to confidence and direction for contextualizing evangelism today. Studying the history of evangelism as a congregation can help groups identify areas of strength and dissatisfactions about how evangelism is to be understood and practiced. Constructing a congregational timeline together is a way to begin that exploration. Our Louisville congregation took time over a summer to remember, to reflect, and to record our own history and outreach efforts. Guidance for creating such a congregational timeline is given in the appendix.

Through the process of creating a timeline, congregations may discover differences in perspective that can enhance the diversity of ways to reach out. They may discover needs that make them want to be served by others so that they can hear the good news in a new way. Partner congregations from poorer neighborhoods or countries can become a source of renewal for congregations in the United States, for example. Perhaps learning African ways of prayer, hearing Malaysian ways of expressing the gospel, or finding out how a partner congregation sees the needs of American Christians can bring good news to a congregation in a US context.

Studying your own congregation's location, geographically and historically, can prepare you for moving into change. Finding out about yourselves as a congregation can help you name difficulties and find unifying common ground. From there, you can move into the future, sharing dreams and visions, creating new paths to sharing good news with others that are rooted in your church's identity and appropriate to your context.

As you create a congregational timeline and do the three exercises in this chapter and the context worksheet from chapter 1, you begin the process of exploring your congregation and finding your way into a win-win situation for evangelism in the here and now. You will probably find that you are doing much already. Your congregation is a dynamic and changing institution, a community called by God to shine as stars in the world. The work you do together is built on a strong foundation of your congregation's history of service and outreach, your spiritual strength and your desire to grow. Assessing your history, context, and identity can renew your energy and provide direction as you work together to craft a graceful evangelism for the twenty-first century, for you, here and now.

PART 4

Can We Craft a Graceful Evangelism?

11

Insights from Contemporary Theologies of Evangelism

Reflecting on the meaning of abundant life, developing a mission statement for evangelism, and analyzing our contemporary contexts in church and society show us the complexities of our current situation. We come to deeper questions here: Can we craft a graceful evangelism? Can theologies of evangelism become more than an individual exercise, a congregational effort, or even a denominational project? Can our theologies of evangelism be inclusive or at least accepting of theologies of others? Can we get beyond the "evangelism wars"?

In this chapter we will identify a number of helpful sources that Christians can use to facilitate a more graceful evangelism, both individually and through their churches (outlined in sidebar 11.1). We can start by utilizing theologies and strategies of evangelism that are currently advocated. We can also reinterpret the situation for evangelism today, focusing on how current conditions can be used by God to further our ministries. We may want to broaden our definition of evangelism to include many activities that are usually split off from the idea of evangelism in our churches or contexts. We can develop spiritual practices, both personal and communal, that deepen our faith and increase our yearning to love others and share the good news with them. We can take a new approach to evangelism, understanding it as blessing what God is already doing in a situation. We can recognize how we ourselves are in need of hearing the gospel, exploring the role of evangelistic preaching for ourselves and our congregations.

And we can develop a style of reflexive evangelism that recognizes the gifts we receive as well as those we give as we reach out to others with the gospel.

Utilizing Current Theologies and Strategies

One way to find support in today's climate for Christian evangelism is to critically appropriate theologies and strategies of evangelism from across the theological spectrum. The contemporary theologies of evangelism presented in chapter 7 can guide churches and individual Christians in that endeavor.

> **Sidebar 11.1 Insights for Contemporary Evangelism**
>
> 1. Utilizing current theologies and strategies
> 2. Reinterpreting the situation for evangelism today
> 3. Broadening definitions of evangelism
> 4. Deepening our spiritual practices
> 5. Seeing evangelism as blessing
> 6. Recognizing the role of evangelistic preaching for the church
> 7. Doing evangelism reflexively

Adapting those approaches to your own context sensitively and critically can boost your evangelism quotient. Some of them can be taken in part, used in connection with others, or mixed and matched. Depending on your theological moorings and your local community sensitivities, one or another strategy may provide a new direction and infuse new energy into your community. For churches that enthusiastically do evangelism in one way, studying other theologies of evangelism can open new vistas for outreach. For others, evangelism can stop being the "E word" and start being something that excites and motivates congregations to gracefully share what God is doing in their lives. Either way, a more graceful evangelism becomes a reality.

You need not agree with an author's evaluation of the current situation; you may not share all of his or her theological viewpoints. Still, you may find nuggets of truth and new approaches that could be useful in your denomination, congregation, or personal life.

For example, Bob Roberts Jr. describes a church-planting method adopted from Asian Christians in his book *The Multiplying Church*. Roberts comes out of a Southern Baptist background. Some may find his views on eschatology and/or roles for women in ministry incompatible with their own. His anti-institutional attitude may raise questions about the use of this approach in denominational settings. His overgeneralizations about the growth of Christianity in Asia may generate skepticism. And his directive entrepreneurial approach may not fit into some settings.

Despite those difficulties, Roberts's fresh approach to church planting can offer something exciting to congregations quite outside his tradition. I often tell my students that, having learned to think critically, they may never again read a book that they totally agree with. One of my students lamented this fact, commenting on Roberts by saying, "I wish I was still a naive reader. I would just love this book."

A critical analysis of Roberts, however, does not negate the helpfulness of his work. His is an approach that takes globalization seriously; Roberts sees the connections between the global economy and the wealth or poverty of specific nations. He recognizes the need for structural changes in those realms and encourages Christians to become part of that change. He utilizes successful small-group evangelistic strategies from the house church movement of China. He insists that numerical growth in churches be accompanied by social transformation. Roberts insightfully shows how the culture of a congregation affects outreach. He suggests that congregations can take a great step forward by developing a church-planting mentality. Roberts dreams big.

Using Roberts's book as a tool, pastors and congregations can also dream big. Here are some suggestions on how to do that: Book study groups can analyze the text, taking the good ideas and ignoring or refocusing those that are not helpful. For example, despite his use of inclusive language, Roberts clearly indicates that men are the church planters and that wives play a supportive role in church-planting ministries. Recognizing this can lead to a discussion of how women's leadership skills are changing the face of the church. Critical readers can separate Roberts's eschatological views from his strategies and identify a multitude of reasons for outreach that are not driven by premillennialism. A helpful comparison here can be found in *Unbinding the Gospel*, Reese's study of mainline denominations, which identifies many of those reasons (2006, 19). Finally, Roberts's overly positive analysis of church growth in Asia can lead congregations to a deeper study of particular Asian countries, resulting in an active prayer ministry for the churches in those places.

In short, the *differences do not have to divide*—they can augment the study and practice of evangelism. Differences can be used to spur Christians on to deeper analysis and more thoughtful appropriation of the good ideas Roberts advocates.

Let's take an example from the other side of the theological divide on evangelism. In *Unbinding the Gospel*, Reese offers hope to mainline churches as she walks us through an evangelism approach based on telling the good news in our churches and beyond them. Her background as a pastor in the Disciples of Christ led her do a study of evangelism in mainline denominations. Rather than encountering enthusiasm about evangelism, she found that many participants in the study saw it in negative terms. Evangelism, dubbed the "E word" by many congregations, was a source of both fear and disdain. At best, some congregations simply sidelined the concept and practices of evangelism.

Rather than judging this stance as "unchristian," Reese shows reasons for the current negativity around traditional forms of evangelism in mainline congregations. She then shows how congregations are already doing evangelism with their children and youth. She offers positive approaches to becoming more comfortable sharing the gospel with various constituencies through both personal and group methods.

Utilizing an approach that draws from multiple viewpoints in a congregation that is divided over its understanding of evangelism can be very helpful. Comparing Reese's approach with Roberts's may offer support to groups on both sides of the issue. For some Christians, preaching the gospel in many settings is simply a biblical mandate. They may find Reese's mild congregation and personal-sharing approach weak. Others, however, focus on the hurt caused by aggressive kinds of evangelism that may be perceived as insensitive or even oppressive by others. They may find Roberts's approach too aggressive. Pairing Reese's gentle approach to finding appropriate strategies of evangelism for different groups with Roberts's adaptation of an Asian church-planting approach may help Christians see the value in approaches that differ from their own, especially in contexts that are foreign to their experience.

Reinterpreting the Situation for Evangelism Today

No one can argue with the fact that church membership is declining in many Protestant churches in the United States today. What we *do* with that fact is another matter.

Elaine Heath, in her book *The Mystic Way of Evangelism*, interprets current church decline in a different light. She argues that the church may be experiencing a "dark night of the soul" as St. John of the Cross and other Christian mystics have described it. Rather than an individual darkness, Heath sees a darkness that affects the church as a whole. She describes a "dryness and fruitlessness" in the American church that results in a loss of vitality. In over-accommodating to culture, churches are afflicted by dysfunctional congregations, insecure clergy, and pathological board members (2008, 33). Those trends could and often do lead to the demise of congregations. But Heath also sees in the current situation the possibility of renewal.

By recognizing and accepting the losses we face in the church and relinquishing our striving ever harder to overcome those losses, Heath suggests that we may lose our desires and begin longing for God in a deeper way. And that yearning may lead to illumination for us as it did for the ancient mystics. God may reveal to us our woundedness and convince us of God's deep love for us. We may find that love, not death, ultimately rules the day, as 1 Corinthians 13 tells us. And seeing God as love, we may begin to believe, with Julian of Norwich, that "all manner of things shall be well" (Heath 2008, 57).

The progression out of the dark night of the soul is not a linear one. Illumination can be occurring even as we are experiencing our loss. This is certainly the experience of many congregations that are finding a deeper spirituality and a clearer vision of outreach even as they grieve the loss of the larger congregations they once experienced. Heath stresses both healing and the importance of giving ourselves away, learning to pray, and becoming one with God's will (2008, part 3). Those activities may seem like an oblique approach to evangelism, but they actually form the roots of it. As our faith deepens, the light of Christ shines out from us. People are attracted to the light and will seek it out. So evangelism results from our acceptance of our situation, our yearning for God, and our growing maturity in Christ.

Broadening Definitions of Evangelism

Sometimes when I do a seminar on evangelism, I find that congregations are doing a great deal of evangelism that they don't recognize. In our age of specialization and with our penchant for delegating assignments, we tend to see evangelism as the purview of the pastor or of a committee of the church. The everyday worship and discipleship that we engage in, our teaching of children, our ministries of support, our graciousness in allowing our buildings to be used for preschool, AA meetings, or health fairs, and so on, are often not even considered in our evaluation of evangelism. And yet all these activities are an outreach, a statement of God's love for others through us, and a witness to the power of God in healing, in personal growth, and in caring. If we broaden our definition of evangelism to include those activities, we suddenly, and rightly, feel that we are not so lax in this important area of Christian life.

William Abraham defines evangelism in the broadest way possible, as "initiation into the kingdom of God" (1989, 95). The church is about inaugurating people into the life of the kingdom. That kingdom is both here and not yet. In our present work as Christians in the world, we strive to exhibit the qualities of the kingdom of God. Our goal as Christians is to invite people into the warmth of God's family.

And we do this all the time, often without realizing it. Instead of castigating ourselves and our denominations, perhaps we should applaud what, by God's Spirit, we are already doing.

Deepening Our Spiritual Practices

Part of recognizing that breadth of evangelism happens as we deepen our spiritual practices. The communion or eucharistic practice of the church is, in a very deep sense, evangelistic. We demonstrate with our communion ritual the death of Christ for the atonement of the world. We remember; we give thanks; we are nourished. We go out into the world as the body of Christ. As our own appreciation for this act of communal worship deepens, so does our witness. Visitors can see our seriousness as we partake of bread and wine; they can feel the depth of our love for God. Our witness becomes bolder and more powerful as we deepen this spiritual practice.

The same is true for other spiritual practices. Our life of prayer can be superficial and even trivial. Or it can grow deeper over the years. We can discover new forms of prayer: devotional reading of the Bible; bringing the day's events to God; asking blessing for ourselves and others; praising God in song, in silence, in service. We can praise God in nature with the psalmist, see God's love in others, search for God's spirit in human courage, delight in God's creativity displayed in scholarship, embrace God's love in the miracle of children. We can see God's hand in the events of history. We can learn to seek God's leading in our relationships, in our professions, in the still, small voice of our heart as we spend time in solitude.

Individual spiritual practices can deepen—and so can communal ones. The habits of our life as a congregation can tend toward distrust and complaining or toward praise and embracing others. Every congregation, like other societal groups, has a culture that becomes distinctive over time. As we look for help in evangelism, assessing our attitudes and practices can help us identify areas that need revamping. Are we an inviting congregation, or do we exclude? Can we tolerate new types of people who visit, or are we subtly discouraging them? Do we see the best in one another, or do we put others down and compete for prominence? Are we concerned about our neighborhood, or do we resent the ways it has changed over time? Do we understand our social and political actions as part of our worship, as activities that glorify God and bring justice? Our practices as a congregation can enhance or detract from our attractiveness to others and thus from our ability to reach out with the good news.

Seeing Evangelism as Blessing

A church that finds itself caught in negative patterns of behavior might re-work its idea of evangelism to help members become more positive with themselves and others. David Fracknell, director of Seminary Consortium for Urban Pastoral Education (SCUPE) in Chicago, develops the idea of *blessing as evangelism*. He uses the Enneagram personality pattern and shows how each different personality type sees evangelism in a different way. In his view, all of the gifts of 1 Corinthians 14 can be utilized and appreciated in the church. Rather than bicker about who does evangelism the correct way, many forms of outreach can be recognized and affirmed as part of our own approach to graceful evangelism.

Fracknell suggests that, besides learning to applaud the various gifts and approaches to evangelism, we try to see how God has gone before us into every situation. So when a Christian or church group enters a new situation, the task before them becomes not to convince others of their point of view but rather to understand what God is already doing. For example, a distraught family, torn apart by internal strife, may also exhibit intense care for one another. To bless them for that care is to bring God's blessing upon their fractured situation. Evangelism as blessing shines a light on how God is working in a situation. As that light becomes clearer through our blessing, people begin to understand that God is with them and is already bringing grace to their lives.

Evangelism to other cultures forms another example. If Christians go with criticism, denigrating the views and practices of another society, the gospel will not be heard. In Thailand, for example, Christianity is still seen as a foreign religion. When Christians reject the cultural practices of other groups, they in turn are seen as outsiders. But as Christians in Thailand go to Buddhist villages with blessing, affirming what God is already doing, they are embraced.

Thai theologians and pastors Nandichi and Ubolwan Mejudhon have developed *meekness evangelism*, an evangelism that asks what villagers need and blesses them with those very things. One village in the northeast Isaan area now has an English school. With the help of Christians, the people celebrate an annual harvest festival. That traditional festival was suspended for lack of funds and transportation. Meek Thai Christians have blessed that village, affirming its harvest festival and introducing the story of Jesus along with it. They have listened to the desire of the villagers to learn English and have supplied the village with a school that teaches English along with healthy sanitation and Christian stories. The responsiveness of Christians is leading to evangelization in this village of Thailand. People are asking, "Why are you blessing us with such goodness?" The Christians answer by saying, "God is blessing you and we are participating in the work God is already doing among you." And so through blessing the good news of the gospel is shared.

Recognizing the Role of Evangelistic Preaching for the Church

Usually we think of evangelistic preaching as something we do for outsiders. But evangelistic preaching plays an important role in the church as well. We all need to hear the gospel, the story that enlivens and heals us. The hymn "Tell Me the Story of Jesus" says it well: "Tell me the story of Jesus, write on my heart every word. Tell me the story most precious, sweetest that ever was heard" (Crosby 1951).

Proclaiming the gospel in our churches does a number of things for the congregation itself. First, it reinforces the authority of the church's leadership. After all, those leaders are describing for us what is wrong with the world and how the gospel can begin to heal those wrongs, both personally and socially. Since the authority and values of the church are not as central to our society as they were one hundred or even fifty years ago, holding up the truth claims and values of Christianity by evangelistic preaching reassures us of the authority of the church (see sidebar 11.2).

Strengthening the church's authority in turn reinforces the hearers in their beliefs and identity as faithful Christians. Congregants are drawn into the evangelistic patterns of preaching in many ways. At St. Stephens African Methodist Episcopal Church in Louisville, Kentucky, congregants that bring visitors to the service are publicly recognized. Central Presbyterian Church in Louisville publicly announces its pro gay and lesbian stance as part of the good news of the gospel. Southeast Christian Church in Louisville provides shuttle buses from its huge, crowded parking lots and sets up information booths and racks of literature that give information and schedules of church activities. At the small Brethren meeting I attended as a child, I usually got my head patted by one of the elders who would say, "How good to see the little lambs here tonight." In these and other ways, followers of the religion are drawn together and given a sense of the solidity of their beliefs.

Another positive effect of evangelistic preaching is that it creates a social space for the church in society. Religious organizations, like political parties, are differentiated entities that perform discreet functions in modern societies. Recognition of religious pluralism and presentation of various claims for meaning-construction and for allegiance create a competition among religious groups.

Sidebar 11.2 Evangelistic Preaching for the Congregation

Benefits:
- Reinforces the authority of the church's leadership
- Reinforces the hearers in our beliefs and identity as faithful Christians
- Creates a social space for the church in society
- Establishes a position for the religious group in societal life
- Strengthens allegiance to the group by demarcating clear and reasonable ideological parameters
- Establishes the church as a respectable cultural entity

Drawbacks:
- Public power of definition also causes dissension and embarrassment
- Unwanted reformulation of beliefs

Antidotes to unwanted effects:
- Advocacy efforts that clearly define views
- Formatting material in new ways in the public sphere (e.g., television)
- Reinforcing beliefs with renewed evangelistic preaching for congregations

The evangelistic service, whether or not it is successful in bringing new followers into the religious fold, establishes a position for the religious group in societal life. At the same time, it encourages followers to strengthen their allegiance to the group by demarcating clear and reasonable ideological parameters. In this way, the religion, although not adhered to by all, establishes itself as a respectable cultural entity.

While playing a positive role for many hearers, in a religion as diverse as Christianity, that public power of definition also causes dissension and embarrassment. The most vocal proponents of Christian beliefs are often those with narrow and pejorative views. Because of the power of ritual speech to define belief, those narrow theologies appear to represent the Christian religion. Reformulations of religious beliefs occur, even if unwanted by a majority of adherents.

An antidote to that unwanted reformulation is for the disaffected groups to engage in similar advocacy efforts that clearly define their own views. This trend can be seen in Christian television programming, which includes viewpoints from many Christian denominations. Some of those presentations are formatted in ways that are very different from traditional evangelistic presentations. Formatting the material in new ways allows the group to advocate its religious beliefs without violating the ritual setting of the traditional evangelistic service. At the same time, through television programming, it distinguishes itself from groups purporting different views of the Christian message.

Understanding the power of evangelistic preaching for both insiders and outsiders can enable a congregation to utilize the evangelistic service in more positive and powerful ways.

Doing Evangelism Reflexively

Understanding evangelism as reaching out and also receiving from others can transform a congregation's view of evangelism. The apostle Paul exemplifies this giving and receiving model in Acts 17.

When he arrived in Athens, Paul didn't immediately begin to preach or reach out to others. Instead, he put himself into a learning mode. He visited the markets and began talking with people. He listened to the philosophers and dialogued with them. He visited the temples to the many gods of the Greek pantheon. And he went even further. He studied the ancient texts of the Greeks, thoroughly familiarizing himself with their thought.

Perhaps Paul already had the idea that God was working among the Athenians long before he arrived on the scene. Perhaps a simple curiosity drove his explorations. Or perhaps he understood that effectively communicating the gospel to others had to be based on understanding the society and culture of those to whom he was sent. Whatever his reasons, Paul avidly soaked up the thinking, mannerisms, and beliefs of the Athenians.

And then he went up to the philosopher's corner to discuss all of this with the seekers there. For, as in any large city, there are usually those who find new ideas and ways of interacting with society to be stimulating and seek them out. So Paul presented the gospel to them there.

It is how he did it that intrigues and informs us (see sidebar 11.3). He began by recognizing their questions. He drew attention to the "unknown god" they worshiped. This was only one of many gods for the Greeks. But for Paul, it provided an entry point to appealing to their curiosity and presenting the good news. He promised to name that unknown God for them. No doubt that got their attention. Next he quoted their wise philosophers to them, finding points in their views that agreed with his own. Rather than take an adversarial position to their beliefs, which he certainly could have done since there was much incompatibility between Paul's understanding of Jesus as the Savior and Greek religious ideas, he found the nuggets of wisdom in their philosophers' thought and spoke that back to them. After affirming their views in ways that he could with integrity, Paul preached the gospel to them. He didn't shy away from the difficult parts but prepared the way with affirmations. The result was one that

Sidebar 11.3 How Paul Did Evangelism in Athens
Acts 17:16–32

1. Paul listens, explores, and experiences Athenian culture.
2. From the beginning, he speaks openly of his faith.
3. He identifies with the Athenians' search for God.
4. He learns their poetry, philosophy, literature, and beliefs.
5. He approaches them not as other but as the same as himself ("you also are religious").
6. He praises them rather than distancing himself, even though some are hostile and critical.
7. He centers on their struggle—relates to their questions of meaning.
8. He includes them in God's family of humanity.
9. He substantiates that inclusiveness through their texts.
10. He builds on their common ground, working out of their questions, their struggle, their texts, their poets. (So far, not one word about Jesus!)
11. Then he uses their own beliefs ("since we are God's offspring") to show that their way of worshiping God is not consistent with who God actually is.
12. Now, he pulls no punches but shows that their ways need to change because in practice they overlook the God whom they are seeking. It is time to change.
13. He brings in Jesus as the demonstration of the truth of his position and understanding of God.

Christians in every age have experienced. Some scoffed, but some believed and were added to the church.

Paul brought the treasure of the gospel to the Athenians that day. But he also received much from them. Those graces had been given to the Athenians by God. Paul learned from them and embraced them. The people and their culture also intrigued Paul, and he spent many days forming relationships, listening and sharing, giving and receiving from those amazing people and their culture.

If we can read the text again, bracketing our adversarial tendency to see other religions as totally wrongheaded, we too might learn to receive gifts from those whose worldview and beliefs differ from our own. Reflexive evangelism recognizes Christians' need and ability to benefit from the wisdom of other people and their views. Rather than a lopsided and proud view of evangelism as what we give to others, we also see what we humbly receive. Our interactions with those we reach out to become a source of grace in our lives. We receive as well as give, listen as well as talk, appreciate as well as receive appreciation. And so the gospel is given and received gracefully, and we are on our way to crafting a graceful evangelism.

12

Challenges to Crafting
a Graceful Evangelism

We have seen in the last few chapters the possibilities of understanding our context and wisely using insights from contemporary evangelism and biblical sources to craft a graceful evangelism. Multiple religions flourish in the United States, and this religious pluralism in today's world presents special challenges. In chapter 5 we asked the question, "How should Christian congregations advocate Christian faith in our free marketplace of religious ideas?" We discussed the doubt that creeps in when Christians and congregations face the presence of diverse "paths to God" in our pluralistic society. This chapter explores the special issues that religious pluralism raises for Christians working to present the gospel in winsome ways.

The situation is reminiscent of a tale told about the abrupt change from persecution to power experienced by the church in St. Augustine's day. Augustine lived in a tumultuous time of social change. Pagan gods had flourished for centuries. Jesus Christ had lived and died. Christianity had swept through the Roman Empire. The age of martyrs saw many people staking their lives on a new loyalty and the promise of a reality beyond their immediate situation (Adeney 1989, 92). Constantine was seeking a religion that could bind the failing empire together. This was a turning point in Western history.

A Tale of Sudden Change

There is a tale that goes something like this: Seven men from Ephesus in early fourth-century Asia Minor hid out in a cave. Having fled from their persecutors, these early Christians fell asleep. As the story goes, they woke up one hundred years later. Fearfully sneaking into town, they were stunned to see crosses on the coins and cathedrals on city corners. The whole of their reality had reversed itself. No longer persecuted, Christians were privileged. The sleepers' perspective on life changed in a moment.

The Protestant church in the United States faces such a moment. But, in contrast, the reversal goes in the opposite direction. We are slowly waking up to the fact that we are no longer in charge and, indeed, have not been in charge for some time now.

One hundred years ago, at the height of the worldwide mission movement, American Christians spearheaded the spread of Christianity to the ends of the earth. Faith in progress and in the superiority of Western civilization combined to lend courage and optimism to Christian missionary efforts.

Today mainline Christians see the world from a different perspective. Churches lament their declining numbers (Coalter, Mulder, and Weeks 1996, 19). Contemporary writers get their biblical facts wrong. Americans turn to other religions in their quest for meaning. Islam, not Christianity, is the fastest growing religion in the United States today. Hindu and Buddhist temples proliferate, and New Age spiritualities enjoy renewed popularity. Christians have become fascinated with world religions. In a series of lectures on Christian topics at the Institute for Ecumenical and Cultural Research in Collegeville, Minnesota, the one lecture that packed the room was a basic explanation of Buddhist beliefs by Father Hand, a Catholic priest. We see more and more books and Web sites on spirituality, Buddhism, and Eastern religious leaders. Seminars and conferences on those topics draw many religious seekers. While interest in other religions grows, mainline Protestants experience aging congregations, face redevelopment problems, or close church doors.

Much has happened during the long sleep, and we are waking up to a different world. We need to readjust our perspective. There is more going on here than an increasing number of empty pews or a forgetfulness of the biblical tradition. Robert Bellah argues that our managerial and therapeutic society may be contributing to a moral impoverishment and loss of community (Bellah et al. 1985, 139). Allan Bloom works to reinforce dominant cultural forms in the face of a multiculturalism that challenges Anglo viewpoints on every side (1987, 42). Hispanics demand education in Spanish for their children. Black Americans want Black English to be respected as a valid linguistic form. Asian Americans assert that their religious holidays should be honored. Native Americans revive religious rituals and resist studying classic Western texts and ideas. Christianity does not hold the center stage in the United States today.

The religions of the world have come home to our urban neighborhoods. Mosques spring up on street corners. Hindu temples, Jewish synagogues, and worship centers of New Age religions are now a prominent feature of urban landscapes. The predicted secularization of American society has not materialized. Instead, fascination with religion grows. "Other religions" seem to be everywhere. Christians who get to know their neighbors from other religious traditions find themselves enriched by those encounters.

While other religions intrigue, Christian history appears oppressive. University education portrays a very different interpretation of Christian activity than white Protestants learned in Sunday school. Postcolonial critiques of Christian mission and appraisals of Christian faith as irrational and misguided pose as "objective" studies of religion. That approach formed a significant part of the American studies curriculum that my daughter studied as an undergraduate at the University of California at Santa Cruz between 1990 and 1994.

In this view, it is clear that the spread of Christianity went hand in hand with Western imperialistic and economic expansion. As Western civilization spread, indigenous cultures were marginalized or, as in the case of Native Americans, destroyed. According to some historians, the genocide of World War II was linked to Christian anti-Semitism. Cornel West picks up that theme when he states, "The European hatred of Jews rests on religious and social grounds—Christian myths of Jews as Christ-killers and resentment over the disproportionate presence of Jews in certain commercial occupations" (1994, 105). Feminist scholars point out that patriarchal practices of Christianity led to a greater oppression of women during this era of cultural imperialism. Paula Cooey analyzes various feminist views and concludes that the role of Christian traditions is ambiguous, not irredeemable. She suggests offering fresh interpretations of inherited Christian doctrines that have liberative power for all oppressed groups (1991, 106–30).

Although Christians have done much good in the last century, we wake up in a world that recognizes the oppression of Western colonialism and its links with Christianity. At the same time, it is a world that acknowledges the presence and insights of other religions. Responding to those insights means changing perspectives on mission and evangelism. Many Christians reject civilizing and Westernizing other culture groups as a part of Christian mission. Governments may also distance themselves from a model of proclamation that some scholars argue was tied to economic and cultural imperialism. Indonesia, for example, refuses to reissue visas for Christian missionaries. In order to maintain control of their own economic and social development, that government limits interaction with Western religions and ideologies through controlling Western immigration. At the same time, the growing edge of the church includes many who see such mission efforts as crucial to the life of the church. Churches that are committed to a view of mission as presence, partnership, or liberation, on the other hand, are finding it difficult to acquire the funding and energy to practice mission in those time-consuming and costly ways. Finding reasonable and productive new perspectives on Christian mission today proves difficult.

Sidebar 12.1 Two Paradoxes

Contemporary Situation	Christian Mandate
Expansionist Christian mission has done harm.	The church must act in missionary ways.
Efforts to show God's love have resulted in economic and cultural harm.	The church must be committed to showing Christ's love for the world.

Questions for Discussion

1. What should we do?
2. How can we find a way to act that spreads God's love to the world without also bringing harm to the peoples that we encounter?
3. How can our commitment to Christ and our historic faith be lived out without oppressing those who walk in other religious paths?

Two Paradoxes

The confusion presented by this situation can be summed up in two paradoxes (see sidebar 12.1). We have seen the harm done by Christian mission combined with an expansionist agenda and a superior attitude. Yet, the church, if it is to be the church, must act in missionary ways. We are called to spread the gospel. We want to educate people to be able to read the Bible and embrace the Christian narrative. Second, we have been humbled by the realization that our genuine efforts to show God's love have resulted in economic and cultural harm. Yet the church, if it is to be the church, must be passionately committed to showing the love of Jesus Christ. Love can be shared only by people and communities that are embodied and culturally formed. We cannot completely shed our cultural heritage.

A Changed Perspective

I suggest that intentionally reforming our perspective on Christian mission can enable the church to discover mission paths that make peace (see sidebar 12.2).

First, recognizing the changed situation for mission allows us to see the church in a time of transition. Transitions require patience as new directions are mapped out and new ways of interacting with others are formed. The transition from a nineteenth-century model of mission to postmodern, twenty-first-century models will take time. We need to be patient with the process, to listen to those with differing points of view, to take time to wake up and adjust ourselves to the new world in which we find ourselves.

Sidebar 12.2 Reforming Our Perspective

1. Transition: recognize the changed situation for mission.
   - New directions take time to formulate.
   - Listen to those with differing points of view.
   - Adjust to the new world in which we find ourselves.
2. Diversity: accept differences among Christians and the society at large.
   - Refrain from imposing litmus tests of theological or political correctness on others.
   - Avoid narrow commitment to noninterference with others.
3. Knowledge: a shift in our understanding of others.
   - Recognize the cultural situatedness of all knowledge.
   - Be humble as we dialogue with others.
   - Realize that every perspective is limited.
   - Do not reject other positions; explore, analyze, and evaluate in conversation with others.

Second, accepting diversity within the church as well as the pluralism in society is crucial. Even as Christians speak of accepting others, the tendency to impose litmus tests of theological or political correctness upon others both within and outside the boundaries of Christianity persists. The other side of the danger is a narrow commitment to noninterference with other religions that can short-circuit the mutual transformation that is at the heart of true dialogue.

Third, a shift in our understanding of knowledge is necessary for true acceptance of diversity and broad-minded teaching about Christian mission. Recognizing the cultural situatedness of all knowledge can foster humility as we dialogue with others. We can hold deep convictions about the church and its mission while embracing the truth of the limitedness of any perspective—its boundedness by history, culture, and social setting. Realizing that every perspective is limited can allow a true conversation to occur. Other points of view are not rejected out of hand, but explored, analyzed, evaluated.

At the same time, convictions about the truth of Christianity need not be compromised but can be the secure center of the focus and meaning of the church. A confessional stand on the belief that God in Christ is redeeming the world forms that strong center. While listening respectfully to those with other convictions, one can hold as universal a cherished conviction about the truth and power of Christianity (Polanyi 1958, 266).

Bringing together epistemological humility with ontological conviction allows mission to happen in an affirming and dialogical way. Christians may argue passionately from their convictions, while realizing the limitedness of their perspective and the possibility that others may have wisdom from a differing point of view. Pastors can take their convictions about mission to their churches without embarrassment, on the one hand, or dogmatic intolerance, on the other. Missionaries can act in congregations, social service organizations, or educational institutions without needing to find agreement with all other Christians on every missiological issue.

Waking Up

The church faces a time of transition in understanding and action in mission and evangelism. We need patience, recognizing our confusion in this time of uncertainty. We need to learn an acceptance of diversity that reaches beneath mere platitudes. We need to develop a view of how knowledge and faith intersect in our understanding and bring that comprehension into our discussion about Christian mission in educational and congregational settings.

We have awakened from a long sleep and find our reality quite changed. We move into the future recognizing that changed context and searching for new perspectives that will result in fitting ways to do mission in a new century.

Challenges of Other Religions for Congregations

Other religions present themselves not only in the news media but in our neighborhoods. Understanding that our own views are heavily influenced by our background and context makes us wonder about the religious views of those brought up in another culture. Finally, we see "religion" more and more as a private issue rather than a public one. So we feel hesitant to "interfere" with the religious views of others.

But sometimes other religions present challenges in our congregations. They come to us, even if we don't go to them. When that happens, we can confidently display our faith in God even as we humbly acknowledge the limitedness of our understanding. And as we do that, we may find that our interactions with persons of other religions increase, changing us and our context even further.

Let's look at a number of challenges that congregations may face as we encounter people of other faiths. We will present them not as problems to be solved, although some of them are that, but as opportunities to expand our own understandings and reach out, giving and receiving gifts, thus presenting a graceful mode of evangelism (see also sidebar 12.3).

Membership in Another Religion

Sometimes a young person from a family in our congregation joins a group espousing a belief other than Christianity. Here is an opportunity for con-

Sidebar 12.3 Congregations Encountering Other Religions

Challenges and Opportunities

1. When congregations encounter people of another religion:
   - They become more aware.
   - They establish ties with people different from themselves.
   - They face the challenge of listening without judgment.
   - There is an opportunity for dialogue of mutual respect.
   - They face issues of acceptance and forgiveness.
   - Leaders seek wisdom as the anxiety of the congregation increases.
   - All can grow through this experience.
2. When the question of interfaith marriage arises:
   - Anxiety is produced.
   - Issues relating to this topic must be addressed.
   - The congregation must face the implications of worshiping with someone of another religion.
   - Congregations must decide how to incorporate the newcomer in congregation.
   - Ideas about education for the congregation and the person from another religion may come to light.
   - Issues of open communication with the interreligious couple arise.
   - Addressing these questions helps develop respect in a difficult situation.
3. Education about other religions:
   - Reduces fear of others that inhibits relationships with people of another religion.
   - Presents uniqueness of Christianity in dialogue with beliefs of other religions.
   - Increases respect for other religious ways.
   - Fosters congregational relationships as religious backgrounds are explored.
   - Promotes community ministries as we understand others better.
   - Increases opportunities for public theology.
   - Promotes interreligious understanding.
   - Clarifies Christian perspectives on theological issues.

gregants to become aware of another religion—its beliefs and practices, its attraction in our society and among people like us. We see someone from our own social, economic, and ethnic group establish ties with people who seem very different from ourselves.

Learning about another religion now becomes more than an intellectual exercise—it becomes a real encounter. Listening to this young person give reasons for joining another religion, showing interest in the worship practices of the other group, and allowing friendships with congregants to continue without censure of the young person are first steps in addressing this challenge.

As the leaders, counselors, and families listen without judgment and open their hearts to the person who has joined another group, issues about his or her past experience with the church or congregation may arise. A dialogue of mutual respect and acceptance may need to occur. Are we willing to forgive an unlovely picture of the church drawn by this young person? Can we respect the person's anger and move toward acceptance of his or her decision? Can we accept the young person even if we don't understand or agree with his or her reasons for leaving the church?

We can also seek forgiveness from the young person for ways in which the congregation has failed him or her. Are we willing also to repent and be forgiven? Can we find ways to be at peace or even unity with this young person as he or she follows a path that is strange to us?

Such an experience may cause anxiety in the congregation. Some may be more willing than others to accept the difference that the encounter with another religion through one of our own engenders. Some may be unwilling to accept critical attitudes toward the church that often precede a young person's joining another group. Rather than learning together, the congregation may become fractured. Wisdom is needed to guide families and the congregation through this process.

Young people often want to experiment with other views and religious practices; this process helps them define their own adult beliefs and attitudes as they separate from their parental home. The more relationship can be maintained with the one who has left and the more Christians can learn about the other religion, the better the outcome will likely be. Although painful at times, if this experience is handled gracefully, everyone can learn and grow through it. Sidebar 12.4 presents a reflection for our congregational leaders as we seek wisdom to address the serious issues that religious pluralism presents to our congregations.

Interfaith Marriage

For some Christians, even more distress occurs when a young person marries someone from another religion. Many of the issues listed above need to be addressed in this situation as well: the encounter with different religious ideas, the possibility of a critical attitude toward Christianity, and the need for listening, confessing, and forgiving. The anxiety engendered by the issues surrounding interfaith marriage can be stressful for both family and congregation. In addition, the location of the interreligious couple in the community must be addressed. Do they want to become members of the congregation? Or will they worship with the other religion's community and follow their practices? The family of the young person and those who counsel them will be the first to explore those issues, but the congregation is unavoidably involved.

Sidebar 12.4 Seeking Wisdom

Listening to Sophia, the Voice of Wisdom

Leader:

> Dear Ones, if you accept my words and store up my instructions within you,
> Turning your ear to wisdom and applying your heart to understanding,
> And if you call out for insight and cry aloud for understanding,
> And if you look for it as for silver and search for it as for hidden treasure,
> Then you will understand reverence for God and find the knowledge of God,
> For God gives wisdom and from God's mouth comes knowledge and understanding.
>
> Blessed is the one who finds wisdom, the one who gains understanding,
> For wisdom is more profitable than silver and yields better returns than gold.
> It is more precious than rubies; nothing you desire can compare with wisdom.
>
> Proverbs 2:1–6; 3:13–15 (NIV, paraphrased)

As leaders we seek wisdom so that we may shepherd God's flock well.

Praying with the Apostle Paul for the Wisdom That Is Rooted in Love

Read together in unison:

> For this reason, we kneel before the Creator, from whom the whole family in heaven and on earth derives its name. We pray that out of God's glorious riches we may be strengthened with power through the Spirit in our inner being, so that Christ may dwell in our hearts through faith.
>
> We pray that we, being rooted and established in love, may have power, together with all the saints, to grasp how wide and long and high and deep is the love of Christ, and may know this love that surpasses knowledge—that we may be filled to the measure of all the fullness of God.
>
> Now to the one who is able to do immeasurably more than all we ask or imagine, according to the power that is at work within us, to God be glory in the church and in Christ Jesus throughout all generations, for ever and ever. Amen.
>
> Ephesians 3:14–21 (NIV, paraphrased)

It may be wise for leaders to discuss the possibility of interreligious marriage and explore the congregation's attitudes toward it before a concrete situation arises. What are the theological implications of worshiping with someone of another religion? What steps toward incorporating them into the life of the church might be appropriate? Can the couple be married in the church if the person of another religion does not desire to convert to Christianity? How could the congregation go about educating someone of another faith in Christian practices with an awareness of the tradition he or she comes out of? Should the congregation learn about the faith of the other as well? How can families learn to celebrate an interreligious marriage, preventing the loss of communication and a breaking of the bonds of love in the family and the congregation?

Graceful evangelism in this situation calls for a loving presence and a gracious attitude on the part of both church leaders and congregants. A respect for other religions and some knowledge of specific practices and beliefs can aid Christians in their attempts to love others as Christ loves us. The gospel communicates wordlessly as persons from outside the family of Christ experience God's love through Christians' behaviors and attitudes toward them.

Education about Other Religions

The issues above underscore the need for congregations, especially those that are active in the community, to become informed about the beliefs and practices of other religions. A prior understanding of the Five Pillars of Islam, an appreciation for the Eightfold Path of Buddhism, or an awareness of the mystical longings inherent in the Sufi path to faith can enhance the congregation's ability to address interfaith marriages or the longings for spiritual reality that may lead a young person to seek a different religious path.

Another advantage of learning about other religions is that it reduces the fear of the other that so often prevents relationships from developing with people from other faiths. In Singapore, students told me that although the government has intentionally housed people of different religions in the same high-rise, they rarely interact with one another. Christians fear accusations of proselytizing among Muslims and punishment by the government. They find little common ground with Hindus, so they don't make friends with them. Although many Christian young people are from Chinese Buddhist families, many told me that they know little about that religion, other than what they see their families practicing on a daily basis.

I suspect that ignorance of other religious traditions results in the same types of fear and hesitations here in the United States. Billboards portraying an angry Khomeini in past years, early suspicions of Muslim involvement in the Oklahoma City bombings, and Muslim extremist terrorist involvement in the 9/11 attacks have given rise to increasing levels of hostility toward Muslim citizens in the United States. Learning about Islam from our Muslim neighbors can balance those fears and bring harmony in our communities.

Religious pluralism and postmodern philosophy, which understands all truths to be situated and relative to context, present challenges for preaching and teaching theology. Christian leaders are called upon to teach others in this changing context of religious pluralism and ethical relativism. Pastors face those challenges as they inform congregants of the uniqueness and universality of the Christian gospel, the value of other religions, and the importance of respect and interaction with those of other faiths.

Such education will also deepen the relationships among Christians of various backgrounds in the congregation. Our histories and prior experiences may vary more than we thought. Learning about Mary of Guadalupe or tai chi or silent meditation may give us access to an understanding of both neighbors and people in our own Christian circles—people we think we already know so well in our own congregations.

Facing the challenges of other religions reaches beyond the threshold of the church. As our congregations grow in their understanding of other religions, they will more easily interface with the organizations of those religions that are present in the community. David Bos's book *Bound Together* calls Christian congregations into community ministries. He gives a sound theological explanation for why such ministries are crucial to the church. We can work with people of other religions for the common good of our communities and society at large.

As our congregations become more informed about other religions and active in community ministries with people of other faiths, pastors face unique challenges. Learning to interact publicly with leaders of other religions, finding a comfortable place in interreligious worship, and attuning public teaching to the importance of interreligious dialogue are a few of those challenges. The pastor will need to develop personal relationships with the leaders of mosques, temples, and synagogues as congregations become more actively engaged with communities of other faiths.

As Christian leaders, we must inform ourselves about the touchy issues relating to religious practice in public places that abound in our pluralistic context. The issue of Muslim women veiling in public places in France is important to Muslims here in the United States. In *Ethics and World Religions*, edited by Regina Wolfe and Christine Gudorf, that question and others are explored from the perspective of persons from different faiths. Intelligently discussing Christian responses to the one-child policy in China, the use of the sacred knife in Sikhism, or other religious practices that have become controversial in our world can further interreligious understanding and provide support for people of minority religions in the United States today.

When Jürgen Moltmann visited our campus a few years ago, he lamented the fact that his students, when visiting a mosque, listened attentively to Islamic explanations of God, the world, and human responsibility. When the Muslims asked the Christian students to describe their Christian beliefs, however, they were dumbfounded. The emphasis on religious tolerance and the relativity of knowledge prevented the students from speaking clearly on behalf of their own faith. The Muslims didn't actually appreciate that very much, since they were interested in interreligious dialogue on theological matters. Learning to articulate our faith, to explain our convictions, and to claim them as our own is a necessary part of relating to people of other faiths responsively and responsibly.

What Church Leaders Can Do

Church leaders face challenges on many levels as members in congregations face interreligious issues, interact with those of other faiths in the community, and address theological issues in changing pluralistic contexts. Both pastors and counselors in our churches need to prepare themselves and their congregants to face these challenges effectively (see sidebar 12.5).

Pastors and Christian counselors need to learn the basic worldviews and practices of major world religions. To make that learning come alive, leaders can visit places of worship, introduce themselves, and form relationships with Hindus, Buddhists, and Muslims. As they learn about other religions, Christian leaders need to study biblical views of other religions and grapple with the theological issues presented (Muck 2005). That study will aid leaders in honoring and articulating their own Christian views. Finally, leaders need to work on listening to others and respecting the views of practitioners and leaders of other religions. That homework will take some time. Since interreligious work is so important to Christians in our society, resources to help with this study can be obtained from denominations and ecumenical groups.

The next chapter outlines some changes taking place in the Christian world that can inspire leaders and congregants to move ahead with interreligious activities and other ways of developing new parameters of graceful evangelism.

> **Sidebar 12.5 Homework for Church Leaders**
>
> 1. Learn the basic worldview and practices of major world religions.
> 2. Visit places of worship, introduce yourself, and form relationships with congregations of other religions.
> 3. Study biblical views of other religions and grapple with theological issues presented.
> 4. Practice honoring and articulating your own Christian views.
> 5. Work on listening to others and respecting the views of practitioners and leaders of other religions.

13

Changes

New Movements and Institutional Re-visionings

As Christians face the challenges of religious pluralism, new movements arise and institutions change. Both contemporary theological insights and historical models of evangelism are utilized to address issues and find points of entry for the gospel. This chapter explores a few of the many ways Christians are reformulating evangelism in today's world.

New Outreach Movements

A number of new movements offer new directions in evangelism that can be instructive for Christians seeking to present the gospel gracefully.

New Monasticism

Since the 1930s in America, Christians have formed committed communities that work with local neighborhoods and address global issues. These Christians typically live together in community, stay in contact with denominations, and form networks with other Christian communities. They use spiritual practices gleaned from historical church traditions, monasticism in particular. They reach out in innovative ways with the gospel, with their presence, with their commitments to social justice, and with their ministries.

Koinonia Farm in Georgia is one of the early manifestations of the new monasticism. Founded by Clarence Jordan in Americus, Georgia, during the Depression era, this group simply lived together in an interracial community that showed dignity to all. Their children played together. They worked side by side in the fields and paid the workers well. They prayed together. It wasn't long before this radical witness in southern Georgia brought the Ku Klux Klan to their doorstep. Conflict ensued, but the radical witness of sharing life together as God's people across racial lines left a deep impression on those who came in contact with the courageous group. Habitat for Humanity is one outgrowth of their prophetic witness.

The Houses of Hospitality begun by Dorothy Day during the same period displayed another type of monastic life. Catholics worked and lived together, poor and rich alike, offering hospitality and discussion of life issues to any who came to their doors. The *Catholic Worker* newspaper proclaimed radical ideas of Christian nonviolence and sharing life with the poor to any who would listen. Day's ministry grew phenomenally through the 1930s and 1940s, influencing many left-wing political advocates, Catholic Christians, and homeless wanderers.

A contemporary form of this movement that calls itself "the new monasticism" has organized Schools for Conversion, which teach the theology and practice of monastic Christianity as a way of life. Many of their classes are held in communities that have been responsible centers of Christian teaching and learning for decades, such as Reba Place Fellowship in Evanston, Illinois, and Koinonia Farm, mentioned above (see www.newmonasticism.org).

Leader Jonathan Wilson-Hartgrove describes going back to the Scriptures to discover graceful ways of interacting with people in the consumeristic context of North America. "We found that Jesus used money to make friends," he declared. "So we do that" (2009). At the conference where I heard him speak, he then proceeded to make a number of books and articles available free to participants, including his book *The Good Life Redefined*. He thus demonstrated his focus on what he calls "God's economy of abundance," which taps into community life and generosity.

The teachings of the church fathers also contribute to the theology and community life of new monasticism. Wilson-Hartgrove frequently refers to the promise of Jonah, a promise that his community embraces. That promise assures its members that God is working with all people, and that those outside faith can, at any time, repent and turn to God. Living in that expectation gives members of the new monasticism a positive outlook on those around them.

This movement also *receives* the good news from those outside the church in North America. One of its resources is Emmanuel Katongole's *Mirror to the Church*. Katongole gives an African Christian perspective on the situation of Christianity in the United States.

Reaching out with hospitality, operating local ministries, hearing good news from vibrant churches from other times and places, and worshiping with

energy and faith show the new monasticism to be a movement of graceful
evangelism that can help Christians formulate new ways and revitalize old
ways of showing forth the good news of the gospel.

Emerging Church

The emerging church movement has many faces. Karen Ward of the Church
of the Apostles in Seattle describes it as "sight seeking wider vision, relationships seeking expanded embrace, and spirituality seeking holistic practice. It
is a 'road of destination' where Christ followers, formerly of divergent pasts,
are meeting up in the missional present and moving together toward God's
future." The intentional vagueness of this description leaves room for creativity and multiple expressions of the emerging church. In a reference to *Alice in
Wonderland*, Ward likens the emerging church to an experience. The emerging
church is "being willing to take the red pill, going down the rabbit hole, and
enjoying the ride" (Gibbs and Bolger 2005, 27).

Although some Christians may find this way of viewing the Christian life too
open-ended, others may be nurtured by that broadness, discovering that new
forms of practicing Christianity can be lifegiving. In Louisville, Kentucky, for
example, a church development project by the Presbyterian Church (USA) sets
up worship and Bible discussions in coffee houses and pubs. The participants
of the resulting worship community make a commitment to one another and
begin to look like a congregation without walls.

Doug Pagitt describes another manifestation of this rather diverse movement
called the emerging church. Solomon's Porch is a church in Minneapolis that
reaches out to young people who consider themselves "postmodern." Their
emphasis has moved from a theological or ecclesiological emphasis to a relational emphasis. What is important as people gather together at Solomon's
Porch are their relationships to one another and to the broader community.

In a lecture to the American Society of Missiology, Pagitt describes how he
and his wife adopted two foster kids from a home in the neighborhood. Rather
than see themselves as rescuers, they asked themselves from the beginning,
"How will our family be changed by the gift of these boys and their inclusion
in our family?" They saw the good news of the gospel as something they would
receive from what we might consider "the least of these."

The worship at Solomon's Porch is anything but traditional. The focus is on
what the community sees as important, be it environmental protection, the care
of widows and orphans, or the community garden. The worship atmosphere
is warmed by the creation of a living-room space in an old church where the
pews have been removed. Worshipers are in their twenties and thirties, and
digital media and modern live music are the order of the day. Rather than allowing tradition to limit and hamper them, the Christians at Solomon's Porch
bring in culturally savvy forms and ideas.

Some believe that a Christocentric approach is central to the emerging church's view of life (Gibbs and Bolger 2005, 115). But clearly churches like Solomon's Porch are moving toward a more relational model of Christian community. What is at the center? Pagitt claims that nothing is at the center (2009, 115). Rather, a web of relationships holds the group together in Minneapolis and throughout the world. This view strains toward an entirely new paradigm of evangelism that finds its center not in theology but in relational networks. The appeal of that relational model to young people who are not attracted to more traditional churches is unmistakable. How will this new emerging church influence society as God's *missio Dei* permeates the culture?

Another form of emerging church is happening in the Philippines. The "Church of McDonald's" consists of Christian evangelicals who have their worship services every Sunday in McDonald's fast-food restaurants in Manila. These Christians have made their ministry one of outreach to any and all who would like to join them for breakfast under the golden arches. They have no buildings or pastors, so they avoid multiple expenses. With the offering money, they buy breakfast for all the congregants and visitors. When their groups become too large, some of them branch off and start meeting at another McDonald's restaurant. Their goal is to establish two new churches each year. Mimi, a church member and accountant for a parachurch organization, told me about this lively church growth movement in the Philippines. She said it was the most energizing factor in her whole life. She had prayed for over thirty years for her husband to come to Christ. He did, and now the couple is active in the McDonald's Church, reaching out to other folks in Manila with the good news of the gospel.

Economic Development as Christian Outreach

Some Christians are beginning to do evangelism that specifically addresses physical poverty. In *Hearts Aflame* (2008), Michael Pucci contends that "the evangelical retreat from engaging physical poverty is a missed opportunity for the gospel to confront and contradict the value system of the world in the economic realm" (207). In response, he advocates owning up to our own spiritual poverty, identifying with the poor, and directly addressing physical poverty. Michael and his wife, Adele, work with Food for the Hungry, setting up study centers in poor countries like Thailand and Rwanda. Those centers are becoming places where Christians from wealthy parts of the globe can learn about poverty in the two-thirds world and begin doing something about it.

Insider Movements

Countries in Southeast Asia are experiencing a new form of outreach that transforms religious communities. People who have been brought up in Muslim or Buddhist communities are finding that they want to follow Jesus. Rather than leave their families and communities, these believers stay in the mosque or continue to attend the temple. But their allegiance has shifted to Jesus. Some Christian evangelists are working with these groups to form Christian enclaves that worship within the traditional religious community. Although the author has firsthand information about this movement, specifics about locations and mission workers doing this work are not available for publication. Controversies about insider movements abound. Some think that syncretism is inevitable, but others see the movements as an expansion of God's kingdom. Either way, people are finding their way to Christ and forging new paths of worship without becoming ostracized from their families and social context.

Institutional Change in the Churches

A number of very noticeable changes in institutional churches also show new models of graceful evangelism developing around the world.

Holy Spirit Focus

From Sweden to Indonesia and in many countries in between, informal worship services held before or after the traditional worship service focus on the work of the Holy Spirit in the lives of individuals and the group. One Lutheran church I visited in Sweden simply paused for a few minutes after the service and then launched into a time of singing and charismatic prayer. Everyone participated in this lively prayer and song service. In Indonesia, the Catholic church in Salatiga made room for a smaller group of parishioners to worship in a similar way after the morning mass.

Inagrace Dietterich, who works in missional church development in the United States, believes that renewal of the church can come about through a new embrace of the role of the Holy Spirit in the church. It is God's Spirit that empowers Christians to live the life of the gospel. As churches open themselves to the movement of the Holy Spirit, all things will be renewed. Signs of the kingdom will proliferate. Rather than develop new programs or new forms of worship, Dietterich is putting her energy into teaching Christians how to recognize where the Spirit of God is working and cooperate with that work.

Healing Ministries

Both within the church and in organizations that work with churches, healing ministries are spreading the gospel. The World Council of Churches document *Mission and Evangelism in Unity Today* states that " 'mission' carries a holistic understanding: the proclamation and sharing of the good news of the gospel, by word (*kerygma*), deed (*diakonia*), prayer and worship (*leiturgia*) and the everyday witness of the Christian life (*martyria*); teaching as building up and strengthening people in their relationship with God and each other; and healing as wholeness and reconciliation into *koinonia*—communion with God, communion with people, and communion with creation as a whole" (Jesudasan and Ruppell 2005). That statement sums up the theology of many evangelical as well as conciliar churches.

Healing and reconciliation characterize Christian ministries in South Africa. For example, healing ministries are growing in number and size as Christians address the physical and emotional suffering of the HIV/AIDS pandemic. An AIDS hospice I visited in South Africa in 2009, run by the Episcopal Church, recently changed its name from *hospice* to *caring center* because so many patients were becoming well enough to return home. The staff attributed the turnabout to a combination of new medicines and the healing touch of Christian staff at the center. Healing of memories also gets attention in South Africa as the wounds of apartheid and the devastating memories of violence still haunt many people. Father Michael Lapsley, the chaplain for the African National Congress during the apartheid years, runs seminars that help others heal. He uses healing techniques that helped him recover from the violence done to him during the conflict. As a victim of a letter bomb that cost him both of his arms, Father Lapsley shares with others the healing that God has accomplished in his own life.

The World Council of Churches tells of other healing ministries around the world. In Ghana, fellowships in factories pray for healing of mismanagement practices. At Alu-Works Ltd., workers both pray and act together for better working conditions (Jesudasan and Ruppell 2005, 30). The healing of society is not left to strident action alone but is linked with prayer. Hospitals around the world also utilize prayer as a path to spiritual as well as physical healing. The Deliverance Church, pastored by E. M. Bulbul, announces prayer services specifically for healing and casting out evil spirits. "Jesus heals the broken-hearted," proclaims the signage announcing services (Jesudasan and Ruppell 2005, 27).

Liturgy Revitalization

Another focus of finding the path toward graceful evangelism is put forward by Catholic historian William Burrows. He argues that a renewed understanding of the *mysteries of the Eucharist* will energize the practices of the church, leading to a vibrancy that will attract others. A rational understanding of the Eucharist is not enough. The mysteries hidden within this ancient and contemporary ritual must be apprehended as Christians partake. And those mysteries will themselves lead to revitalization of the church. A renewed church will have a vibrant witness and draw others into the circle of worshiping God (Burrows 2009). The Eucharist also gives healing to many as Christians are brought together in unity across social, linguistic, and cultural barriers (Jesudasan and Ruppell 2005, 59).

The Rise of Pentecostalism

Pentecostal Christians attest to "an experience of the presence and power of the resurrected Christ and of the Holy Spirit as the source of life and hope, the power to make it through each new day, and the guarantee of victory over demonic forces" (Shaull and Cesar 2000, 145). Those promises motivate the largest growing Christian church movement on the planet. In fact, Karla Poewe argues that the resurgent charismatic forms of Christianity *are* the new global Christianity, remaining marginalized no longer (Kalu 2008, 8n12). In South America, poverty-stricken people flock to services that preach that the human problem is one of fallenness from an original state of goodness. The solution to that problem is God's free gift of forgiveness and justification. And that solution is available to all through the death of Christ on the cross (Shaull and Cesar 2000, 144). While worship services don't specifically address the poverty issue, congregants find encouragement and empowerment through experiencing the presence and power of the Holy Spirit. Lives are changed by the gospel.

In Brazil, through the work of Cheryl Bridges Johns, Pentecostals are being exposed to the pedagogical insights of Paulo Freire's work *Pedagogy of the Oppressed* (Shaull and Cesar 2000, 223). Johns gets Pentecostals involved by raising people's awareness and aiming at radical change in society. She links her efforts at conscientization to those of Freire and many Latin American base communities that focus on political change through faith-based efforts. Through bringing those frames of reference together, Johns hopes to see a new kind of spiritual formation occurring among Pentecostals. "Each has a contribution to make to the other," she declares (Shaull and Cesar 2000, 223).

Missional Churches

Changes in American culture and a decline in mainline church membership have led some scholars to suggest that Christendom, the dominance of Christianity in Western culture, is coming to an end (Van Gelder 1996, 41; Guder 2000, xii). Like the seven Christians from Ephesus in the legend discussed in chapter 12, Christians need to wake up to the fact that their context has radically changed. Churches today need to recognize that fact and realize that their neighborhoods and communities are mission fields. Churches respond to the decentralization of the place of Christianity in American culture by developing theologies that suit this new context and by forming new evangelism strategies. The Gospel and Our Culture Network does much work in this area, presenting cogent theologies that address contemporary issues with the gospel.

Congregational Centers for Mission

As churches develop the idea that they need to become a missionary force in their context, mission becomes focused more in congregations. Denominations are responding to that shift by helping congregations with their mission efforts.

The Presbyterian Church (USA) provides an example of a denomination that is paying attention to this shift from denominationally based missions to missions that begin in the congregation. In fact, new relationships between congregations, mission workers, and denominational leaders around mission are revitalizing the face of mission in the PC(USA). Recognizing the energy and motivation of many congregations to be actively involved in outreach, Hunter Farrell, director of Worldwide Ministries, encourages congregational outreach and provides multiple sources of support for those programs. Mission Crossroads, an online informational service, shares data on mission efforts around the world. Denominational coordinators working with this PC(USA) service advise and connect congregations with national church workers on every continent. Presbyterian mission coworkers return to the United States, work with a yearly national mission conference event, and from there spread out across US Presbyterian congregations to share what is happening in mission across the planet. Presbyterian Young Adult Volunteers venture out from congregations for year-long mission work in other countries. The Office of International Evangelism works hand in hand with the Worldwide Ministries division to facilitate evangelistic outreach from congregations. The increasing emphasis on congregational outreach now connects denominational resources and contacts that enrich the spread of the gospel across the world.

Prophetic Voices in the Church

Whenever cultures or religions seem to be in decline, prophets arise to call the religion back to its ideals and its roots. The journal *Sojourners* and the community of Jonah House in Washington DC call American culture to reevaluate nuclear arms and our nation's military status. Ron Sider and Tony Campolo call Christians to turn from our materialistic culture and witness more truly to the good news of Jesus Christ. Thomas Merton and Dorothy Day addressed political issues from a gospel point of view. Some new prophets see the decline of Protestantism in the West as a wake-up call for churches to become missional and prophetic in their witness.

Charles Fensham, raised in South Africa and now living in Canada, sees church decline related to a coming "dark age." Fensham states that "the ecological crisis, the exhaustion of fossil fuel, the outbreak of global pandemics, and the loss of quality of life and health will profoundly affect the church in North America" (2008, 8). He traces the cultural history of North America and speaks of the digital age contributing to a loss of memory, wisdom, and ethic of the reign of God (9).

Into that rather dark projected scenario, Fensham combines the ideas of the emerging church as a free-form development *outside* denominations that would contribute to denominational revitalization. He works from the theologies of Karl Barth, David Bosch, and Lesslie Newbigin to argue for the missional nature of the church and its role in bringing wholeness to creation (2008, 148). He focuses on reading the Bible in the present context to develop a stronger understanding of mission, of the poor and marginalized, and of the Enlightenment and our technological culture (9).

We see many of Fensham's emphases arising in multiple networks of Christians and churches. Digital media have enhanced communication among those networks. The Gospel and Our Culture Network; Progressive Christianity; networks of immigrant churches from Indonesia, Ghana, Brazil, and other countries; informal networks of people in mission and evangelism; Internet networking sites; and countless others offer enriching theological perspectives and models of evangelism.

The changes described above show different paths to a reenergized church that can become more effective in reaching out and reaching in with the good news. Not every group will be drawn to all these approaches, but as Christians follow the call to faithful living, all these models of renewal can have positive effects on contemporary society. Developing a graceful evangelism, however, entails working hard to *appreciate* various approaches in their contexts. Finding value in the beliefs and patterns of witness of others continues to challenge us as Christians. In the next chapter, we will present a way to approach those differences with a goal of understanding, so that our understanding of evangelism can become open and broad enough to include voices different from our own.

14

Seeing through Their Eyes

A Spiral of Knowledge Acquisition

In the last chapter we outlined a number of movements and changes in the church that point to new directions in evangelism. Despite those signs of hope for Christianity in our society and in our world, we as Christians often find it hard to appreciate the views of others when it comes to announcing the good news of the gospel.

It is especially difficult to appreciate the views of other Christians with whom we disagree on methods of outreach. But crafting a graceful evangelism means accepting the diversity of approaches we find in the church. In this chapter we will outline an approach to learning about views that differ from ours in such a way that appreciation and even perhaps complementarity will result from the process.

Social theorist Jürgen Habermas speaks of two realms of society: the systems and the lifeworld (1984, 1:72). In political and economic systems, communication is geared to amassing money and power. So when we hear a sales pitch, we know that the salesperson is styling our interaction with the goal of making a sale. Money controls communication. Likewise in political speeches, the goal is to get the audience to accept one's views so that one can proceed with decisions based on power granted by the people.

In the lifeworld, communication has a different function. In social settings, families, communities, churches, and cultural events, communication is geared to understanding. We talk with the goal of getting our thoughts communicated clearly so that they can be understood. We listen, believing that the person communicating with us is speaking truthfully and sincerely and that he or she will behave morally in our interaction. The goals in talking and in listening in the systems or the lifeworld are quite different.

Evangelism happens in the lifeworld, as does Christian fellowship. Our attempts to communicate with others who do evangelism in ways different than ours, and perhaps in contradiction to our ways, is geared to understanding. For example, I want to understand the reasons that Charles Fensham sees a dark age coming in the West and why he recommends a theology of social trinity to draw others to Christ. I want to understand how Pastor E. M. Bulbul understands deliverance through Christ for the brokenhearted. I want to know how Michael Pucci understands relieving physical suffering to be part of responsible Christian evangelism. In each of those cases, my communication with the people involved is geared not to amassing money or power but to gaining understanding.

How can we better understand those whose evangelism theologies and strategies differ from our own? We need to venture toward those viewpoints with fresh eyes and open hearts. We need to gain knowledge about their theologies, their contexts, and their methods. We need to understand why certain aspects of their view of evangelism set the pattern for their actions. To do that, we need to spend time trying to understand them and their worldview, their

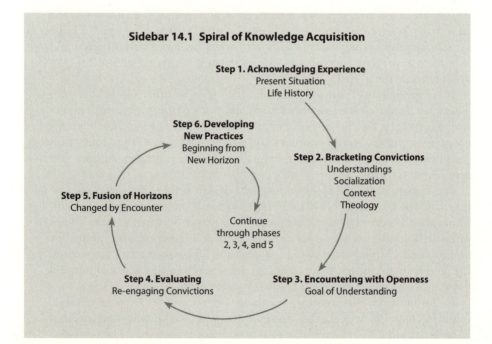

Sidebar 14.1 Spiral of Knowledge Acquisition

Step 1. Acknowledging Experience
Present Situation
Life History

Step 6. Developing New Practices
Beginning from New Horizon

Step 2. Bracketing Convictions
Understandings
Socialization
Context
Theology

Step 5. Fusion of Horizons
Changed by Encounter

Continue through phases 2, 3, 4, and 5

Step 4. Evaluating
Re-engaging Convictions

Step 3. Encountering with Openness
Goal of Understanding

situation, and the way they understand it. The model for this process can be envisioned as a spiral of knowledge acquisition. Although we are constantly engaging every step of this spiral, it is easier to picture in terms of six steps to understanding (see sidebar 14.1).

—————○—————

Some Christians are contextually sensitive because they intuit what is appropriate in a particular situation. Such intuition might be described as a spiritual gift. But even without that talent, one can learn to understand a particular context for evangelism and develop insights and strategies that relevantly address it. We can learn to interact positively with the surrounding culture and religion and bring the good news of the Christian gospel to bear on that situation. And we can learn to understand and appreciate the evangelistic strategies of others and how they relate to their particular setting. We do this by interacting with them with the goal of understanding, not with the goal of seeking power over them or gaining something from them.

We can begin to understand other strategies by acquiring knowledge that breaks through stereotypes, sees the situation in fresh ways, evaluates the context with a critical standard of God's truth, and forms new understandings that lead to healing and renewal. Through engaging in that process of knowledge acquisition, a Christian changes the surrounding context and is also changed by that context. Opening up to the wisdom in the strangeness of the other's situation and approach to evangelism leads to an interaction that revolutionizes both you and the people you are trying to understand. The *missio Dei*, God's mission, breaks into the situation and the good news is right there—in our face—to be apprehended by all, strangers and locals alike.

Something like this happened in Acts 10 when Peter received a vision from God about eating what was considered, in his local context of the Jewish religion, to be unclean. That vision led him to receive the messengers from Cornelius—gentiles—and have them as houseguests in Joppa. Cornelius had a vision at about the same time—a vision that Peter would come to his home and instruct him more perfectly in the ways of God. Cornelius, a Roman who probably worshiped the emperor, was, nonetheless, according to the text, a God-fearing and righteous person. Peter went to Cornelius's house, enjoyed the hospitality of Cornelius, ate unclean food, and watched as the Holy Spirit descended on all in that place. Gentiles were baptized and a whole new era began—the beginnings of a church that would span the globe. Peter was open to the strange culture of the Roman household of Cornelius. God had prepared him to be open. He was changed by that encounter and by the good news that God accepts all who fear God and do right. Peter's boundaries of inclusion broke through significant barriers that day. God and Cornelius rocked Peter's world, and the world itself was forever changed.

Step 1: Acknowledging Experience

Peter's innovative evangelistic work was possible because he opened himself up to the strangeness of Roman culture. He stood in the Jewish tradition. All his experience up to that point had been in the secure world of the synagogue. The Jewish world was his world—the only world that he knew. Presumably, he had not been unhappy in that world. He did not seek a different path. Even his interaction with Jesus confirmed his beliefs and worldview. Understanding our own situation and experience is the first step in acquiring knowledge of how someone else sees the world.

Jesus's death had, of course, been a shock. It presented a huge anomaly in his secure paradigm. Other anomalies had been building up as Peter followed Jesus—when he called Zacchaeus the tax collector down from the tree and went to his house for dinner, when he allowed a woman to come straight into his dinner party from the street and anoint his feet with perfume, when he touched the child Tabitha lying on her death bed, when he talked theology in the heat of the day with a Samaritan woman at the well.

But now suddenly Peter was thrown into a situation that he couldn't possibly comprehend with his old paradigm, a situation that demanded personal action on his part. His vision shattered his old paradigm by instructing him to be open—open enough to receive the unclean.

Step 2: Bracketing Convictions

So Peter set aside a lifetime of experience, defied the rules of etiquette and religious purity that he had so long embraced, and on the thin evidence of a dream, went forward. Peter bracketed his convictions and opened the door to Cornelius. Peter invited Cornelius to stay with him in the home of his friend Simon the tanner. Peter clearly stated that this behavior went against centuries of tradition that instructed Jews not to associate with gentiles (Acts 10:27–28; 11:8). But walking with Jesus, witnessing a resurrected Christ, and associating with a community of Jesus's followers had prepared him for new encounters. Anomalies to his old paradigm were accumulating. His vision was further evidence that a new way of interacting with gentiles was part of God's plan for the world. Peter bracketed his convictions. He opened the door.

Peter's story shows us the first two steps for the Christian attempting to understand the strange evangelism theologies and strategies of others: step one is recognizing our own experience and how it predisposes us to see things in a particular way. Our beliefs in universal truths are expressed in cultural/

religious forms. For Peter, the rules about avoiding unclean food were particular forms that enabled the Jews to preserve their culture, carrying God's truth through the centuries in a pluralistic world. Understanding the particularity of our life experience is the first step in understanding others. Accepting that we are Western post-Enlightenment people practicing our beliefs in the universal truths of Christianity in particular ways is our first step.

Other Christians may practice their belief in the graciousness of God in sending Christ to the world in different ways. They may approach people with the story of the gospel in ways we wouldn't dream of. Or perhaps in ways that we have experienced and were hurt by. Or perhaps in ways that we've learned from our own church study or university education are colonialistic and culture destroying. We begin our journey by recognizing that our own experience of evangelism and our convictions about it are just as culturally contained and socially managed as those of others.

Step two is bracketing those convictions so that we can open ourselves up to wisdom from other sources. Peter's vision gave him the courage to set aside his convictions about unclean food and unclean people, and open the door to Cornelius. Just as Peter had to bracket his dearly held convictions about how God works in the world, so we need to bracket our convictions about the best and worst ways to practice evangelism. Only then are we ready to live out a graceful evangelism ourselves.

Christians and Christian communities today also receive messages from God about how to interact with others. Paula Tibbs, one of our graduates, worked with the Presbyterian Church in the Democratic Republic of Congo during a field education experience. She felt awkward every time she received the greeting "Muoyo mutoke" (Hello, white woman). Rather than react by withdrawing or criticizing, Paula bracketed her discomfort, which was based on her experiences as a Caucasian American. She also set aside her convictions about how a missionary "should" interact with the Congolese. Were there particular forms of outreach expected of her? She laid them aside. Instead, she began seeking understanding of how the Congolese interpreted that greeting. Through open conversations with the Christians there, she concluded that the greeting carried racist overtones for both the local people and the mission workers. Something was wrong with the interaction that didn't result in good news on either side. Through her work and the work of her Congolese counterparts, a new paradigm of interaction between mission workers and local church people is developing. This new paradigm moves beyond the superiority/inferiority assumptions of the old Western missionary paradigm. Bracketing one's convictions makes way for attention to intuitions, certain Scripture passages, interactions with local people, and counsel from local Christians that provide nudges by the Holy Spirit to those God is sending to new situations. Recognizing the limitations of her own perspective and bracketing her convictions opened Tibbs up to a new understanding of missionary/culture interaction that she could not have otherwise understood.

Step 3: Encountering the Strange Situation with Openness

Recognizing the particularity of our life experience and bracketing the convictions that we have developed over the course of that experience prepare us for the third step in learning a graceful evangelism: encountering the new situation with *openness*. Missionaries leave the security of their home, their church, and their cultural context, embarking on a journey to encounter the strangeness of another culture. This can happen to any Christian who travels to another country or walks down the street to a mosque or community center in her or his own neighborhood. Strange customs offend one's sense of etiquette; strange sights and odors assault the senses; strange religions confuse the mind. A different religion or perhaps many different religions with odd practices and ideas confront the Christian. How to interact with that new situation presents multiple challenges.

Sometimes challenges to understanding are even greater within the church. A comfortable middle-class American Christian may have difficulty appreciating a prison ministry evangelism that centers on "being saved." Trying to appreciate a direct conversion approach if one is socialized into a gradual coming to Christ through education in the church can be very difficult. Richard Mouw responded with an open approach in this situation when while working at a restaurant during his seminary years he encountered a customer who insistently and repeatedly told him that he must know the moment that he was "saved." Since Richard had been raised in a Christian home and had come to faith as he grew, he found this a jarring approach. But he kept listening to Mick, he kept his mind open, and in the end, he learned to appreciate Mick's theology, although he never adopted it.

His openness led to an understanding that would not have occurred if he had simply explained to Mick that he didn't accept his theology. Instead, Mouw came to a realization that the center of theology, when it comes to conversion, is this: "Conversion is something that happens when we respond to something that God has done" (2008, 167). Opening oneself up to the strange is a crucial step if we are to learn to gracefully appreciate the evangelistic techniques of others.

In other words, we can respond by using the frameworks of a lifetime of experience (responding as usual) or we can respond with openness, exploring the new situation and its strangeness like a child encounters new experiences. Curiosity, fear, and delight are a few of the responses that openness generates.

Evangelism may look very different in a new setting. The first Advent season I spent in Java, Indonesia, sent me into a whirlwind of confusion. I couldn't wait; I couldn't worship; I felt I was losing my faith. Then I realized that all my usual cues for worship during Advent were missing. Instead of the crisp cold air of December, I was drenched in perspiration in the wet heat of the tropics. Instead of the scent of evergreen boughs and Christmas lights in the sanctuary, I was stunned by the sight of plastic red roses adorning a huge white cross above the altar. Instead of merry English Christmas caroling and hot chocolate, we sang songs in the Indonesian language and drank lychee juice. How humbled I was to realize that my worship was so culturally conditioned that I felt lost without my usual cues.

By the second Christmas, I was able to respond more positively to the Advent celebrations in Indonesia. I had learned that cold weather wasn't the only cue for waiting and welcoming the Christ child. I had begun to appreciate a sense of beauty that contrasted bright red roses with a white cross behind the altar instead of green trees adorned with Christmas lights. I had learned the centrality of the cross even in Advent worship for the church in Java. By opening myself to the strange worship cues around me, I found that, rather than losing my faith, my faith was stretched and strengthened by my interaction with expressions of Advent worship in Indonesia. Encountering the strangeness of the Indonesian culture with openness brought me to new levels of understanding Christianity in my mission setting.

Barriers and Doors to Openness

The barriers I came up against in the process of opening myself to Indonesian culture were many. The cultural cues from my own experience were a major barrier. Another barrier was the sense of beauty that valued different materials, color schemes, and kinds of hymns than I was used to. A third barrier was the religious milieu in Java. The church there is a minority, struggling to maintain a strong presence and a theological depth in an Islamic society that is layered with Hindu and Buddhist cultural forms. Consequently it emphasized basic Christian doctrines, especially a theology of the cross. The idea of waiting for Christ to break into one's life during Advent wasn't nearly as important as a strong sense of the depth of love that Christ showed the world in dying on the cross. Although not present in Christian worship itself, the strength of the presence of other religions in the society influenced the whole process of teaching and worship during Advent in the church. The evangelistic side of Advent worship had escaped me at first. It was not until I opened myself up to the strange ways of worship in that setting that I began to understand (see sidebar 14.2).

Encountering the cultural situation with openness helped me to identify those barriers and go beyond them. I could not hang on to my own sense of Advent worship. I had to let it go. Developing respect for the values and habits of the local people helped me with that letting go. Rather than maintaining a negative attitude toward plastic flowers, I listened attentively to the admiring comments about the Advent sanctuary decorations. Rather than maintaining my own sense of the church year and what was appropriate for meditation at Advent, I opened my heart to the messages of God's love in

> ## Sidebar 14.2 Openness to Cultural Differences
>
> **Barriers to Openness:**
>
> - Lack of cultural cues from one's experience
> - Aesthetic differences
> - Differences in religious milieu
> - Focus on different doctrines
> - Yearning for home
>
> **Doors into Openness:**
>
> - Letting go of one's expectations
> - Developing respect for the values and habits of the local people
> - Attentive listening
> - Opening one's heart to the messages of God's love expressed in that culture
> - Embracing the new situation

sending Christ to the world, not just to be born, but to die for our sins. Rather than holding on to a feeling that cold weather and Christmas go together, I tried to embrace the life-giving sun and heat and the lush greenery of the mountains of Java.

These actions may sound trivial to someone who has never been away from the comfortable cues of his or her own milieu at Advent. To those who have, you will recognize the deep impact of cultural forms on our worship and attitudes toward others. Encountering the strangeness of a new place, different people, and alien cultural forms with openness is a difficult and central step in acquiring knowledge that will enable a mission worker to become loving and effective in her or his new setting.

The same might be said of a middle-class Christian beginning to do prison ministry. Opening oneself up to the prison culture, the lived experience of the incarcerated, the forms of worship that Christian ministers in prison use can each be a step in understanding the reasons for the "strange" form of evangelism that works effectively in that setting.

Gifts and Dangers of Openness

As a Christian continues to interact with the strangeness of a new situation, more and better reasons for the behavior of the people become clear. One begins to understand why villagers don't like to go out alone at night, or why drums or gamelans are not used in Christian worship, or why it is unseemly for women to rush to class, arriving drenched with perspiration. One begins to respect an evangelistic service performed with only Christians present as a faith strengthener for Christians in a Muslim context. Those were some of the lessons I learned in Java through understanding the particularity of my own former experience, bracketing my convictions, and encountering the strange culture of Java with openness.

As I went along that path, I learned much. I also discovered that I was becoming more and more like the people whom I lived with. I became more indirect in the ways that I communicated with people, mirroring the Javanese style of communication. I began to wear dresses when I went shopping, instead of sauntering to the store in jeans and a T-shirt. I walked more slowly to class, avoiding embarrassing my students by arriving drenched with perspiration. I forgot about the waiting focus in Advent worship. And I didn't long for cold weather quite as much.

I was becoming like the people around me. But what was happening to *me*? Where were *my* convictions, my cues for worship, my sense of beauty, my communication style, my love for strenuous exercise? Was my identity being compromised? Was I losing my theological focus? Was I losing myself?

In opening oneself to a new culture and different forms of life, one runs the danger of becoming a chameleon. Quite the opposite danger to holding on tightly to one's past experience, here is the danger of forgetting one's roots and convictions. In opening oneself to the strangeness of another culture and bracketing one's own convictions, one gains tremendous new knowledge. Embracing new ideas, taking new perspectives, absorbing new frameworks, and engaging in new practices expands one's horizons. One is able to gain understandings of others that would be impossible without such openness, but the new knowledge one gains influences behavior. And one's behaviors become part of one's sense of self. The danger of losing one's own identity now confronts the person who has opened up to new ways of perceiving the world.

If we open ourselves to every form of evangelism, will we become theologically wishy-washy in our own views? Can we appreciate the theologies of others without losing our own focus?

A lesson from missionary experience might be helpful here. One of the best gifts a missionary brings to a new culture is his or her very strangeness—his or her difference. People see themselves in distinction to others. One's uniqueness is highlighted by the strangeness of someone from another culture. To simply adopt all of the views and behaviors of the community one enters denies those who welcome the missionary the very difference that can produce positive change. By accepting our strangeness, we show vulnerability, indicate our openness, and learn to cooperate with others *where they are* (Gittins 1989, 132–33). Although one must be open to the new culture to acquire the knowledge necessary for giving and receiving the gifts of the gospel, one also needs to evaluate the new culture and offer insights that may allow the gospel to be more fully present in that place. It is our open attitude that will allow us to be heard.

We certainly won't adopt every evangelism strategy that we study or encounter. But we can learn to accept the presence of contradictory theologies and the importance of varying contexts.

Step 4: Evaluating the Strange Culture

The fourth step in the spiral of knowledge acquisition, then, is to bring back all of one's past experience and those bracketed convictions that were set aside in order to foster the openness necessary for understanding a different culture or religion. We have struggled with the strangeness of a new culture or a different view of evangelism with openness. Now is the time to step back and evaluate the cultural forms one has encountered using one's own cultural and theological lenses.

Now that some understanding based on the ways of the new culture has been acquired, the Christian reengages his or her past experience and cultural and theological convictions. We may have accompanied evangelists to the prison to do ministry. We may have seen their direct approach and learned to value it in that setting. Now, we step back and critically evaluate that method of evangelism. That critical reengagement is crucial for two reasons. First, by simply accepting everything in the new culture—embracing the ideas and practicing all the cultural forms—one's own values and beliefs become muted and begin to disappear. This compromises one's identity. Second, by *not* reengaging one's own convictions, the message of love and peace inherent in the gospel story may also become lost.

For example, if missionaries to China one hundred years ago had simply adopted all the cultural forms of Chinese society, they would have had to affirm the practice of footbinding among upper-class families. What would happen to a mission worker who believed that foot-binding is wrong because it cripples a healthy body made in God's image? Which is more important—sensitivity to culture or the value of the unhindered growth of a child? How can this difference in values be navigated between the missionaries and the local people?

Missionaries faced this real dilemma. The China Inland Mission, led by Hudson Taylor in the late nineteenth century, required missionaries to adopt Chinese dress and practice Chinese customs with the people. A story, most likely having a basis in real experience, tells of a girl with an infection in one of her bound feet who came to a missionary for help. The missionary unbound the foot of the child, salved it with ointment, and instructed the mother to leave the foot unbound until it healed. When that treatment cured the child, the mother brought her back for further examination. The missionary examined the foot and without comment unbound the other foot. The mother seemed surprised but went away without objecting. In the weeks that followed many other mothers brought their baby girls to the missionary, asking her to unbind the feet of their children. What they could not do themselves due to cultural prohibitions, they could receive from the hand of the foreigner. Reengaging one's convictions can have a powerful effect on a community, especially if they already perceive that the stranger wants to understand them.

Reengaging one's convictions is also critical for the missionary who is interacting with customs that are not only strange but sometimes abhorrent. The impact of "living with" practices that go against deep theological or moral convictions can have a devastating effect on a Christian. Reengaging one's convictions helps one find a way to accept what is compatible with one's own convictions and turn away from practices or beliefs that are contrary to one's deep convictions.

At the same time, one's openness to the foreign culture or strange way of doing evangelism has an impact on the person seeking understanding. That openness allows one's convictions to change by encountering the other. An example from my own mission experience might help here. When I arrived in Java, I began hearing loud speakers chanting strange Arabic phrases in very odd-sounding tones every few hours. Five times a day, mosques everywhere in Indonesia send out the call to prayer, one man's chanting voice magnified many times over with a loudspeaker system. This reminder sends men and women to their knees in their homes, in their fields, and in the mosques. "Allah Akbar—God is great!"

Set prayers are recited at dawn and throughout the day, ending with evening prayers at dusk. The call to prayer emanating from the mosques reminds devout Muslims that it is time to pray. Hearing this reminder five times a day for nearly six years had the effect of reminding me to pray. It also made me realize how deeply many Indonesians felt about praising God and bowing down to the One God who created all things. Because I was open to learning from Indonesians and their cultural forms, their ways of practicing belief in God, and their daily habits, I came to appreciate the call to prayer.

That was not the case for some of my Christian missionary acquaintances in Indonesia. Some felt the call to prayer was an intrusion on their daily life, a disruption to children's classes at the local Christian school. Some even heard the call to prayer as a demonic force keeping Indonesia in spiritual darkness. How very different this reaction was from my reaction based on practicing openness toward Indonesian culture.

Openness to Muslim culture didn't turn me into a Muslim though. Through reengaging my convictions about Jesus Christ as the Son of God and Redeemer of the world, I remained wholeheartedly committed to Christianity. But my attitudes toward Islam changed greatly.

Step 5: Fusion of Horizons

The next step in the spiral of knowledge acquisition often happens without conscious effort. In my case, my own experience and convictions changed because of the influence of the knowledge I gained in Indonesia. My attitude toward Islam is one example. Through learning about Islam; through hearing and responding openly to the call to prayer; through making friends with a Muslim family from Pakistan; through participating in Ramadan, the month of fasting; and celebrating Idul Fitri, the end of fasting, with Muslim friends and neighbors, my own thinking and behavior toward Islam changed. My past experience and the new experiences I had in Indonesia with Muslims came together. My understanding of Islam deepened. My horizons broadened. I changed.

The Christian who is open to those of different convictions changes in this way. The barriers between the Christian and the culture encountered fall away as openness brings understanding and as evaluating the culture brings clarity to one's identity and broadens his or her horizon of knowledge. People of very different persuasions find, at this point, a great deal of mutuality and care for one another. Differences no longer threaten but enrich relationships. Gifts of care and respect are given and received. Knowledge of the other's culture changes both the mission worker and the local people. The good news is heard and received by both.

John Ng describes this process as he works to evangelize CEOs. By listening and sharing his own struggles, Ng discovered that business people who are not Christian are both realistic and pragmatic. He identifies with the human struggles, needs, and failures that he shares with "pre-Christians" (2008, 67). This fusion of horizons with those he ministers to draws people to Christ as Ng becomes more like the people he serves and authentically shares those similarities with them.

Step 6: Developing New Practices

Such encounters change both the Christian and those he or she reaches out to. A new platform of understanding has been built through the process of openness and evaluation. Consequently, the actions of the Christians change. Rather than do evangelism in the way they had thought would be their modus operandi when they entered the situation, Christians find themselves ready to work with the people in different ways. Those ways are more sensitive to the needs and aspirations of the people since time has been spent in learning to understand them and their ways. In John Ng's case, he found himself resonating with the religious Buddhists he met and empathizing with their dedication to their religion. He went further in his relationship with those of other religions, speaking of his own Christian experience, sharing his weaknesses, and building trust over the long haul (2008, 643–67).

As common struggles are shared, the Christian doesn't go ahead of others but walks with them. Plans are developed together. A give-and-take arises that springs from deeper understanding on both sides. The shape those plans take differs from context to context.

Carrie Maples, a Southern Baptist missionary who went to Kenya in 1998, recounts her own surprise when she found herself working with African women for basic human rights. She hadn't come to Africa to do that. But through acquiring knowledge of her setting and the people there, she found herself working with the women on the issues that were important to them, rather than staying with her own agenda (Bergner 2006, 7).

Was that mission strategy less evangelistic because she worked on human rights and agriculture? Not at all. The gospel became real in Ng's and Maples's situations because they learned from the society they encountered, identified the problems faced by the people, and developed innovative ways to address those needs. Each of them took the path of recognizing the limitedness of their own experience, setting aside their convictions in order to listen openly to the people, learning from those encounters, evaluating the culture, and fusing their interests and ultimately their knowledge with those of the local people. And *voila*—their practices changed. They appreciated both the problems and the possibilities of the people. They began to do evangelism in new ways.

Their new knowledge changed their practice. Both their theology and actions changed through moving through the spiral of knowledge acquisition. But a spiral doesn't end. So Christians begin again, with new experience, and traverse the spiral again from a brand-new starting point. As they move up the spiral over and over again, they learn to do evangelism more gracefully. And so can we.

15

Radical Habits

Practices for Evangelism Today

In the previous chapters, we have discussed ways to address the unique and complex situation for evangelism that we face in the twenty-first century. We develop new theologies to suit particular contexts. We recognize how very different our religiously pluralistic context is and face the challenges of other religions. We study new movements and institutional changes that can help Christians and congregations to tailor evangelism to their situation. We try to see through others' eyes, acquiring knowledge of how those different from ourselves understand evangelism.

Addressing the "evangelism wars" creatively in the churches today requires all those approaches. With so much variance in content, context, and method, doing evangelism gracefully is a task no one person or church can accomplish alone. Individually, none of us will solve all the problems presented by contexts and theologies of evangelism today.

One thing we can do is develop a way to live. Creative Christians through the centuries have developed "radical habits" that enhanced their interaction with others. Christians and churches can develop those same practices to ensure that a patient and graceful evangelism results in our context from whatever methods we deem appropriate. Focusing on habits or practices rather than content, contexts, and methods allows us to develop a disciplined way of interacting with others that supports the message of love of the gospel. The ways we interact with others and the qualities of character and attitudes that radiate from our lives may be a stronger witness than the theologies and strategies of evangelism we advocate.

This chapter describes seven practices that are not only consistent with the gospel but actually further the cause of the gospel through a witness of grace and love toward others. Missionaries through the centuries have developed these innovative practices that have furthered the gospel in many places. The practices described here are based upon the lives of those missionaries detailed in *Christianity Encountering World Religions: The Practice of Mission in the Twenty-first Century*. Practicing these radical habits will lend a biblical consistency to the outreach of both individuals and communities of Christ's followers.

A few crucial assumptions undergird these practices for graceful evangelism. First, we assume that God has gone before us and is currently working with

> **Sidebar 15.1 Assumptions Undergirding Graceful Evangelism**
>
> 1. God has gone before us and is currently working with those with whom we long to share the good news of Christ's gospel; God's grace is never limited to Christian interaction but infuses life in all parts of the world.
> 2. Graceful evangelism is neither competitive nor cooperative but is reflexive—a giving and receiving of gifts to and from those with whom we interact.
> 3. Listening and identifying with the people to whom we are sent forms the basis of developing these practices in a particular setting.

those with whom we long to share the good news of Christ's gospel. God's grace is never limited to Christian interaction but infuses life in all parts of the world. Second, graceful evangelism is neither competitive nor cooperative but is reflexive—a giving and receiving of gifts to and from those with whom we interact. Third, listening and identifying with the people to whom we are sent forms the basis of developing these practices in a particular setting (see sidebar 15.1).

The Metaphor of Gift

Giving and receiving gifts is a perfect metaphor for a graceful evangelism. The evangelist is a witness to God's grace and to the wonderful gift of salvation in Jesus Christ. The *giftive mission* metaphor emphasizes the appropriateness of giving and receiving gifts as part of that witness (see sidebar 15.2). The radical habits of each missionary below illustrate that in giving, in sharing the gospel, gifts are exchanged between the missionary and the people to whom he or she was called.

Reasons for using the metaphor of gift are many. To begin with, Scripture uses it. Missionaries have traditionally seen themselves as bearers of gifts, especially the free gift of the gospel. And Christians attempt to imitate God in

Sidebar 15.2 Characteristics of Giftive Mission

1. Recognizing God's gifts to others (Ps. 119:30; Prov. 3:34; Acts 15:9–10)
2. Giving to others (Matt. 19:21; 2 Cor. 8:7)
3. Receiving gifts from others (Matt. 7:11; 1 Cor. 11:13; 12:31; Phil. 2:25)
4. Awareness of receiving through giving (Prov. 11:24; 15:23)
5. Giving as a spiritual practice (Prov. 11:25; Matt. 6:4)
6. Seeing Christ in those who receive (Luke 6:20; John 17:10; James 2:5)

giving gifts, thus moving beyond the excesses of confrontation and competition in mission. Thinking about evangelism as a giving and receiving of gifts also highlights the positive practices that we are already using in our evangelistic efforts. Seeing ourselves as bearers and receivers of gifts improves our relationships with people of other religions and, at the same time, counters antimission forces of distrust, self-aggrandizement, and comparing the best of Christianity with the worst of other religions. Giving and receiving gifts in culturally appropriate ways shows that Christians desire to honor both the culture they are called to serve and the individuals in it. When we use the giftive mission metaphor, we discover hints of the free gift of God's love in other cultures (Muck and Adeney 2009, 354).

The metaphor of gift is appropriate for our twenty-first-century context for a number of reasons. First, Christians today are in contact with people of other cultures who hold different beliefs frequently and inevitably. Through travel, getting to know neighbors of other faiths, Internet information and acquaintances, and education about cultures, Christians are positioned for intercultural interaction. Second, people from many sectors of society feel a need for a spiritual alternative to economic globalization and a materialistic lifestyle. Whether we are rich or poor, the focus on ever-increasing material benefits invariably becomes empty. The metaphor of gift puts relationship ahead of making a sale. The world is looking for a way to counter coercive power with communication that leads to mutual understanding and peace. The thought of receiving and giving gifts with those far from us or different from us can give us hope that military might will not ultimately destroy our world. The two-way interaction of giving and receiving gifts leads Christians into better relationships with those of other religions and reflects how God acts toward us—freely and with grace, just like a gift.

Radical Habits for Graceful Evangelism

How does giftive mission express itself in terms of practices—radical habits of Christians? Would missionaries down through the centuries recognize giftive mission as a useful and effective way to gracefully speak of God's mission?

The examples that follow show how a number of innovative missionaries did just that. In every generation, missionaries have made innovations that tailored the gospel message to the times.

The approach of those innovators involved a give-and-take—a giving and receiving of gifts. They developed radical habits in their unique situations—habits that showed the graceful ways that God gives gifts to people and the graceful ways that missionaries found themselves receiving gifts from others, within and outside of the church. The giftive practices those missionaries developed were not peripheral to their ministry. Instead the attitudes and habits of each practice were central in the life of a particular missionary. By learning from these exemplars, we can become innovators ourselves, giving and receiving gifts that fit Christian evangelism to global contexts in the twenty-first century. And it is this sort of innovation that will move us beyond "evangelism wars."

Paul: The Universality of the Gospel

The apostle Paul highlighted the universality of the gospel story (see sidebar 15.3). Paul saw the task of the church's mission in a wider frame of reference than anyone before him. He was the focal figure in following up on Jesus's insistence that God's gracious gift was for all people (he called them gentiles), not just the Jewish people. Paul and Apollos spent hours talking about how to share the story of Jesus with the Corinthians who had never heard it, never heard it persuasively, or just plain heard it wrong.

Paul believed that all people benefited from the story of Jesus and needed to be told about it. Jesus came that the whole world might be saved. That has become the paradigm for Christian mission ever since—a paradigm that is compatible with the giftive mission metaphor. All cultures, all people, need to hear the gospel of Jesus Christ's redemptive work. All people have an understanding of giving and receiving gifts. Most cultures have an explicit understanding of free gift, even if they are not always successful in modeling this ideal. In encouraging the Corinthian church members, Paul insisted that they excel in gift giving, specifically giving the gift of grace. For Paul, giving God's grace to others was an indispensable sign of Christian maturity (2 Cor. 8).

> **Sidebar 15.3 Universality**
>
> ***Reaching Out to All, Including Christians***
>
> - Mission exemplar: Apostle Paul
> - Location: Asia Minor, Rome
> - Audience: Gentiles
> - Time: First century
> - Features of Paul's universal gospel:
>   *Compatibility* with Jewish understanding of El Shaddai
>   *Universality* beyond ethnicity, birth, and religious rituals
>   *Simplicity* of a gift-giving God
>   *Trialability*—"come and see"
>   *Observability*—evidence shown in changed lives

Giftive mission, like Paul's reflexive evangelism, went in two directions. Paul groomed the church in Jerusalem and later in Antioch to accept the gift of God's grace through Jesus and to remove some of the Jewish constraints of circumcision and membership in its ethnic group. That, for Paul, was *mission interna*, or in-reach. Paul's mission to reach those in the church in Jerusalem models for us some ways that we can give and receive gifts of gospel grace with other Christians. Paul also encouraged Christians to move out in mission to others. He trained Apollos and others to do *mission externa*—outreach toward the gentiles in Asia Minor. The gospel was for all. We might ask ourselves in developing the radical habit of reaching out to all, "Who are the gentiles of our day?" From oddballs to stressed-out people to cynics—they are everywhere.

How did Paul share this universal message of the free gift of the gospel? There are five features of Paul's universal gospel message. First, compatibility with the Jewish understanding of El Shaddai: Paul began with the Jews and their understanding of their own religion. Second, universality: from the known context of Jewish religion, Paul moved to a wider universality beyond the boundaries of Jewish practice. Third, he kept it simple: God gives the gift of life through grace. Fourth, trialability: Paul encouraged people to try out the free gift of life in Christ. All people, whoever they were, and whatever their religion, could "come and see." Finally, observability: Paul pointed to the observable evidence of those who had received God's gift of grace in Jesus. Lives changed and the evidence of that was visible in new groups of gentile Christians. God's gift of grace made a difference in the lives of anyone who accepted it.

St. Patrick: Fellowship with All

St. Patrick, who lived in the fifth century, displayed another radical habit we can develop in sharing the gospel. Patrick's whole life was a gift to others. From the day he was kidnapped and taken to Ireland, he determined to spend the rest of his life as a gift to the Celts, the very people who had torn him from home and family. His gift to the Irish, however, was even more specific than that. He focused on a practice that is universally useful. Creating the conditions of fellowship for all, regardless of their spiritual status, enabled him to gain a foothold in a difficult culture and eventually to witness to the gospel by his very presence. The monasteries Patrick established throughout Ireland demonstrated the centrality of the radical habit of hospitality that Patrick's life exuded. Patrick's idea of free gift was that there are no strings attached to fellowship and Christian love, not even the crucial strings of orthodoxy (see sidebar 15.4).

The first step in Patrick's evangelistic outreach strategy was welcoming a person into the community. Hospitality was provided; life stories were exchanged; work began to be shared. Trust was built with that exchange of gifts, and acceptance was key. Later, as questions about the Christian faith of those in the community began to arise, the newcomer began behaving like the Christians in the community. Last, beliefs were embraced by the newcomer and he became part of the monastic community, sharing all of life with the others.

Patrick believed that the basis of true mission is community. Belonging to a community of people trying to find out what it meant to be part of God's great story was a gift of grace that Patrick and his monastic friends offered to anyone who was interested. That is a radical habit that fits perfectly with the idea of graceful evangelism. For Patrick, becoming members of Christ's body meant becoming a community bound together despite differences.

> **Sidebar 15.4 Fellowship**
>
> *Belonging Precedes Believing*
>
> - Mission exemplar: St. Patrick
> - Location: Europe, Great Britain, Ireland
> - Audience: Indigenous Celts
> - Time: Fifth century
> - Basis of true mission is community:
>   Step 1: Belonging
>   Step 2: Trusting
>   Step 3: Behaving
>   Step 4: Believing

Bartholomé de Las Casas: Defender of Freedom

In championing the cause of Christ to the indigenous populations of Latin America, Bartholomé de Las Casas found himself defending a principle that one would not think a Christian mission worker would have to defend. The principle that all human beings are equally able to love and glorify God was under attack. Many Spaniards considered the Indians incapable of rational thought. They were considered a subhuman species that needed to be coerced and civilized before they could accept the good news of the gospel. So Las Casas had to argue that the native populations of Latin America were capable of receiving the gift of the gospel.

By arguing for the full humanity of the Indians, Las Casas prefigured the human rights emphasis on the freedom to choose one's religion. He influenced his fellow monastic brothers, the Dominicans and the Franciscans, to reject the notion of the inferiority of native populations. He influenced the philosophies as well as the theologies of the day as the West moved toward a more inclusive view of human rights. The Spanish Crown and the colonies it subjugated also eventually conformed to Las Casas's more enlightened view of humanity. Human flourishing was given a huge boost by Las Casas's practice of honoring the freedom of religious choice (see sidebar 15.5).

Las Casas's battle for the rights of the Indians to choose their religion sprang from his personal experience with the idea of gift. As a teenager, Las Casas was "given" a slave from the colonies by his seafaring father. Bartholomé and

Sidebar 15.5 Freedom

Honoring Free Choice in Religion

• Mission exemplar: Bartholomé de Las Casas
• Location: South America, Latin America
• Audience: Indigenous tribes
• Time: Sixteenth century
• Las Casas's argument with the Crown:
   Indians are rational humans.
   They have freedom to choose religion.
   They must not be enslaved.
• Who listened?
   The church (Dominicans and Franciscans)
   European philosophy/Christianity debates
   Spanish Crown
   Colonies
   Legal system
   Human rights movement

this young boy became fast friends before Queen Isabella sent all the imported slaves back to the New World. The loss of this friend influenced Las Casas's life journey so profoundly that years later he found himself freeing the slaves that he had "earned" through his conquests and arguing for their full humanity. Gifts can be given and received in the grace of God, but a person, made in God's image, can never be considered a gift, to be owned by another person. Las Casas's radical habit of insisting on the freedom of religious choice for all deeply influenced the course of colonialism and Christianity in South America and Latin America.

Catherine Booth: Bringing the Gospel to both Rich and Poor

Catherine Booth and her husband, William, cared for the poor. As a co-founder of the Salvation Army, Booth spent her life convincing Christians that giving to the poor, providing medicine for the sick, and helping the disadvantaged were as much a part of mission as was preaching the good news of Christ's gospel. She did both. But she wanted to make sure she lived her life committed to giving all the gifts of the gospel, not just a select few that some group had decided were the most important.

Consequently, she developed a number of different strategies for reaching different constituencies in her nineteenth-century English world (see sidebar 15.6). To the wealthy women of the churches, she preached giving of one's income and time to take good news to the poor. She trained women to go into the ghettos of London's East End with food and clothing. She and William utilized the popular cultural symbols of military might to communicate with the rough crowds of working poor. They rented dance halls, played popular band music, and preached about God's redemptive grace. Booth insisted that Scripture shows that anyone called by God could work in public ministry. Furthermore, she convinced others that the wealthy needed to experience God's grace in Christ as much as the poor. The churches needed to stop aggravating the plight of the poor and instead come to their aid.

Sidebar 15.6 Variety

Communicating the Gospel in Many Forms, Verbal and Nonverbal

- Mission exemplar: Catherine Booth
- Location: Europe, England
- Audience: Christians and the working poor
- Time: Nineteenth century
- Convictions that spawned variety in evangelistic strategies:
    Scripture shows that anyone called by God can work in public ministry.
    Sexual equality is a God-given right.
    God cares about the poverty-stricken people of London's East End.
    The church's lack of response to the needs of the poor aggravate their plight.
    The wealthy need to hear the good news as much as do the poor.
    Exploitation of women and children cannot be ignored by the churches.
- Steps in Catherine Booth's evangelistic approach:
    Step 1: Getting their attention
    Step 2: Filling a need
    Step 3: Striking a chord with the culture
    Step 4: Going to where the poor live
    Step 5: Entertainment as a mode of preaching
    Step 6: Being practical and doing what works

Catherine Booth's evangelistic approach began with getting the attention of those in need, whether rich or poor. Filling that need by engaging them in ministry or giving charitable gifts was the next step. The Booths struck a chord with the culture, delivering relevant and entertaining messages. They went to where the poor lived. Their preaching came alive with contemporary music and entertainment. And they insisted on doing what was effective and dispensing with traditional approaches that didn't seem to move people. Imagination and determination energized the radical habit of Catherine Booth to preach the gospel in a variety of ways.

As Christians study new theologies of evangelism, gain knowledge of how others are *doing* evangelism, and see the changes that movements and institutions are making to bring the gospel to contemporary society, a variety of evangelistic outreach models can be utilized in reaching people around the world.

William Sheppard: Honoring Others

William Sheppard did effective ministry in the late nineteenth century by focusing on the importance of mission to African traditional religionists.

As the first African American Presbyterian missionary to Africa, Sheppard made deep connections with the leaders of the Kasai tribe in the Congo. He hunted with the kings, saved the gifts of artifacts from the culture, and provided dental services to the villagers. Later in his ministry, Sheppard struggled against the atrocities that managers were perpetuating on their rubber plantations (Adeney 2006). Sheppard was intent on reaching the people with the good news of God's grace. He treated all with respect, never disparaging the views of the Congolese and rejecting their religious practices only when they conflicted with his Christian views of human rights (see sidebar 15.7). For him the importance of this mission superseded all the difficulties of being an African American attempting to gain support in a mission that had traditionally been all white.

Besides honoring the natives with tremendous respect, Sheppard also honored the white denomination that had sent him to the Congo. He had a gift to give, and he gave it with respect—even if he did not receive the gift of respect in return from those who "supported" him. On some occasions, he could not even sit down for a meal with members of the American churches that he was

---

Sidebar 15.7 Respect

Not Disparaging Others to Champion Your Own;
Not Disparaging Your Own to Respect Others

- Mission exemplar: William Sheppard
- Location: Belgian Congo, Africa
- Audience: African traditional religions and home churches in the United States
- Time: Nineteenth to twentieth century
- Sheppard's gift: Respecting the culture
    He was the first African American Presbyterian missionary (1891).
    His ministry itself was an innovation.
    He received gifts from Kasai people: artifacts, inclusion in hunting expeditions, hospitality of the king.
    He never disparaged or looked down on Africans.
    He only objected to their religious practices when human rights were violated.
- Results of Sheppard's ministry:
    African Americans were sent as missionaries.
    The church grew in the Congo.
    His respect for culture led to anthropological work and later the indigenization of the church.
    His early critique of colonial oppression influenced others to address exploitation.
    He brought attention to racism in the United States.

reporting to (Adeney 2006). Yet he continued to show respect for both himself and those who supported his faithful service. For Sheppard, how one gave the gift was as important as the gift itself, and this translated into all the mission practices he used in Africa.

The results of Sheppard's respect for others made a mark on mission history. African Americans began to be sent out as missionaries. Despite a slow start, with only a few followers of Christ in the first five years, the church grew in the Congo. Sheppard's work was followed by further anthropological work with natives in all parts of the world. And the respect he showed the native people may have influenced the later indigenization of the Congolese church. Sheppard's early critique of colonial oppression also sent a strong message to the world about addressing colonial exploitation. Finally, Sheppard's fine work with the Congolese and his respect for the people who had sent him to do mission work in Africa brought attention to racism in the United States. Sheppard had a radical habit of not disparaging others or disrespecting himself. And it led to graceful evangelism.

Mother Teresa: Giving the Gift of Love

Mother Teresa was certainly not a quid pro quo gift giver. She measured her gift to the Hindus of India not by how many came for help but by how Christians treated the ones who did come to get the services the Sisters of Charity offered. She once said that she did mathematics differently than most people. She didn't worry about the incredibly small percentages of Indian Hindus she and her colleagues were able to treat medically. Her mathematics considered the one she was loving right now as the total of God's universe at that moment. That kind of care can only come with gospel love.

Mother Teresa developed a radical habit of loving the people to whom she witnessed (see sidebar 15.8). She did this first by initiating contact with them. No one in the city of Calcutta wanted to lift the dying off the dirty streets. A belief that each person has to experience the results of misdeeds in his or her past lives fosters a "live and let live" attitude toward suffering. Changing the situation of one who suffers may actually result in hurting

Sidebar 15.8 Charity

Loving the People to Whom We Witness

- Mission exemplar: Mother Teresa
- Location: India, with global scope
- Audience: Hindus
- Time: Twentieth century
- Habits for loving those to whom we witness:
  - Initiate contact.
  - Pay attention to the response.
  - Affirm the other person.
  - Appreciate the other person for himself or herself.
  - Act for the good of the other.
  - Pay special attention to the weak.
  - Receive gifts.

her or his spiritual progress for the next life in the never-ending cycle of rebirth. So for strongly held reasons, many were left to die on the streets. Mother Teresa couldn't do that. She felt a deep Christian love for those people and began to help them one by one. She lifted them off the street, washed them, and gave them a dry pallet to sleep on and nourishing food to eat. She held each one in her arms and blessed him or her. She paid attention to how each one responded to her, and she affirmed each, appreciating each one for himself or herself. Then she acted for their good, paying special attention to the weakest.

On top of all of this, Mother Teresa received gifts. She was blessed by the dying poor, seeing in each one the face of Christ. She received gifts from temple leaders and government officials—places to house and nourish the dying. She graciously received gifts from Christians all over the world, though she never asked for funds for her ministry. So her witness grew from serving the poor to impressing the wealthy with the graceful winsomeness of the gospel. Her radical habit of loving those to whom she witnessed bore fruit throughout the world. Mother Teresa's influence on global culture is unrivaled, and centers in many parts of the world now receive the dying poor, giving and receiving gifts with them.

Billy Graham: Uniting Believers

Ironically, Billy Graham's gift to the church, as a twentieth-century evangelical evangelist, was the gift of ecumenism. He insisted not only that all churches everywhere should be involved in evangelism, but also that they should partner together to do it. The metaphor of gift giving illumines this insistence. Ideally when people give gifts, they should not be trying to outdo one another like some modern-day Pharisee, but should be giving with a loving, open, and humble heart. During much of the nineteenth and twentieth centuries, many churches did work together on evangelism. Somewhere along the way, however, evangelism lost its ecumenical focus. Billy Graham's radical habit of working with the churches in his citywide evangelistic meetings kept his work from fragmenting and overlapping with efforts of others in the same locale.

Graham told the gospel story in a way that united rather than divided people (see sidebar 15.9). In a world of competing global, secular, and religious interests, Graham brought people together around a common theme. "Just As I Am, Without One Plea," his signature hymn, brings a message that unites people. All people are equal in their need for forgiveness, in their longing to make peace with others and with themselves. Graham was a master at focusing that longing on a single religious story as the true one while recognizing that the story takes many cultural forms.

But Graham did not bring that message as an individualistic evangelist. His commitment to worldwide evangelism also stressed intra-Christian interactions. He would not preach in a city unless all the major churches agreed to come together, participate in the meetings, sing in the choir, and do follow-up with those who accepted Christ.

During his long career, Graham also fostered other unities. His work on Judeo-Christian interactions, interreligious interactions, and racial-religious identity also sent strong ecumenical messages to the church and society. His stance against nuclear weapons proliferation displayed a profound respect for the dignity and unity of the human family. Although sometimes caricatured as a preacher with narrow views, Graham actually fostered unity among many sectors of society. Never divisive in his approach, he practiced a radical habit of ecumenical relations within and beyond the church.

Conclusion

We've made an excursion into the history and development of evangelism in this book. We asked the question, "Where did we come from?" and found that evangelism has presented itself in many forms through the long centuries of Christian history. We asked, "Where are we now?" and realized that many of the dilemmas we see in our contemporary situation have corresponding advantages. We asked, "Where are we going?" and ascertained that in aiming for abundant life, Christians seek the welfare of all

> ### Sidebar 15.9 Missional Ecumenicity
>
> *Practicing Mission as the Joint Project of the Churches, Not an Occasion for Competition*
>
> - Mission exemplar: Billy Graham
> - Location: United States, with global scope
> - Audience: Secularists
> - Time: Twentieth century
> - Preaching the gospel story in a way that unites rather than divides:
>   Today's world is one of competing global, secular, and religious interests.
>   Graham focused on a single religious story as the true one while recognizing that the story takes many cultural forms.
>   His commitment to worldwide evangelism also stressed intra-Christian interactions, Judeo-Christian interactions, interreligious interactions, and racial-religious identity.

people and find God going ahead of us with grace to every place. Finally, we asked, "Can we craft a graceful evangelism?" and here we saw that contemporary theologies of evangelism can help us and that with courage we can face the challenges of our religiously pluralistic environment today. We analyzed new movements that bring life to evangelism and discussed ways that church institutions are making headway in devising relevant cultural forms for contemporary evangelism. We outlined a model of learning that brings us knowledge of difference and fosters our ability to accept others with their differing perspectives and experiences. And we researched history to find the radical habits of innovators who have gone before us, bringing good news to the world. As we continue to put all of this together, we are discovering graceful evangelism.

Appendix

Constructing a Congregational Timeline

ADAPTED FROM AMMERMAN ET AL. 1998, 43–46; 209–10

Use the following instructions to make a timeline focused on evangelism in the history of the congregation. This exercise should be done in a leisurely way, during an evening or afternoon. It may take about two hours—or longer if a meal or coffee hour is included.

What Is a Congregational Timeline?

A congregational timeline is a historical rendering of the life of the congregation as recalled by its members. This collective effort of history-telling includes multiple perspectives on events and processes brought about by demographic, cultural, and organizational changes.

A time-space network of the congregation as a human institution includes three parts:

Locating the congregation in history from its founding to the present.

Locating the congregation geographically.

Locating the congregation in the lives of its members as members create network "maps" of their lives.

187

What Are the Goals of Constructing a Timeline?

The main goal in constructing a timeline is to understand how the congregation is situated within an inclusive conception of its history—local, denominational, national, and global.

> The timeline can become a tool for uncovering links between external demographic, cultural, and organizational shifts and internal stresses experienced by the congregation.
>
> The timeline can help the congregation understand its biases and predispositions to see things in certain ways—more than one perspective sometimes pervades the congregation. Reasons for varying perspectives are often discovered in a congregation's history.

Who Is Equipped to Construct a Congregational Timeline?

The experts on the location of the congregation are the congregants themselves.

> Collective reflection on the past can be done by a diverse group from the congregation, including youngsters, old-timers, women and men, those currently serving on committees, and those less involved or retired from heavy involvement.
>
> This structured reflection can be done in an evening, along with a potluck, creating a social occasion with a goal of better understanding the ecology of the congregation.

Can We Focus the Timeline on Our History in Evangelism?

Some reasons for focusing on evangelism:

> Looking back on the congregation's history of worship, outreach, mission efforts, and presence in the community with an eye toward understanding how those facets of congregational life have had an evangelistic impact on congregants and the wider community can shed light on present views.
>
> It is hard to understand current views without a historical grasp of how those views came to be held.
>
> Understanding the history of the congregation can help the group to avoid unnecessary conflict and identify strengths and weaknesses that contribute to or hinder evangelistic efforts.

Putting the congregation's knowledge together to form a historical view of the group thus helps direct evangelism in a positive way.

How Do We Make a Congregational Timeline?

1. Write a paragraph of invitation so that participants will understand the purpose of the exercise: to recall how evangelism has been understood and practiced in the congregation's history, with a view to continuing and reshaping those traditions in a transformative way.
2. Invite a cross section of congregational members to spend an evening or afternoon on this structured, collective reflection on the past, for example, ten to thirty people of diverse backgrounds, including those with different duties and levels of involvement in the congregation. Make sure they understand the focus of the history-telling venture.
3. Prepare for the event by doing the following:
   - Gather the necessary materials, including markers, legal paper, and a long piece of three-foot-wide butcher paper. Tape this paper on the wall of the fellowship hall or some more public area of the church building.
   - Draw a horizontal line from one end to the other about halfway from the top edge of the butcher paper. Mark the number of years appropriate to the congregation's history and the study's purpose (e.g., evangelism).
   - If a large group is gathering, plan to divide into small groups of four or five, using legal paper for recollecting historical events, and then regroup to do a larger timeline.
   - Someone can tape-record the event so that fuller details can be included in the final study. Alternatively, someone can volunteer to take notes.
4. Once participants have gathered, explain the exercise and how it fits into the congregation's study of its context and focus on evangelism.
   - One or two study group members can volunteer to record facts about the congregation above the horizontal line and recollections about facts external to the congregation can be recorded below the horizontal line. Place the data at the appropriate year demarcated on the butcher paper. Recollections can then be recorded when suggested, not necessarily only in chronological order.
   - Begin by encouraging members to identify when they or their families joined the church or to recall their earliest memories of congregational life. Each participant may initial the point on the timeline for his or her entry into congregational history.

- Invite people to relate important events in the congregation's past, for example, when new clergy came, when building additions were made, when ministry directions changed, or when controversies occurred.
- Ask participants to reflect on one or two significant moments in their lives as members of the congregation—moments that brought "good news" to them or others, for example, aid after loss, children entering Sunday school, accompanying youth groups on mission trips, or hosting international students or missionaries. Title these events and write them on the butcher paper according to when they occurred.
- Reflect also on significant events in community history in the region and nation, in the world and the denomination. Note political changes, new leaders, natural disasters, and so on.
- Spend the most time on local events but don't neglect larger patterns or events.
- Encourage participation of all—allow people to jog each other's memories. Discourage "historical experts" who want to speak for the whole group.

5. Follow-up possibilities:
  - Leave the timeline up in a public space for a week or two so that others can share in the exercise. Post instructions for others to add their memories of events.
  - The congregation can go on to construct a comprehensive congregational history based on this exercise, thereby expanding its understanding of the church in its context.
  - A scaled-down version of the timeline can be distributed in the congregation's newsletter or bulletin.
  - This focused history of evangelism can be added to other historical documents of the congregation.
  - Most importantly, this study can be used as a basis for evaluating present views and practices of evangelism in the congregation and for imagining future plans for evangelism in the congregation.

Bibliography

Abraham, William J. 1989. *The Logic of Evangelism*. Grand Rapids: Eerdmans.

———. 2003. *The Logic of Renewal*. Grand Rapids: Eerdmans.

Adams, James R. 1994. *So You Can't Stand Evangelism? A Thinking Person's Guide to Church Growth*. Boston: Cowley.

Adeney, Frances S. 1989. *Citizenship Ethics: Contributions of Classical Virtue Theory and Responsibility Ethics*. Ann Arbor, MI: University Microfilms International.

———. 1994. "A Framework for Knowledge, a Source for Ethics, and a Vision of Justice." In *The Unique Christ in Our Pluralist World*, edited by Bruce J. Nicholls, 119–27. Carlisle, UK: Paternoster (for World Evangelical Fellowship); Grand Rapids: Baker Books.

———. 2000. "Reflexive Evangelism: The Give and Take of Growing Churches." Paper presented at National Presbytery Leaders training event, St. Simon's Island, Georgia, February 19.

———. 2001. "Is Mission Impossible?" *Dialog: A Journal of Theology* 40 (2): 105–7.

———. 2003. *Christian Women in Indonesia: A Narrative Study of Gender and Religion*. Syracuse: Syracuse University Press.

———. 2005. "Factors in the Rise of Women Leaders in the Sulawesi Protestant Churches." In *Een vakkracht in het Koninkrijk: Kerk- en zendingshistorische opstellen*, edited by Chr. G. F. de Jong, 18–32. Netherlands: Uitgeverij Groen–Heerenveen.

———. 2006. Introduction to *Pioneers in Congo*, by William Sheppard, 13–27. Wilmore, KY: Wood Hill Books.

———. 2007. "Human Rights and Responsibilities: Christian Perspectives." In Adeney and Sharma, *Christianity and Human Rights*, 19–39.

———. 2008. "Christian Evangelistic Preaching as Ritual Speech in a Buddhist Context." In *Communicating Christ through Story and Song: Orality in Buddhist Contexts*, edited by Paul H. De Neui, 60–76. Pasadena, CA: William Carey Library.

———. 2009. "Why Biography? Contributions of Biography to Mission Theology and Theory." *Mission Studies* 26 (2): 153–72.

Adeney, Frances S., and Arvind Sharma, eds. 2007. *Christianity and Human Rights: Influences and Issues*. Albany: State University of New York Press.

Ammerman, Nancy T., Jackson W. Carroll, Carl S. Dudley, and William McKinney, eds. 1998. *Studying Congregations: A New Handbook*. Nashville: Abingdon.

Anderson, Gerald H., ed. 1998. *Biographical Dictionary of Christian Missions*. New York: Macmillan Reference USA.

Andrews, William L, ed. 1986. *Sisters of the Spirit: Three Black Women's Autobiographies of the Nineteenth Century*. Bloomington: Indiana University Press.

Augustine. 1949. *The Confessions of St. Augustine*. New York: E. P. Dutton.

———. 1952. *The City of God*. Translated by Marcus Dods. Edited by Robert Maynard Hutchins. Great Books of the Western World, 18. Chicago: Encyclopedia Britannica.

———. 1967. Sermon 24,6. In *Augustine of Hippo: A Biography*, by Peter R. L. Brown. Berkeley: University of California Press.

Barrett, David B., and Todd M. Johnson, eds. 2001. *World Christian Trends: AD 30–AD 220*. Pasadena, CA: William Carey Library.

Barrett, David B., George T. Kurian, and Todd M. Johnson. 2001. *World Christian Encyclopedia: A Comparative Survey of Churches and Religions in the Modern World*. 2 vols. New York: Oxford University Press.

Bednarowski, Mary. 1999. *The Religious Imagination of American Women*. Bloomington: Indiana University Press.

Bell, Lynda S., Andrew J. Nathan, and Ilan Peleg, eds. 2001. *Negotiating Culture and Human Rights*. New York: Columbia University Press.

Bellah, Robert N. 1973. *Beyond Belief: Essays on Religion in a Post-Traditional World*. New York: Harper & Row.

Bellah, Robert N., Richard Madsen, William M. Sullivan, Ann Swidler, and Steven M. Tipton. 1985. *Habits of the Heart: Individualism and Commitment in American Life*. 2nd ed. Berkeley: University of California Press.

———. 1988. *Individualism and Commitment in American Life: Readings on the Themes of Habits of the Heart*. New York: Harper & Row.

Berger, Peter L. 1969. *The Sacred Canopy: Elements of a Sociological Theory of Religion*. New York: Doubleday Anchor Books.

————. 1993. *A Far Glory: The Quest for Faith in an Age of Credulity.* New York: Doubleday Anchor Books.

Bergner, Daniel. 2006. "The Call." *New York Times Magazine*, January 29. http://www.nytimes.com/2006/01/29/magazine/29missionaries.html.

Bevans, Stephen B., SVD, and Roger P. Schroeder, SVD. 2004. *Constants in Context: A Theology of Mission for Today.* Maryknoll, NY: Orbis Books.

Bloom, Allan. 1987. *The Closing of the American Mind.* New York: Simon & Schuster.

Booth, Michael. [2003.] *Briars in the Cotton Patch: The Story of Koinonia Farm.* DVD. Produced and directed by Faith Fuller. Americus, GA: Koinonia Partners. http://briarsdocumentary.com.

Boots, Steven. 1989. *Living the Vision: Congregational Transformation.* Louisville: Mission Interpretation and Promotion for Evangelism and Church Development Ministries of the General Assembly Council, Presbyterian Church (USA).

Bosch, David J. 1991. *Transforming Mission: Paradigm Shifts in Theology of Mission.* Maryknoll, NY: Orbis Books.

Bourdieu, Peter. 1991. *Language and Symbolic Power.* Translated by Gino Raymond and Matthew Adamson. Cambridge, MA: Doubleday.

Bos, David. 2005. *Bound Together: A Theology for Ecumenical Community Ministry.* Cleveland: Pilgrim.

Brown, Peter. 1967. *Augustine of Hippo: A Biography.* Berkeley: University of California Press.

Brunner, Emil. 1947. *The Divine Imperative.* Philadelphia: Westminster Press.

Burrows, William, SJ. 2009. Presidential address at the annual meeting of the Society of Missiology, Chicago, IL, June 20.

Campolo, Tony. 1985. "Tony Campolo Interview." *Wittenburg Door Magazine* 85, July.

————. 1995. *Can Mainline Denominations Make a Comeback?* Valley Forge, PA: Judson.

Cannon, Katie. 2003. *Katie's Canon: Womanism and the Soul of the Black Community.* New York: Continuum.

Chang, Curtis. 2000. *Engaging Unbelief: A Captivating Strategy from Augustine and Aquinas.* Downers Grove, IL: InterVarsity.

Chilcote, Paul W., and Laceye C. Warner, eds. 2008. *The Study of Evangelism: Exploring a Missional Practice of the Church.* Grand Rapids: Eerdmans.

Clarke, Susanna. 2004. *Jonathan Strange and Mr. Norrell.* New York: Bloomsbury.

Coalter, Milton J., John M. Mulder, and Louis B. Weeks. 1996. *Vital Signs: The Promise of Mainstream Protestantism.* Grand Rapids: Eerdmans.

Coleman, Robert E. 1993. *The Master Plan of Evangelism*. Grand Rapids: Revell.

Coleman, John, SJ. 1985. Lecture presented in ethics course, Graduate Theological Union, April.

Cooey, Paula M. 1991. "The Redemption of the Body: Post-Patriarchal Reconstruction of Inherited Christian Doctrine." In *After Patriarchy: Feminist Transformations of the World Religions*, edited by William R. Eakin and Jay B. McDaniel, 106–30. Maryknoll, NY: Orbis Books.

Covey, Stephen R. 1989. *The Seven Habits of Highly Effective People: Powerful Lessons in Personal Change*. New York: Simon & Schuster.

Cracknell, Kenneth. 1995. *Justice, Courtesy and Love: Theologians Encountering World Religions, 1846–1914*. London: Epworth.

Crandall, Ronald K. 2001. *Witness: Exploring and Sharing Your Christian Faith* and *My Witness Journal*. Nashville: Discipleship Resources, United Methodist Church.

Crosby, Fanny J. 1951. "Tell Me the Story of Jesus." In *Praise and Worship: The Nazarene Hymnal*, no. 177. Kansas City, MO: Nazarene Publishing House, 1951.

Cuddihy, John Murray. 1978. *No Offense: Civil Religion and Protestant Taste*. New York: Seabury.

Davies, Horton, and R. H. W. Shepherd. 1954. *South African Missions, 1800–1950*. London: Thomas Nelson and Sons.

Day, Dorothy. 1952. *The Long Loneliness*. San Francisco: Harper & Row.

Dietterich, Inagrace. 2009. "A Vision for the Sending of the Church in North America—Ten Years On." Paper presented at the annual meeting of the American Society of Missiology, Chicago, June 20.

Donovan, Vincent J. 2002. *Christianity Rediscovered*. Maryknoll, NY: Orbis Books.

Durkheim, Emile. 1995. *The Elementary Forms of Religious Life*. Translated by Karen E. Fields. New York: Free Press.

Elliot, Elisabeth. 1958. *Shadow of the Almighty: The Life and Testament of Jim Elliot*. New York: Harper & Row.

Ernst, Eldon. 1987. *Without Help or Hindrance: Religious Identity in American Culture*. 2nd ed. Philadelphia: Westminster.

Fensham, Charles. 2008. *Emerging from the Dark Age Ahead: The Future of the North American Church*. Toronto: Novalis.

Fracknell, David. 2008. "Evangelism as Blessing." Lecture presented in evangelism course, Louisville Presbyterian Theological Seminary, April.

Gadamer, Hans-Georg. 1996. *Truth and Method*. 2nd ed. Translation revised by Joel Weinsheimer and Donald G. Marshall. New York: Continuum.

Geertz, Clifford. 1973. "Ideology as a Cultural System." In *The Interpretation of Cultures*, 193–233. New York: HarperCollins Basic Books.

George, Sherron. 2004. *Called as Partners in Christ's Service: The Practice of God's Mission*. Louisville: Geneva.

Gerth, H. H., and C. Wright Mills. 1946. *From Max Weber: Essays in Sociology*. New York: Oxford University Press.

Gibbs, Eddie, and Ryan K. Bolger. 2005. *Emerging Churches: Creating Christian Community in Postmodern Cultures*. Grand Rapids: Baker Academic.

Gittins, Anthony. 1989. *Gifts and Strangers: Meeting the Challenge of Inculturation*. New York: Paulist Press.

Glendon, Mary Ann. 2001. *A World Made New: Eleanor Roosevelt and the Universal Declaration of Human Rights*. New York: Random House.

Grant, Jacquelyn. 1989. *White Women's Christ and Black Women's Jesus: Feminist Christology and Womanist Response*. Atlanta: Scholars Press.

Grunder, Horst. 2002. "Christian Mission and Colonial Expansion—Historical and Structural Connections." *Mission Studies* 12 (1): 18–29.

Guder, Darrell, ed. 1998. *Missional Church: A Vision for the Sending of the Church in North America*. Grand Rapids: Eerdmans.

————. 2000. *The Continuing Conversion of the Church*. Grand Rapids: Eerdmans.

Guralnik, David B., ed. 1966. *Webster's New World Dictionary of the American Language*. New York: World.

Guthrie, Shirley. 2002. "Evangelism in a Pluralistic Society: A Reformed Perspective." Paper presented at the Covenant Network Conference, November 8.

Habermas, Jürgen. 1984. *The Theory of Communicative Action: Reason and the Rationalization of Society*. Vol. 1. Translated by Thomas McCarthy. Boston: Beacon.

Hand, Thomas, SJ. 1996. "The Basics of Buddhism." Lecture presented at the Institute for Cultural and Ecumenical Research, St. John's University, Collegeville, MN, November 15.

Haney, Marsha Snulligan. 2007. *Evangelism among African American Presbyterians: Making Plain the Sacred Journey*. New York: University Press of America.

Heath, Elaine A. 2008. *The Mystic Way of Evangelism: A Contemplative Vision for Christian Outreach*. Grand Rapids: Baker Academic.

Hiebert, Paul G. 2008. *Transforming Worldviews: An Anthropological Understanding of How People Change*. Grand Rapids: Baker Academic.

Howland, Courtney W. 1999. *Religious Fundamentalism and the Human Rights of Women*. New York: St. Martin's.

Hunsberger, George R., and Craig Van Gelder, eds. 1996. *The Church between Gospel and Culture: The Emerging Mission in North America*. Grand Rapids: Eerdmans.

Hunter, George G., III. 2000. *The Celtic Way of Evangelism: How Christianity Can Reach the West . . . Again*. Nashville: Abingdon.

Hutchinson, William R. 1987. *Errand to the World: American Protestant Thought and Foreign Missions*. Chicago: University of Chicago Press.

Isasi-Diaz, Ada Maria. 2004. *En La Lucha (In the Struggle): Elaborating a Mujerista Theology*. Minneapolis: Fortress.

Jesudasan, Usha, and Gert Ruppell. 2005. "The Role of the Community in Healing." In *Healing as Empowerment: Discovering Grace in Community*, 55–78. Geneva: World Council of Churches.

Johns, Cheryl Bridges. 1993. *Pentecostal Formation: A Pedagogy among the Oppressed*. Sheffield, UK: Sheffield Academic Press.

Jones, Scott J. 2003. *The Evangelistic Love of God and Neighbor: A Theology of Witness and Discipleship*. Nashville: Abingdon.

Kalu, Ogbu U., ed. 2008. *Interpreting Contemporary Christianity: Global Processes and Local Identities*. Grand Rapids: Eerdmans.

Katongole, Emmanuel M., and Jonathan Wilson-Hartgrove. 2009. *Mirror to the Church: Resurrecting Faith after Genocide in Rwanda*. Grand Rapids: Zondervan.

King, Martin Luther, Jr. 1963. *Strength to Love*. New York: Harper & Row.

Kingsolver, Barbara. 1999. *The Poisonwood Bible: A Novel*. New York: HarperPerennial.

Lapsley, Michael. 2009. Group conversation about healing of memories with Louisville Presbyterian Theological Seminary Travel Seminar group, Capetown, South Africa, January.

Lindbeck, George A. 1984. *The Nature of Doctrine: Religion and Theology in a Postliberal Age*. Louisville: Westminster John Knox.

Little, Paul E. 1966. *How to Give Away Your Faith*. Downers Grove, IL: InterVarsity.

Lloyd-Sidel, Patricia, and Bonnie Sue Lewis, eds. 2001. *Teaching Mission in a Global Context*. Louisville: Geneva.

MacIntyre, Alisdair. 1981. *After Virtue: A Study in Moral Theology*. Notre Dame, IN: University of Notre Dame Press.

Marshall, George, and David Poling. 1971. *Schweitzer: A Biography*. New York: Albert Schweitzer Foundation; printed by Pillar Books, Doubleday.

McClendon, James. 1980. *Systematic Theology*. Vol. 1, *Ethics*. Nashville: Abingdon.

McFague, Sallie. 2001. *Life Abundant: Rethinking Theology and Economy for a Planet in Peril*. Minneapolis: Augsburg Fortress.

McGavran, Donald A. 1970. *Understanding Church Growth*. Grand Rapids: Eerdmans.

Mead, George Herbert. 1934. *Mind, Self, and Society from the Standpoint of a Social Behaviorist*. Vol. 1. Chicago: University of Chicago Press.

Meiring, Pieter. 1999. *Chronicle of the Truth Commission: A Journey through the Past and Present—Into the Future of South Africa.* Vijlpark, South Africa: Carpe Diem Books.

Mejudhon, Ubolwan. 1997. "The Way of Meekness: Being Christian and Thai in the Thai Way." Doctor of Missiology diss., Asbury Theological Seminary, Wilmore, KY.

Merk, Frederick, with Lois Bannister Merk. 1966. *Manifest Destiny and Mission in American History: A Reinterpretation.* New York: Random House.

Metcalf, Stephen. 2007. "The God Illusion." *New York Times Book Review,* April 22, p. 11.

Milbank, John. 1990. *Theology and Social Theory: Beyond Secular Reason.* Oxford: Blackwell.

Moltmann, Jürgen. 2000. "The Sabbath: Feast of Creation." Chapel sermon at Louisville Presbyterian Theological Seminary, April 5.

Montgomery, Robert L. 1999. *An Introduction to the Sociology of Missions.* Westport, CT: Praeger, Greenwood.

Morison, Frank. 1930. *Who Moved the Stone?* London: Faber & Faber.

Mouw, Richard. 2008. "What Conversion Is All About." In Tan, *Hearts Aflame,* 165–75.

Muck, Terry. 2005. *Faith in Action Study Bible: Living God's Word in a Changing World.* Grand Rapids: Zondervan.

———. 2006. "That All May Be One: John 17 in the Context of World Religions." Paper presented at the Mountain States Wee Kirk Conference, Santa Fe, NM, May 10.

———. 2007. *How to Study Religions.* Wilmore, KY: Wood Hill Books.

Muck, Terry, and Frances S. Adeney. 2009. *Christianity Encountering World Religions: The Practice of Mission in the Twenty-first Century.* Grand Rapids: Baker Academic.

Ng, John. 2008. "Business, the Good Life, and No Time. . . . How to Share Christ with CEOs." In Tan, *Hearts Aflame,* 61–71.

Niebuhr, H. Richard. 1960. *The Meaning of Revelation.* New York: Macmillan.

———. 1989. *Faith on Earth: An Inquiry into the Structure of Human Faith.* New Haven: Yale University Press.

Njoroge, Nyambura J. 2000. *Kiama Kia Ngo: An African Christian Feminist Ethic of Resistance and Transformation.* Accra, Ghana: Asempa.

Nussbaum, Stan. 2005. *A Reader's Guide to Transforming Mission.* Maryknoll, NY: Orbis Books.

Oduyoye, Mercy Amba. 2008. "Unity and Mission: The Emerging Ecumenical Vision." In Chilcote and Warner, *Study of Evangelism,* 328–39.

Pagitt, Douglas. 2009. "Emerging Church." Paper presented at the annual meeting of the American Society of Missiology, Chicago, June 20.

Peterson, Mikuel. 2009. "'Led By the Spirit': The Missiological Influence of Alice Eveline Luce." Doctor of Missiology diss., Asbury Theological Seminary, Wilmore, KY.

Phipps, William E. 2002. *William Sheppard: Congo's African American Livingstone*. Louisville: Geneva.

Pierson, Robert D. 2006. *Needs-Based Evangelism: Becoming a Good Samaritan Church*. Nashville: Abingdon.

Piper, John, Jr. 2000. *Robert E. Speer: Prophet of the American Church*. Louisville: Geneva.

Pippert, Rebecca Manley. 1979. *Out of the Salt Shaker and into the World: Evangelism as a Way of Life*. Downers Grove, IL: InterVarsity.

Polanyi, Michael. 1958. *Personal Knowledge: Toward a Post-Critical Philosophy*. Chicago: University of Chicago Press. Repr., 1962.

Presbyterian Church (USA). 2001. *The Presbyterians: Part 2; History and Tradition*. VHS. DMS#70310–943–016. Louisville: Presbyterian Church (USA).

———. 2003a. *Connecting in Diversity: Race, Class, Gender, Religion*. VHS. Louisville: Presbyterian Church (USA).

———. 2003. *Presbyterians Do Mission in Partnership*. Louisville: Presbyterian Church (USA), Worldwide Ministries Division. Adopted by the 215th General Assembly.

Pucci, Michael. 2008. "The Gospel and Human Poverty." In Tan, *Hearts Aflame*, 199–230.

Putnam, Robert D. 2001. *Bowling Alone*. New York: Simon & Schuster.

Raiser, Konrad. 1997. *To Be the Church: Challenges and Hopes for a New Millennium*. Geneva: WCC Publications.

Rauschenbusch, Walter. 1945. *A Theology for the Social Gospel*. Nashville: Abingdon.

Ray, Stephen. 2007. "The End of Man." In Adeney and Sharma, *Christianity and Human Rights*, 117–38.

Reese, Martha Grace. 2006. *Unbinding the Gospel: Real Life Evangelism*. St. Louis: Chalice.

Reuther, Rosemary Radford, and Rosemary Skinner Keller, eds. 1981. *Women and Religion in America*. 2 vols. San Francisco: Harper & Row.

Riegle, Rosalie G. 2003. *Dorothy Day: Portraits by Those Who Knew Her*. Maryknoll, NY: Orbis Books.

Robert, Dana. 1997. *American Women in Mission: A Social History of Their Thought and Practice*. Macon, GA: Mercer University Press.

———. 2008. "Shifting Southward: Global Christianity since 1945." In Chilcote and Warner, *Study of Evangelism*, 117–34.

Roberts, Bob, Jr. 2008. *The Multiplying Church: The New Math for Starting New Churches*. Grand Rapids: Zondervan.

Rogers, June Ramage, ed. 1998. *And God Gave the Increase: Stories of How the Presbyterian Church (USA) Has Helped in the Education of Christian Leaders around the World*. Louisville: Presbyterian Church (USA).

Royce, Josiah. 1913. *The Problem of Christianity: The Christian Doctrine of Life*. Vol. 1. New York: Macmillan.

Russell, Letty. 2008. "Liberation and Evangelization: A Feminist Perspective." In Chilcote and Warner, *Study of Evangelism*, 416–23.

Sanneh, Lamin. 1989. *Translating the Message: The Missionary Impact on Culture*. Maryknoll, NY: Orbis Books.

Scherer, James A., and Stephen B. Bevans. 1992. *New Directions in Mission and Evangelization 1: Basic Statements 1974–1991*. Maryknoll, NY: Orbis Books.

Shaull, Richard, and Waldo Cesar. 2000. *Pentecostalism and the Future of the Christian Churches: Promises, Limitations, Challenges*. Grand Rapids: Eerdmans.

Sheppard, William. 2006. *Pioneers in Congo*. Wilmore, KY: Wood Hill Books. (Orig. pub. 1917.)

Sider, Ronald. 1997. *Rich Christians in an Age of Hunger*. 2nd. ed. London: Hodder.

Smith, Archie, Jr. 1982. *The Relational Self: Ethics and Therapy from a Black Church Perspective*. Nashville: Abingdon.

Smith, J. Alfred, Sr. 2006. *Speak until Justice Wakes: Prophetic Reflections from J. Alfred Smith Sr*. Valley Forge, PA: Judson.

Smith, Susan E. 2007. *Women in Mission: From the New Testament to Today*. Maryknoll, NY: Orbis Books.

Stone, Bryan. 2007. *Evangelism after Christendom: The Theology and Practice of Christian Witness*. Grand Rapids: Brazos.

Tan, Michael, ed. 2008. *Hearts Aflame: Living the Passion for Evangelism*. Singapore: Eagles Communication.

Taylor, Charles. 1985. *Philosophical Papers II*. Cambridge: Cambridge University Press.

Thomas Aquinas. 1975. *Summa Contra Gentiles*. Translated by Anton C. Pegis. Notre Dame, IN: University of Notre Dame Press.

Thomas, Margaret O. 2007. "Changing One's Religion: A Supported Right?" In Adeney and Sharma, *Christianity and Human Rights*, 161–81.

Thoreau, Henry David. 2005. *Walden*. Boston: Beacon.

Torrey, R. A., et al., eds. 1972. *The Fundamentals*. Vol. 1. Grand Rapids: Baker Books.

Tutu, Desmond. 1999. *No Future without Forgiveness*. New York: Doubleday.

Van Gelder, Craig. 1996. "Defining the Center—Finding the Boundaries: The Challenge of Re-Visioning the Church in North America for the Twenty-first Century." In Hunsberger and Van Gelder, *Church between Gospel and Culture*, 26–51.

Van Wijk-Bos, Johanna. 2005. *Making Wise the Simple: The Torah in Christian Faith and Practice*. Grand Rapids: Eerdmans.

Walls, Andrew. 2002. "The Multiple Conversions of Timothy Richards." In *The Cross-Cultural Process in Christian History*, 236–58. Maryknoll, NY: Orbis Books.

Webber, Robert E. 1986. *Liturgical Evangelism*. Harrisburg, PA: Morehouse.

Weber, Max. 1946. "The Social Psychology of the World Religions." In *From Max Weber: Essays in Sociology*, edited by H. H. Gerth and C. Wright Mills, 267–301. New York: Oxford University Press.

West, Cornel. 1994. *Race Matters*. New York: Random House, Vintage Books.

White, Paula, 2007. "The Seven Promises of the Atonement." Television show aired on KQED in Louisville, KY, September 19.

Whitman, Walt. 2006. *Leaves of Grass*. New York: Pocket Books. (Orig. pub. 1855.)

Wierenga, Dirk. 2000. *Presbyterians: A Spiritual Journey*. Louisville: Geneva.

Wilmore, Gayraud S. 1984. *Black Religion and Black Radicalism*. 2nd ed. Maryknoll, NY: Orbis Books.

Wilson-Hartgrove, Jonathan. 2008. *New Monasticism: What It Has to Say to Today's Church*. Grand Rapids: Brazos.

———. 2009. "The New Monastics: Mission through Communities of Justice and Peace." Paper presented at the annual meeting of the American Society of Missiology, Chicago, IL, June 20.

Winthrop, John. 1630. "A Model of Christian Charity." In Bellah et al., *Individualism and Commitment in American Life* (1988), 22–27.

Wolfe, Regina Wentzel, and Christine E. Gudorf, eds. 1999. *Ethics and World Religions: Cross-Cultural Case Studies*. Maryknoll, NY: Orbis Books.

World Council of Churches. *Baptism, Eucharist and Ministry*. Geneva: WCC Publications.

———. *Missions and Evangelism: An Ecumenical Statement*. Geneva: WCC Publications.

Yeoman, Barry. 2002. "The Stealth Crusade." *Mother Jones*, May/June, 42–49.

Zahl, Paul F. M. 2001. *Five Women of the English Reformation*. Grand Rapids: Eerdmans.

Zoba, Wendy Murray. 1999. "Missions Improbably." *Books & Culture* (September/October): 36–37.

Index